TALKING LIKE CHILDREN

OXFORD STUDIES IN THE ANTHROPOLOGY OF LANGUAGE

Series Editor: Alessandro Duranti, University of California at Los Angeles

This series is devoted to works from a wide array of scholarly traditions that treat linguistic practices as forms of social action.

Thank You for Dying for Our Country: Commemorative Texts and Performances in Jerusalem

Chaim Noy

Singular and Plural: Ideologies of Linguistic Authority in 21st Century Catalonia

Kathryn A. Woolard

Linguistic Rivalries: Tamil Migrants and Anglo-Franco Conflicts

Sonia Neela Das

The Monologic Imagination

Edited by Matt Tomlinson and Julian Millie

Looking like a Language, Sounding like a Race: Raciolinguistic Ideologies and the Learning of Latinidad

Jonathan Rosa

Talking Like Children: Language and the Production of Age in the Marshall Islands

Elise Berman

TALKING LIKE CHILDREN

Language and the Production of Age in the Marshall Islands

Elise Berman

OXFORD
UNIVERSITY PRESS

Oxford University Press is a department of the University of Oxford. It furthers the University's objective of excellence in research, scholarship, and education by publishing worldwide. Oxford is a registered trade mark of Oxford University Press in the UK and certain other countries.

Published in the United States of America by Oxford University Press
198 Madison Avenue, New York, NY 10016, United States of America.

Library of Congress Cataloging-in-Publication Data
Names: Berman, Elise, author.
Title: Talking like children: language and the production of age in the marshall islands / Elise Berman.
Description: New York, NY, United States of America : Oxford University Press, [2018] |
Series: Oxford studies in anthropology of language |
Includes bibliographical references and index.
Identifiers: LCCN 2018018334 (print) | LCCN 2018034197 (ebook) |
ISBN 9780190876999 (updf) | ISBN 9780190877002 (epub) |
ISBN 9780190877019 (online content) | ISBN 9780190876982 (pbk. : alk. paper) |
ISBN 9780190876975 (cloth : alk. paper)
Subjects: LCSH: Intergenerational communication—Marshall Islands. |
Age groups—Marshall Islands. | Exchange—Social aspects—Marshall Islands. |
Marshall Islands—Social life and customs.
Classification: LCC DU710 (ebook) | LCC DU710 .B47 2018 (print) |
DDC 996.8/3—dc23
LC record available at https://lccn.loc.gov/2018018334

CONTENTS

TABLES AND FIGURES

Table

Figures

ACKNOWLEDGMENTS

M̧oktata, ikōņaan kam̧m̧oolol baam̧le in M̧ajeļ eo aō. Ikōņaan kile er im lelok juon kam̧m̧oolol eļap ñan er kōn jipañ ko aer, mōñā ko aer, im jouj ko aer. Kom̧m̧ool ñan mama im papa in M̧ajeļ ro aō, jatū in M̧ajeļ ro aō, im aolep nukū ro jet. Āliktata, ibar kōņaan joļo̧k aō bōd ñe ewōr bōd kōn naan ko. Bar juon alen, leļo̧k kam̧m̧oolol eļap.

I am deeply grateful to the many people who made this book possible. First and foremost, I thank the many people in the Republic of the Marshall Islands (RMI) who allowed me into their lives. Like everything in the RMI, this book is a collective project that depended on them as much as, or more than, me. To protect their privacy I have used pseudonyms, but I wish I could thank them by name. My family on Jajikon accepted me as a daughter, watched over me, and fed me even while I was not as attentive to my chores as daughters should be. My research assistants were not only workers but also friends who provided new and unique insights into Marshallese ways of life. The assistant whom I can name, Tata Kalles, helped me transcribe and answered my innumerable questions. Everybody on Jajikon became kin and accepted me as such. They talked to me and let me videotape their lives. Some members of this adopted family who moved to the United States worked with me on transcription and translation. Others speak with me on Facebook, continuing to help me make sense of their lives. All of the children in Jajikon opened up their hearts, and their generosity with me is displayed on the pages that follow. I hope that I have represented them well and that people reading these pages learn to love the people in the Marshall Islands as much as I do. To all of my Marshallese readers, I have tried to present an accurate and sensitive account of life in the RMI. But I am sure that there are errors here, and things that I have misunderstood or misrepresented. I deeply apologize for these errors and hope that, if you are willing, you will contact me and tell me about them.

This book benefited from a dedicated and thought-provoking committee at the University of Chicago and a supportive anthropology department at the

University of North Carolina (UNC) at Charlotte. John Lucy sparked my fascination with language and middle childhood. His detailed comments refined my ideas, while his support helped me weather the many challenges of graduate school and fieldwork. Jennifer Cole's insights into ethnographic writing sharpened my prose, and her analysis of youth helped me to think deeply about the relationship between age and culture. Don Kulick's analysis of language socialization and Oceania proved invaluable, and he encouraged me to refine my thoughts and reconsider their implications. Richard Shweder consistently provided support throughout the years and forced me to reconsider my arguments. After the University of Chicago, my department and colleagues at UNC Charlotte encouraged my work and helped me think through the relationship between language, age, and culture. I also spent time at the Institute of Advanced Study in Notre Dame, which allowed me to refine my work. Some of my many colleagues at Chicago, Notre Dame, and UNC Charlotte read or commented on various parts of this book, including Robin Shoaps, Naomi Quinn, Katherine Ewing, Richard Taub, Eugene Raikhel, Bert Cohler, Allison Fasoli, Jacob Hickman, Teofilo Reyes, Julia Kowalski, Les Beldo, Talia Weiner, Jon Marks, Peta Katz, Nicole Peterson, Susan Blum, Tanya Luhrmann, Christine El Ouardani, Eric Hoenes del Pinal, Rebecca Roeder, Elizabeth Miller, Pilar Garcès-Conejos Blitvitch, Lydia Light, Andrea Freidus, Sara Jeungst, and Cecily Garber.

I am also grateful to my series editor Laura Ahearn, the linguistics editors Hallie Stebbins and Hannah Doyle at Oxford University Press, and the three anonymous reviewers who provided detailed feedback. Laura Ahearn read through my work and encouraged me in my writing style, Hallie Stebbins and Hannah Doyle answered innumerable questions and helped me through the revision process, and the advice of the reviewers was invaluable toward refining the final manuscript.

Finally, I thank my family. I am indebted to my parents for supporting me through the trials and tribulations of graduate school and fieldwork. They helped me deal with sicknesses, transported large solar panels over the Pacific Ocean, and put up with only being able to reach me via satellite phone. I thank my husband, Trevor Pearce, for supporting my research, encouraging me when I faltered, and painstakingly editing multiple drafts of the entire book. I could not have done this without him.

Work on this project was supported by funds provided by the Wenner-Gren Foundation (grant numbers 7947, 8924), the National Science Foundation (grant number 0920857), the Lemelson Fund and the Society for Psychological Anthropology, the Notre Dame Institute for Advanced Study, the University of

North Carolina at Charlotte, and the University of Chicago. I presented portions of this work at the American Anthropological Association annual conferences, the Association for Social Anthropology in Oceania annual conferences, and the Society for Psychological Anthropology biennial conferences between 2008 and 2017.

NOTE ON MARSHALLESE LANGUAGE AND ORTHOGRAPHY

Marshallese is a Micronesian language in the Oceanic branch of the Austronesian family (Willson 2008). Unlike some other languages in the Pacific, it is not, at the moment, endangered. All Marshallese people in the RMI learn Marshallese as their first and native language, although this may change if climate change forces a vast emigration from the nation. There are two main dialects that correspond with the two island chains—Ratak and Ralik. These two dialects are mutually comprehensible.

Both Marshallese and English are official languages in the RMI. Many textbooks are in English; English is the language of the high school entrance tests; most people in the government speak passable or excellent English. People also watch English movies. Nonetheless, outside of government settings and school most people do not use English on a daily basis. Some people do not speak English at all, although I suspect that many of them are capable of speaking English but choose not to. Consequently, during my research I spoke to everyone almost exclusively in Marshallese. I did occasionally speak English with some research assistants and government officials in the capital.

Historically, there have been two different ways of writing Marshallese—the orthography used by the previous version of the Marshallese translation of the Bible and the substantially different orthography used by the *Marshallese-English Online Dictionary* (Abo et al. 2018; Bender 1963). In practice, people move back and forth between not only these two orthographies but numerous other (often individual) ones. I have seen words spelled multiple ways within one article in the nation's newspaper, the *Marshall Islands Journal.*

In 2010 the Marshallese government passed the Marshallese Language Orthography (Standard Spelling) Act requiring all government bodies to conform to a single standard orthography, the one set out by the Marshallese-English Dictionary. Following this standard, for the most part I use this official orthography in the recent online version of the dictionary (Abo et al. 2018). However, place-names often depart from this standard, even on maps and papers produced by government agencies. Consequently, I spell the names of atolls as they are typically spelled on maps. In addition, I use the keyboard produced by the Department of Marshallese Studies (2017) at the College of the Marshall Island. Thus, while the dictionary uses the characters ḷ, ṃ, ṇ, ọ and ñ, I have written l̨, m̧, ņ, o̧, and n̄. There are some words that do not appear in the dictionary. I have tried to fit them into the orthography presented here as best I can. I have reproduced the orthography in Table N.1.

Table N.1 Orthography

Orthography	International Phonetic Alphabet	Description
a	[ɑ]	A low back unrounded vowel
ā	[æ]	A low front vowel
b	[bᶭ]	A heavy bilabial stop
d	[ɹ]	A light retroflex trill
e	[e] or [ɛ]	A mid front vowel
i	[i]	A high front vowel
j	[tʸ] or [c]	A light dental stop or affricate
k	[k] or [kʷ]	A velar stop, unrounded or rounded
l	[lʸ]	A light lateral
l̨	[lᶭ] or [lʷ]	A heavy lateral, unrounded or rounded
m	[mʸ]	A light bilabial nasal
m̧	[mᶭ]	A heavy bilabial nasal
n	[nʸ]	A light dental nasal
ņ	[nᶭ] or [nʷ]	A heavy dental nasal, unrounded or rounded
n̄	[ŋ] or [ŋʷ]	A velar nasal, unrounded or rounded
o	[o] or [ɔ]	A mid back rounded vowel
o̧	[ɒ]	A low back rounded vowel
ō	[ə] or [ʌ]	A mid back unrounded vowel
p	[pʸ]	A light bilabial stop
r	[rᶭ] or [rʷ]	A heavy retroflex trill, unrounded or rounded
t	[tᶭ]	A heavy dental stop
u	[u]	A high back rounded vowel
ū	[ɯ]	A high back unrounded vowel
w	[w]	A rounded velar glide
y	[y]	An unrounded palatal glide

Source: Adapted from Abo et al. 2018.

TALKING LIKE CHILDREN

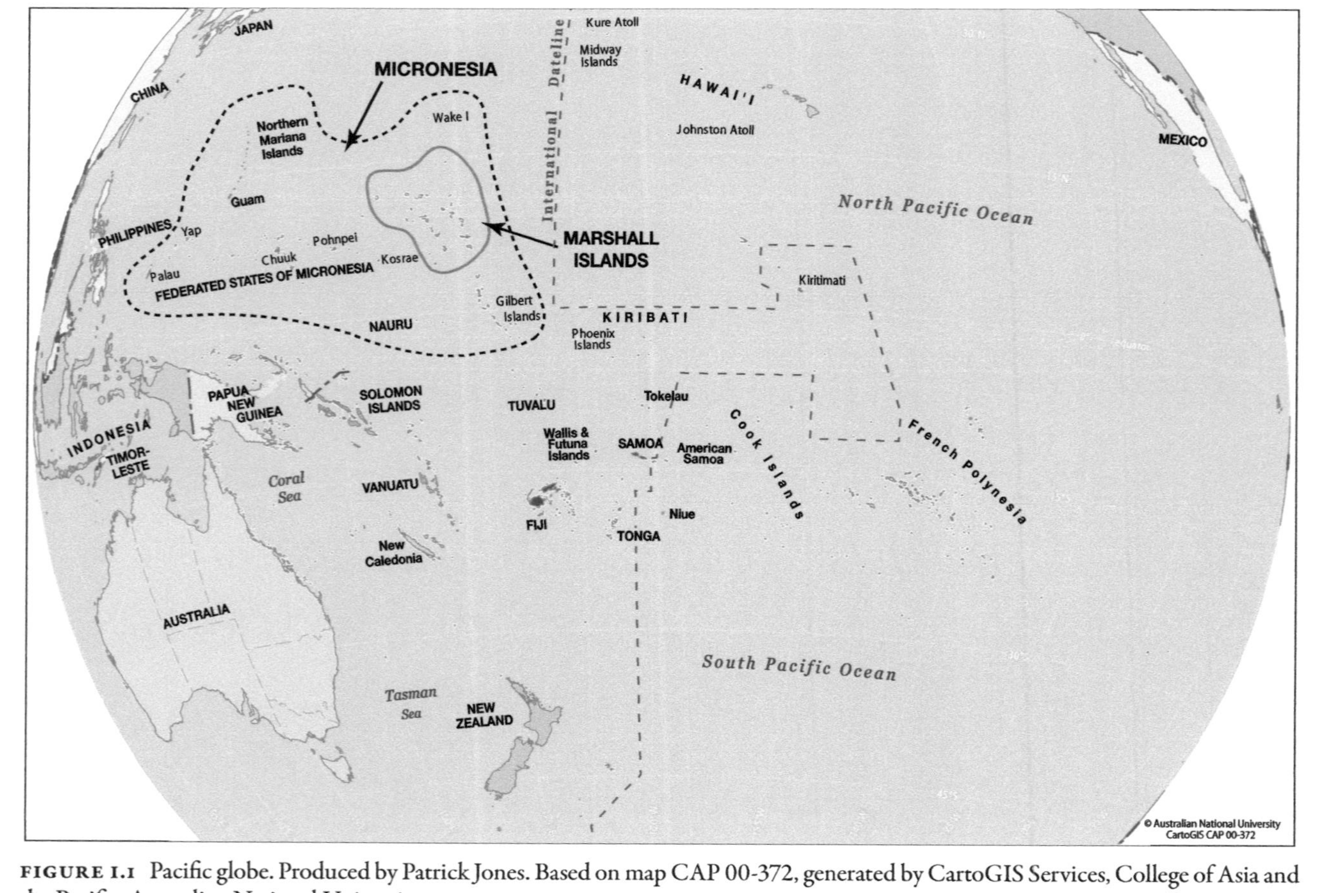

FIGURE I.1 Pacific globe. Produced by Patrick Jones. Based on map CAP 00-372, generated by CartoGIS Services, College of Asia and the Pacific, Australian National University.

INTRODUCTION

BECOMING DIFFERENT

"Mama!" Kori called. "I don't have any pants! I only have a shirt!"

"Go and wear the pants that are in the house!"

"Huh?"

"Go and wear the pants in the house with grandma, because there are pants there! And take grandma and grandpa their food!"

Kori hesitated. "Go there naked?"

"Yes. Walk naked and go and put on your pants."

A couple of minutes later, accompanied by a younger sibling and still lacking pants, Kori started off down the sandy road. He carried a large pink bowl on his head.

Kori lived on one of the smallest human land habitats on earth, a coral atoll. Groups of long, narrow coral islets arranged in a rough oval pattern around a saltwater lagoon, archipelagos of atolls are scattered all across the western Pacific Ocean in an area aptly called Micronesia or "little islands." Within Micronesia lies the Republic of the Marshall Islands (RMI), a nation composed of two atoll chains (see Figures I.1 and I.2). Unlike the large and high islands that characterize much of Polynesia to the south, atolls have no mountains, hills, rivers, or lakes. Averaging only seven feet above sea level, the largest islets in the RMI are a mile square, and the smallest disappear at high tide (see Figure I.3). Added together, these islands occupy around seventy square miles of land, roughly the same size as Washington, D.C. Unlike Washington, D.C., however, the land in the RMI is distributed across 750,000 square miles of ocean (RMI Biodiversity Project 2000, 8–9).

Within the next century, climate change may render the RMI uninhabitable (Australian Government 2011; Barnett and Adger 2003; Rudiak-Gould 2013). For the time being, however, around fifty thousand people live in this independent nation (EPPSO

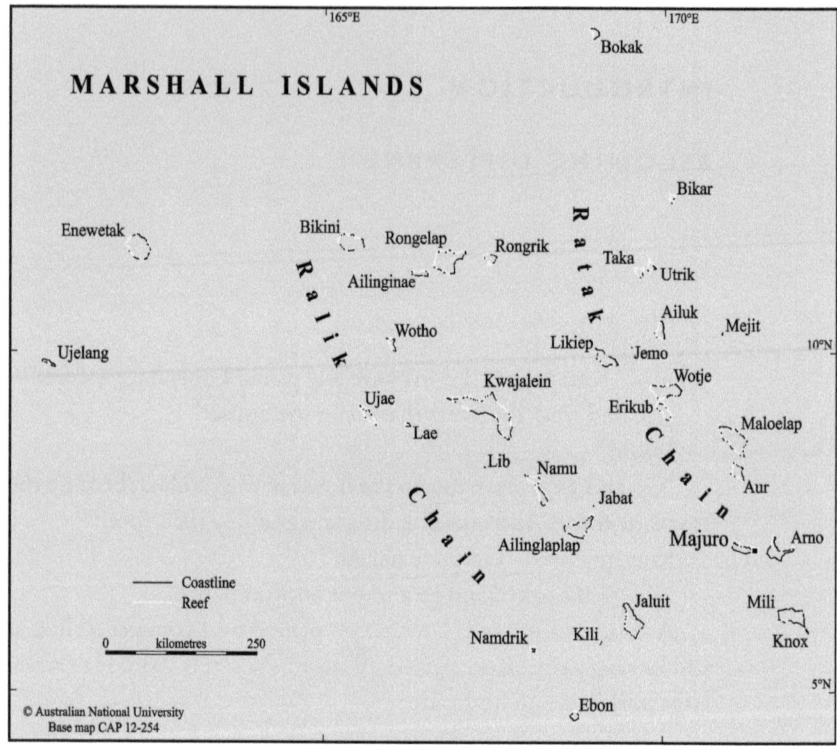

FIGURE I.2 Map of the Republic of the Marshall Islands. Produced by Patrick Jones. Based on map CAP 12-254, generated by CartoGIS Services, College of Asia and the Pacific, Australian National University.

2012). Most residents are indigenous Marshall Islanders, more than half of whom live in two overcrowded urban centers.[1] The rest, like Kori, live in villages located on rural or semirural atolls. In 2009, Kori's hometown, Jajikon, had roughly 250 people. It rested on a sliver of land four hundred yards across at its widest point.

Kori's short two-minute journey to his grandparents' house along Jajikon's single sandy road involved two social faux pas (Figure I.4). The first is obvious: he was half naked. Several women sitting in a nearby cookhouse laughed delightedly when they saw Kori pass by. "They are not wearing pants!" one of the women exclaimed.

His second faux pas was more specific to Jajikon and less obvious: he was carrying food. One of the other women in the cookhouse pointed out the problem: "Those two are carrying a bowl on top of their heads."

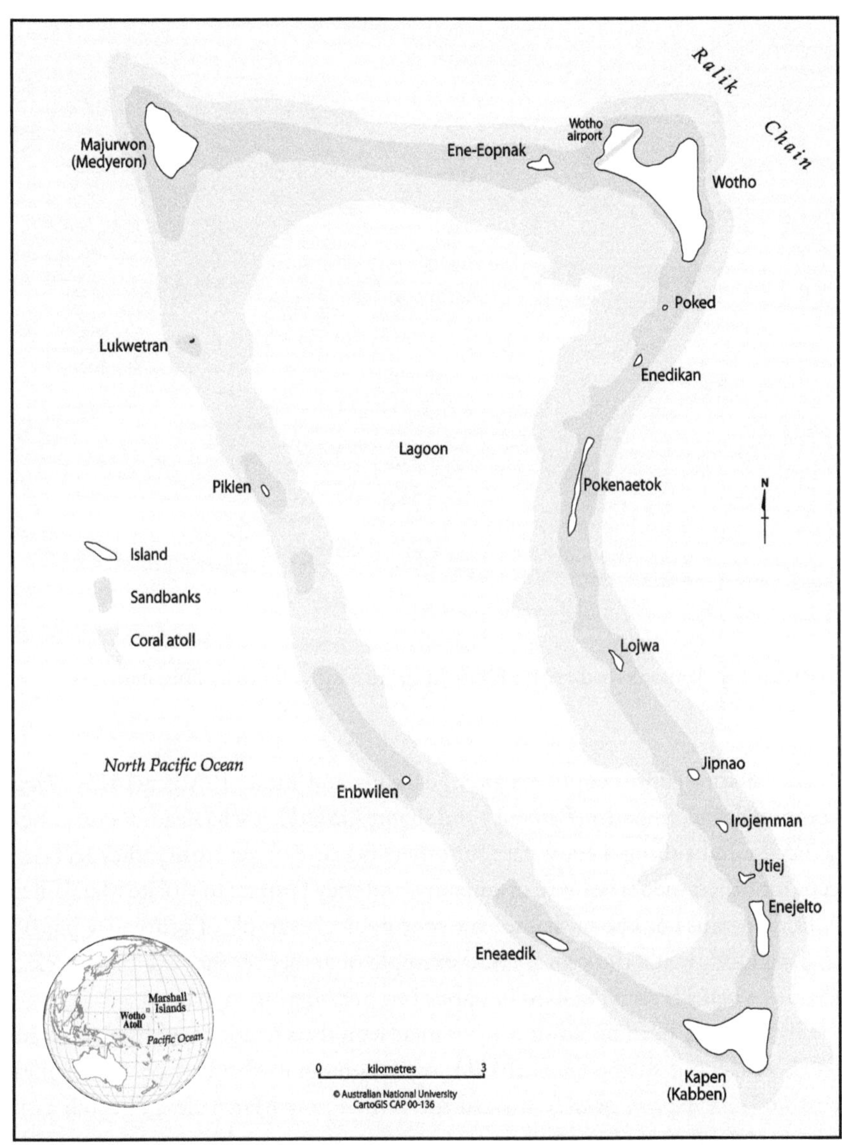

FIGURE I.3 Example of an atoll. Map of Wotho atoll in the northern Marshalls. Some of the areas marked as sandbanks emerge from the water during low tide and retreat during high tide. Map CAP 00-254, generated by CartoGIS Services, College of Asia and the Pacific, Australian National University.

FIGURE I.4 Jajikon's road, with a house in the distance. Photo by Elise Berman.

In Jajikon, good people are *jouj*, generous and kind. This generosity (*jouj*), combined with empathy (*būroṃōj*) and shame (*āliklik*), is what leads moral people to do the right thing. People care for others because of generosity, they feel concern for others' needs because of empathy, and they hesitate to violate Marshallese cultural norms because of shame. The prototypical example of generosity (*jouj*) is sharing food, while the prototypical example of an action that exhibits a lack of shame (*āliklik*) is carrying food in public but not offering to share.

If Kori had been an adult, the women would have criticized him as greedy (*tōr*), as lacking shame (*ñak āliklik*), or as someone who violates Marshallese custom (*ñak m̄antin Ṃajeḷ*). Instead the women, my Marshallese research assistant explained, found Kori's lack of shame not reprehensible but amusing. Kori was a child, after all, and he was supposed to be different from adults. Marshallese children, I was told, "have no shame."

Learning Immaturity and Producing Age

Why not? Why did Kori have no shame? Why was he different from adults?

The rest of this book answers these questions. Most Marshallese adults, and I suspect many readers, would say that children's lack of shame stems from their natural immaturity. Like Kori, Marshallese children constantly did things that their elders avoided. Most adults said that children speak and act differently than adults because they "do not have any thoughts in their brain" and are too "small" to feel shame.

Kori violated adult expectations, however, not because he was too young to do otherwise but because his mother commanded him to do so. Children in the RMI do not naturally disregard adult cultural and moral codes. Rather, they have to learn to ignore them. They are taught to do things that adults avoid: to be rude, inappropriate, and immature. They are socialized to be children who are different from adults.

This book is an analysis of the significance, use, and production of difference in the RMI. Typically, studies of social differences focus on race, gender, or class. I focus instead on another difference that is just as common but less often studied: age. We know, thanks to decades of research, that childhood is a cultural phenomenon and that children in the RMI are different from children elsewhere (James and Prout 1997a; Lancy 2015; LeVine 2007; Rogoff 2003). Scholars, however, rarely study how children learn to be different not from other children but from their elders; that is, few have focused on the interactional production of age itself.

Everyone accepts, of course, that children *are* different from adults. But just as people used to think that racial and gender differences were biologically based, people tend to think of age differences as biologically driven. Some age differences are clearly the result of biological influences: Kori and his sibling were both shorter than the women who laughed at them. Similarly, newly born infants' inability to walk clearly stems from the physical constraints of human infancy. But I propose that other age differences, such as Kori's lack of shame, are at least partly cultural and produced through everyday interactions. As an analogy, consider the supposed feminine characteristic of conciliatory speech (Blum 1997; Moir and Jessel 1991; Moir and Moir 1999). Many believe that biological differences between women's and men's brains create differences in their speech and that women naturally interrupt less, speak more indirectly, and speak more about relationships and feelings than men. However, research shows that gender differences in speech vary across cultures and contexts and suggests that almost all such differences, if they exist at all, are socialized (Cameron 2007; Cameron, McAlinden, and O'Leary 1988; Hyde 2005; Keenan 1974; Kulick 1993).[2] Women and men are not born speaking differently from each other; they learn to be different. I will demonstrate that Marshallese children and adults learn to be different from each other. Specifically, I examine how different people—Marshallese children and adults—and their characteristics—immaturity and maturity—are socially produced.

Everywhere in the world, children do things that their elders do not. By definition, children are people who are not adults. But cross-cultural research on childhood has shown that the nature of such differences can either overlap or vary widely. In much of the United States, children have imaginary friends and believe in fantastic creatures such as the tooth fairy, while elders do not (Clark 1995). In contrast, among the Manus of New Guinea adults talk to and fear spirits, while their children "reject the supernatural in favor of the natural" (Mead 1930, 79). Japanese children ask for things directly instead of indirectly like their elders, while Kaluli children in Papua New Guinea indirectly demand goods by staring at them (Clancy 1986; Schieffelin 1990). Such stares are considered rude, and as Kaluli children grow, they learn to ask directly like adults.

The differences that I discuss, therefore, are particular to the RMI. Moreover, although Marshallese children and adults differ from each other in a number of ways—dress, daily habits, time spent in play—I focus specifically on how Marshallese children and adults in Jajikon differentially use both words and goods. Adults in Jajikon tended to conceal goods that they could not give and use indirect speech to mask requests, refusals, and criticisms. They claimed that they conceal and speak indirectly because of shame (*āliklik*). In contrast, children were more likely to transport food and other goods in public and directly criticize, refuse, and demand things from their peers. All of these differences were contextually specific: adults also occasionally displayed or demanded things, while children sometimes hid food or indirectly refused to give. But the contexts and interpretations of their speech and actions differed. For example, adults often carried food in public to transport it to a feast but avoided displaying a single bowl of food as Kori did. Similarly, children often lied about food in their houses, but when they did so others frequently interpreted them as simply obeying the commands of elders. Indeed, the presence among both children and adults of both revealing and hiding shows that children's displays are tied not to their developmental abilities but, rather, to their social status as children in specific interactional contexts, as well as to the subjective reactions prompted by that status. In similar situations, Marshallese children and adults in Jajikon said, did, and felt different things.

By moving around goods and words, children and adults produced age differences in several ways. First, when children and adults did different things with goods and words, they created symbolic relationships between childhood, adulthood, and specific ways of being, speaking, and giving; they created Marshallese ideas and signs of maturity and immaturity. Second, relative age relationships in the RMI were closely tied to what people said and did with goods. Consequently, when people gave or withheld goods and words, they established who was older and who was younger. Finally, through various interactions, including adults explicitly telling children to do things that adults should not, children learned to speak, act, and feel differently than adults. They learned to be immature.

My analysis of how children and adults produce themselves as different from one another has implications for how anthropologists think about issues as diverse as agency, economics, socialization, and social change. First, children are important social and economic actors in Jajikon not in spite of, but rather precisely because of, their childishness. Children are different from adults and can do different things; they have what I call "aged agency." Children's crucial roles imply that past research on exchange in Oceania, insofar as it ignores children or age, is either incorrect or incomplete, revealing the relevance of age to anthropological theory and ethnography. Second, seemingly paradoxically, children in Jajikon eventually take on mature forms of interaction through doing things that are inappropriate for adults. Therefore, socialization should not be seen as a movement from novice to expert but, rather, as the process of constantly taking on and discarding age specific modes of being and speaking. In other words, socialization is the process of producing oneself as different from others, both those who are younger and those who are older. Finally, cultural continuity and cultural change are often seen as opposed to each other: the former static while the latter is dynamic, the former stable while the latter is constantly shifting. But if we see socialization as a process in which people move through ways of differentiating themselves from others, then cultural reproduction is itself a dynamic form of social change.

Learning about Marshallese Life

I first went to the RMI as a volunteer elementary school teacher in 2003. As a teacher, I found myself confused by many things my students did and particularly by the way they used speech. I decided to return to conduct research. I ultimately found my way to the village I call Jajikon, located on an atoll I call Rōrin. Both are pseudonyms that I use to protect people's anonymity. Rōrin is a southern atoll in the eastern archipelago, relatively close to the capital (see Figure I.2). To protect people's identities, I have also occasionally changed some features of the characters in this book, such as their gender or the number of their siblings.

Although as a teacher I lived in a separate house with several other American teachers, on Jajikon I lived with a family. This living arrangement was both inevitable and purposeful. I had no choice but to live with a family because in Jajikon there is nowhere else to live. At the same time, like many anthropologists, I thought that living with a family would allow me to more fully participate in everyday life. I was right: I eventually became a daughter of my host family, and as a result, I had a kinship relationship with everyone in the village. I will always be thankful to my host family for taking me in and allowing me to study and record them, and I know that I can never pay back their generosity.

The stories I tell here and the words that I reproduce come from observations, audio and video recordings, and interviews compiled over twenty-four total months of living in the RMI and fifteen months of research in Jajikon.[3] Everybody spoke Marshallese almost all the time, including during transcription sessions, although occasionally people would code-switch into English.[4] I spent much of my time with either children or adult women. I followed children around, played with them, and also occasionally attended their classes in school. I helped adult women with their work, sat and talked with them at night, sang with them in church events, and employed several of them as research assistants. Although children did often play by themselves, other interactions were not age-stratified: during meals, work, and simply relaxing at night I often observed and recorded children and adults together. Adult interactions were often gender-segregated, so I spoke with men less frequently. I typically took quick notes during and immediately after interactions and then wrote up these notes as more extensive field notes every night. I carried around an audio recorder and often turned it on when interesting or relevant things seemed to be happening. I also interviewed twenty-five elementary school–age children twice and twenty adults once with two different interview formats: unstructured talk about family and relationships and structured interviews with hypothetical stories to which I asked people to respond. The children drew as they talked, representing their family and friends with crayons and paper.

Finally, building on language socialization techniques of filming focal children (Ochs 1988; Paugh 2012b; Schieffelin 1990), I also filmed eight elementary school–age children once a month for a year as well as twenty-one infants and little children once each. I used both a standard video camera and a smaller video camera that the children could wear on their heads, as shown in Figure I.5. I eventually started using only this head camera because of the freedom of movement it allowed and its less obtrusive nature—children often forgot they were wearing it (Berman 2013). After I put the camera on children's heads, they would run off and go about their lives. After roughly a half hour I would set off in search of them, sometimes finding them in the same place and other times finding them on the other side of the village.[5]

FIGURE I.5 Boy putting on a headband with the video camera. Photo by Elise Berman.

Organization of the Book

Each chapter is focused around a single story that I either experienced or recorded. I move back and forth between the main story, secondary data, and theoretical and ethnographic explanations.

I use this structure for two reasons. The first is rhetorical: people learn through narrative (Miller, Koven, and Lin 2012). I hope to help readers remember the Marshall Islands by engaging them in Pinla's efforts to keep her child, and I hope to convince students of the malleability of age by detailing Jackie's struggle to be young. Anthropological and linguistic data are filled with stories. We can use them to immerse readers in different ways of life, to make the strange familiar and the familiar strange.

The second reason is theoretical. Linguistic anthropologists view meaning not as set in stone but, rather, as coproduced over time and over the course of an interaction (Duranti 1997, 314–21). Through such interactions, people are socialized into and take on cultural practices, forms of speech, identities, and relationships (Ochs and Schieffelin 2012). These identities and relationships are also coproduced, negotiated, and malleable. In the beginning of an interaction people may present themselves as children, while as the interaction goes on they may be reinterpreted as adults. Through telling stories, I show how people coproduce, negotiate, and change their aged identities over time, including over the course of a face-to-face interaction.

The result is a book that may be too narrative for the anthropologist and too analytical for the student, but I have tried to meld the two genres to make both the stories and the theory comprehensible. With the exception of chapter 2, each chapter uses a story to show how people in Jajikon produce different aspects of age through interaction. Chapter 1 tells the story of Pinla's effort to keep her child and also reveals that in Jajikon age is power and power is age. Chapters 3 and 4 contrast adult and child modes of giving and avoiding giving through the story of my comical attempt to go drink soda with a friend in a nearby village and the story of three children's efforts to get a younger boy to share his lollipop. These chapters also reveal the indexical relationships between maturity and indirection, on the one hand, and childhood and directness, on the other, as well as how children coproduce relative age relationships. Chapter 5 tells the story of an alleged incident in which an adult harmed a child—showing that people's status as children or adults affected how others interpreted their words and whether or not harm actually occurred. Finally, chapter 6 focuses on the story of a girl who, given an errand that she felt too mature to carry out, tried to outsource it to younger siblings. In describing her struggle to complete the errand, I analyze in detail the process of socialization and how age is produced.

All of the standard parts of an ethnography are here, but in different places than one might expect. Anthropologists who are looking for the classic ethnographic introduction to the Marshall Islands will find that in Pinla's effort to keep her child, the story that I tell throughout chapter 1. Rather than reporting on Marshallese power structures, kinship relationships, and history, I weave that information into Pinla's narrative. Although I embed theoretical analysis into each chapter, I also have a focused theoretical discussion of age and language socialization in chapter 2: "What Is Age and Where Does It Come From?" Readers more interested in the ethnography of life in the RMI should skip that chapter and move right on to chapter 3. Linguists looking for a description of Marshallese or transcripts of recorded speech will find that information in the "Note on Marshallese Language and Orthography" as well as in the appendix. In the chapters themselves I transform recorded speech into dialogue: single quotation marks (' . . . ') enclose speech that I heard and wrote down in my notes but did not record; double quotation marks (" . . . ") enclose speech that I recorded and transcribed. In the appendix, I include the Marshallese transcripts, with English translations, that are the basis for the stories in this introduction, chapter 4, and chapter 6.

Finally, because chronological age often has little meaning in the RMI, I do not include children's chronological ages. Instead, I describe children's status relationally—as older or younger than others—and as stemming from their height and abilities—such as whether they walk and talk, how much work they do around the house, and where they are in school. Such methods of describing age are consistent with how people talked in Jajikon.

Kori's younger sibling Simpson stood next to him on the road, also pantsless. He tugged at Kori's shirt. Time to go.

Together, they walked down the road.

They had another household to pass before they reached their destination. If they were adults, this would have been a problem. Even fully clothed, an adult would not walk past a crowded household carrying food that should be shared.

But Simpson and Kori were not adults; they were children. They had learned to feel no shame.

Notes

1. The two urban centers are Majuro and Ebeye. Majuro atoll is the capital of the RMI. Ebeye is a small islet in Kwajalein atoll. The largest islet in Kwajalein atoll, also called Kwajalein, has served as a U.S. military base since 1944. Only U.S. citizens are allowed to live on the base itself. The many Marshallese who work on the base, therefore, must commute from Ebeye. The living conditions on Ebeye are substantially inferior to the living conditions on Kwajalein. One of the more densely populated islands in the world, with 46,000 people per square kilometer, Ebeye often lacks clean water, electricity, and good health care, conditions that lead to epidemics of diseases such as cholera (Gorenflo and Levin 1989; McClennen 2007; Yamada and Palmer 2007).
2. In many cases supposed gender differences do not exist at all: for example, the myth that women speak more than men (Mehl et al. 2007). In other cases, supposed gender differences may exist but are often tied more closely to social status than to gender itself. For example, tag questions ("That works, doesn't it?") are often tied more closely to a person's conversational role than to gender. Presenters, teachers, and doctors, whose jobs are to facilitate conversation and get people to speak, use tag questions more than patients and students (Cameron, McAlinden, and O'Leary 1988).
3. I have more than fifteen hundred pages of field notes, thirty-one recorded interviews with adults, fifty-eight recorded interviews with children in middle childhood (two interviews with each child), and more than eighty hours of audio and video recordings of naturally occurring conversations and ritual activities. Forty-two hours of naturally occurring speech and all interviews are transcribed.

4. I worked with local research assistants to transcribe my recordings. My assistants transcribed by hand, I typed the transcription into the computer, and then we listened together and corrected the transcription. In Majuro, bilingual assistants helped me translate difficult sections of some recordings. I also recorded our transcription sessions, as my assistants' interpretations of events helped me to understand much about people's language and their actions.
5. This camera also had some limitations: for example, it filmed whatever the child happened to be looking at, which was not always what I was interested in seeing when I transcribed and analyzed the recordings.

1 "GIVE ME MY CHILD"

AN ETHNOGRAPHIC INTRODUCTION TO THE POWER OF AGE IN MARSHALLESE SOCIAL LIFE

A sharp pain ripped through Pinla's stomach, dragging her to the floor. Marshallese women are so strong-willed that even during labor they rarely make a sound. Or so Pinla's grandmother once told me, the twinkle in her eye reflecting either her joy at pulling my leg or her amused reaction to my account of American women whose screams fill the hospital halls. Regardless, Pinla, only six months pregnant with her first child, needed a hospital. She braved the rough windy-season seas and got on a boat that took her from Jajikon to the capital of the RMI, Majuro (see Figure 1.1).

Like many things in the RMI, Majuro's current nature has been shaped by its history as a U.S. colony. After the U.S. military conquered Micronesia during World War II, they tried to erase any trace of the region's former colonial overlords—the Japanese. (Japan took the islands from Germany during World War I.) The Americans expatriated more than a hundred thousand Japanese nationals, many of whom left behind spouses and children. They also bulldozed any remaining Japanese buildings and built their administrative center on an atoll that had previously played a negligible role in the Japanese government—Majuro. The military then rapidly built cheap, identical wood and metal buildings and began Majuro as it is today—a crowded urban center to which people from around the world and Marshallese from every atoll migrate (Hezel 1995, 251; Poyer, Falgout, and Carucci 2001, 300–301). Between 1944 and 2011 Majuro's population grew from seven hundred to 28,000 people, half the population of the entire nation (EPPSO 2012, 13–17; Mason 1947, 10).

Much of Majuro's population is relatively transient. Like Pinla, people from outer atolls or the United States travel to Majuro for

FIGURE 1.1 Downtown Majuro from the air. Photo by Brian Cowden.

weeks, months, or even years to visit relatives, attend school, or access the hospital. Also like Pinla, many of these more transient residents do not have a house in Majuro. What they do have are relatives. Hospitality—stretching anywhere from a couple of days to a couple of years—is one of the many things that kin give to each other in the RMI.

Pinla found her haven with Terij, her grandmother. An older woman with a round face, a big smile, and an oversized personality, Terij had a well-built house close to the Majuro lagoon.

Pinla lived with Terij for the rest of her pregnancy. I never found out exactly what had ailed Pinla—whether it was preterm labor, a stomach illness, or something else. Whatever it was, due to either access to the hospital or the mere passage of time, on Majuro her condition stabilized. Eventually Pinla gave birth to a healthy baby girl.

Terij and her partner had only one child, a boy. They wanted a girl. Suddenly, an infant girl was in their house. The infant's mother (Pinla) was bound to them through the deference due to elders, the rules of kinship, and the hospitality that Pinla had enjoyed for the last three months.

I do not know the exact words that Terij spoke. Requests for children in the RMI, despite their regularity, are somewhat difficult affairs and tend to take place in private. I suspect, therefore, that people use indirect forms of speech. When people report on such requests, however, they tend to use the same phrase: "Give me my child."

Terij's request was not at all unusual. Family in the RMI regularly ask each other for almost everything—food and flashlights, young pigs and mosquito coils, money and clothing, water and coconuts, labor and hospitality, and infants (Berman 2014a). Adoption (*kaajiriri* or *kōkaajiriri*) is extremely common in the RMI, as it is throughout the Pacific (Brady 1976; Carroll 1970; Carucci 2008; Dickerson-Putnam and Schachter 2008; Roby and Matsumura 2002; Rynkiewich 1976; Walsh 1999). In 2009–10, 90 percent of households in Jajikon included someone adopted in or out. Twenty-six percent of children under fifteen years old in Jajikon were adopted.[1] Contrary to Western expectations that adoption is the last resort of a mother under duress, the majority of these adoptions take place not because birth parents try to give their children away but because their kin ask.

But although Terij's request was not unusual, it was also not destined to be successful. On the one hand, in theory birth parents have an obligation to agree (see also Peterson 1993). As a woman told me, "in Marshallese culture" when relatives say, "Give me my child," people give. On the other hand, people frequently manage to hold onto their children (Berman 2014a). For example, of the nine infants born in Jajikon between 2009 and 2010, kin members asked for at least five of them, but only three were actually adopted. One infant was requested by at least three different people but ultimately given to none of them. Requests such as Terij's are simply the start of often extensive negotiations.

This chapter tells the story of Terij and Pinla's negotiation for this infant girl. Through telling the story, I introduce Marshallese history and social life. Understanding this girl's fate requires understanding Marshallese kinship relationships, economic practices, the power of age, and the way both kinship and age are expressed, negotiated, and created through interaction. As I discuss different aspects of Marshallese society and history, we will see that kin and age relationships not only affected but were themselves transformed by these negotiations for an infant girl. Age is power in the RMI, a power that influenced who ultimately kept this child.

Marshallese Families

Like most people in the RMI, Pinla loved babies. She smothered her young relatives in hugs and affection and grabbed every opportunity to hold a baby in her arms. She tracked babies' eyes, grinning when they laughed as she threw them in the air. She relished giving small children food, one of the main ways that many Marshallese express love. After her daughter was born everything that Pinla said and did indicated that she wanted to keep her infant.

Mothers

Luckily for Pinla, she had an inalienable bond with and claim to the baby. As in many places, the process of giving birth creates a connection between mother and child. Many Marshallese say that this connection comes from not the transfer of genes or blood but, rather, the *bwije-*, the navel or umbilical cord: "The reason there are any men or women at all is because of *bwij*. Life comes from *bwij*" (quoted in McArthur 1996). Pinla passed food from herself to the infant along her umbilical cord during her pregnancy. This sustenance tied the child to Pinla, producing Pinla as her mother.

Symbolically, the umbilical cord ties not only women to their children but also all family members together as well as people to their land and material goods. The umbilical cord (*bwije-*) is the semantic root and symbolic basis of the matrilineage *bwij* and is also related to the term for land, *bwidej*. The RMI, like many places in Micronesia, is a largely matrilineal society (Peterson 2009). Not only nourishment but also inheritance—of land and the goods that rest on or are produced by land—supposedly pass through one's mother, metaphorically along the umbilical cord. Land ownership in the RMI is historically a two-tiered system. First, in theory, members of different matrilineages (*bwij*) have rights to live and work on specific land parcels. On outer atolls, these parcels tend to divide up an island in parallel chunks, thereby giving their dwellers access to the lagoon, solid land, and ocean (see Figure 1.2). Lineage membership and access to the land supposedly pass from mother to child. Second, most land parcels, as well as the people who live and work on them, are under the control of chiefs. Chiefs get tithes—often now in the form of taxes—from the land and grant matrilineages the right to live and work on that land. This chiefly power also often passes through the mother's line. Although historically men have held public positions of power, ideally that power comes from their mothers and sisters and passes on to their sister's children. "These islands belong to women [*an kōrā aelōñ kein*]" because, as people told me, women "give birth" to children (Mason 1947; McArthur 1996, 122; Peterson 2009; Rynkiewich 1972; Spoehr 1949; Stege 2008; Tobin 1958; Walsh 2003, 123). Consequently, however far Marshallese children may roam and regardless of with whom they live, they are always tied to their birth mothers.

Pinla herself was tied to her own birth mother, Lijin. Like many other people in Jajikon, Pinla was adopted (see Figure 1.3). Her case was slightly unusual, at least as Pinla's mother Deina told the story.

"The two of us did not ask [for Pinla], but they . . . they . . . it's like if [I] fill a plate of food and give you your food."

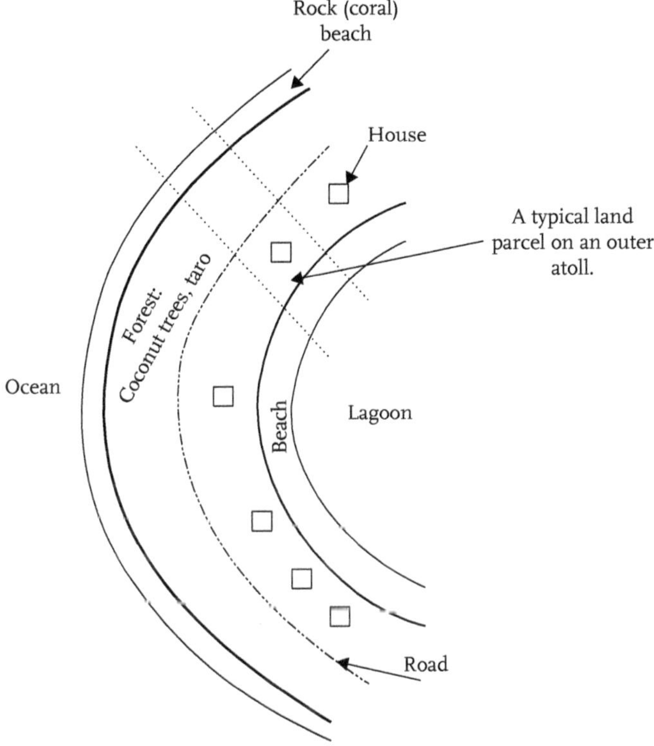

FIGURE 1.2 Typical organization of space in a Marshallese village.

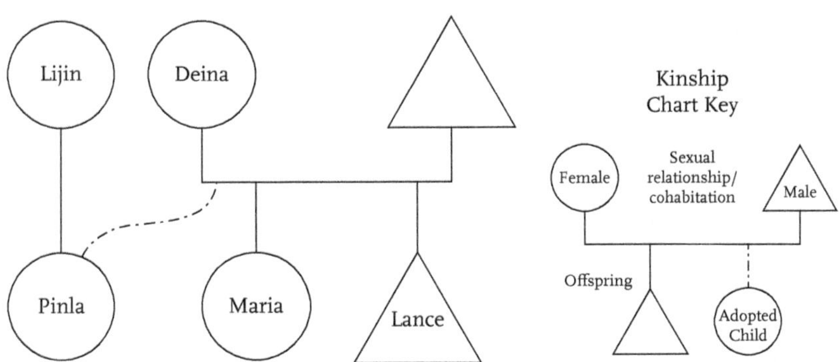

FIGURE 1.3 Pinla's family.

I laughed.

"They shared her with us just like food."

"And why did you take her?"

"Because they asked us to. And we asked our parents, we asked them, and they said it was fine." Other relatives agreed with this interpretation, describing pregnant Lijin as a young and flighty woman who was not ready to settle down. She 'drank too much,' Pinla's brother Lance muttered.

Such stories should be taken with a grain of salt. Younger than Pinla, Lance clearly did not have firsthand knowledge of the exchange. I suspect that if I were to ask Lijin herself (unfortunately I never met her), she would tell a story similar to that of many birth mothers with whom I spoke. These mothers claimed that they gave only under pressure from kin and were terribly saddened by the loss of their child.

Regardless of how the exchange took place, like all parents Lijin never entirely relinquished her rights to Pinla.[2] Birth parents are expected to be concerned with their children's well-being and, by the time these children are grown, to be at least a small part of their lives. A ten-year-old girl's adoptive family lived right next door to her birth mother. She constantly ran between the households; her birth mother often gave her chores that she did not readily give to other nonresident children. A grown woman on Majuro lived with her adoptive parents but occasionally went to visit her birth mother, who lived ten minutes away.

When pregnant Pinla boarded the boat to go to Majuro, Pinla's adoptive sister Maria called Lijin. Lijin was living on Majuro at the time, and Maria thought that Lijin would be concerned for Pinla's health.

Maria was right—Lijin was concerned. In fact, she was so concerned that, as Maria told the story, Lijin met Pinla at the Majuro dock. Then she took Pinla away.

'Why?' I asked.

'She was angry that Pinla was sick,' Maria said.

Illness, according to many Marshallese, can come from a number of different sources: first, dangerous activities such as swimming or eating poisoned fish. Parents regularly told their children not to swim so that they would not get sick. Another source is sadness. "Sickness comes from sadness," a friend told me when I had the stomach flu. If you show your sadness, Maria explained, first you get sick and then you "immediately die." A third source is negative spiritual intervention. This, apparently, is what Pinla's partner thought was the problem. According to two women whom I overheard talking, he said that a ghost came "out of the water and walked toward [Pinla] and entered the window and said, 'Pinla!'" Another source involves poor care. This was Lijin's explanation. Pinla was sick because her adoptive family did not adequately care for her.

If, indeed, Pinla's illness came from poor care, then Lijin had a duty to take Pinla away. Marshallese children are a classic example of Weiner's (1992) notion of inalienable goods that circulate but always belong to their original possessor. Children may be adopted or fostered, and they may live with different relatives and move to different atolls. Now, increasingly, children migrate to the United States. But regardless of with whom they live, children are always tied to those who birthed them. Lijin would always be Pinla's mother.

Similarly, Pinla's new baby was hers and always would be. But the baby was not *only* Pinla's. Quite the contrary, the original ties created by pregnancy that connect children (and land and other things) to mothers spiral out to touch fathers, grandparents, siblings, and other kin. After all, Pinla did not nurture or create her daughter by herself. Nor does anyone create anything themselves, be it the fish men catch, the mats women weave, or the trucks people buy. Many others are involved—people whose work ties them to the things they create.

Fathers

First, there are fathers. One day, around two months before Pinla collapsed in pain and six months before she gave birth, a strange man unexpectedly arrived in Jajikon. Pinla's adoptive mother Deina told me the news.

'Pinla is at grandfather's house with her friend.'

'Who?'

'Her friend.' Deina repeated, confusing me by her subtle use of the word *mōttan*, which frequently marks a nonromantic relationship—common between children of opposite genders but not typical among adults. Deina laughed at my confusion. 'He came to ask Pinla's father to be *koba*. We are really surprised.'

Koba literally means "together" and is a partnership between a man and woman. Becoming *koba* involves no ceremonies or signatures. In the RMI people become *koba* immediately after spending the night together. Or rather, a couple becomes *koba* immediately after spending the night together in a visible way (Pollock 2003, 87). Pinla had clearly slept with someone months before her "friend" arrived in town. But those actions were hidden and never publicly acknowledged. Indeed, even years later Pinla maintained her claim that she had not slept with her friend before he arrived. In contrast to such illicit assignations, *koba* is a visible public statement. The friend's act of spending the night was a sign that communicated, without any need for words or ceremonies, that Pinla's family endorsed their joining. Typically, people become *koba* only when sexual relationships can no longer be hidden—that is, when a woman becomes pregnant.

'Is it okay?' I asked Deina, wondering what she thought about the situation and the new man.

'He has already come, how can I say it is bad?' she responded, revealing the brilliance of the man's ambush. It is difficult to send someone away who has already arrived, especially if the boat on which he came already left.

'What is his name?' I asked Deina.

'I don't know. I haven't talked to him yet.'

Over the next couple of weeks as the man settled into his new household, Deina learned his name: Thomas (see Figure 1.4). She even talked to him once or twice. Introductions take time, and there was no rush. In other parts of the world people talk to newcomers to become comfortable with them. In contrast, in Jajikon people become comfortable with each other and only then do they speak.[3]

This enigmatic stranger is the one who presumably contributed the necessary blood (*bōtōktōk*) that Pinla took and channeled to her child. Symbolically, just as one's matrilineal connections come through the umbilical cord (*bwije-*), one's patrilineal connections come from blood (*bōtōktōk*). Moreover, although in theory both relationships and inheritance pass along the women's line, in practice claims can also pass paternally. These fluid practices are partly the result of historical and geographic variation and partly the result of how kinship and inheritance rules are often much more flexible in practice than in ideology. First, people have always had the right to live on (albeit not inherit) their father's land. Second, on some atolls and within some lineages patrilineal claims have always predominated. Third, throughout history male lineage heads have occasionally transferred land to their children instead of their sister's children, while chiefs have also sometimes gifted land to male lines. Fourth, German, Japanese, and American colonial administrators strengthened the power of some chiefs

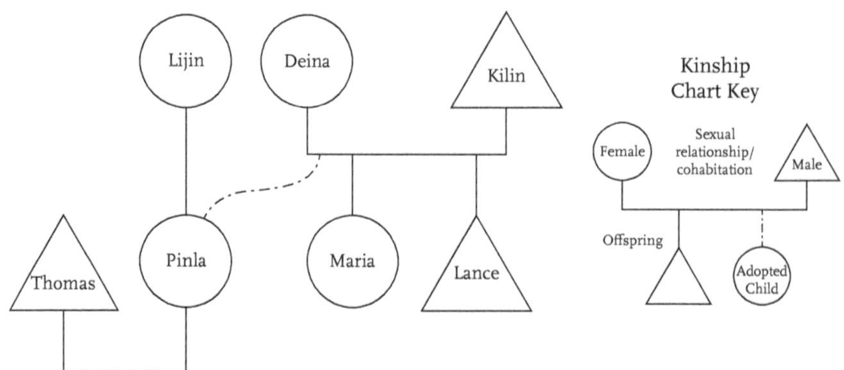

FIGURE 1.4 Pinla's family expanded.

and changed some inheritance rights to patrilineal claims. Finally, urbanization has led to increasing numbers of people renting nonlineage land, while some landowners have formed corporate entities such as those typical in the United States (Carucci 1988, 1997a; Poyer, Falgout, and Carucci 2001, 19; Rynkiewich 1972; Stege 2008, 13–20; Tobin 1958).

Thomas's gifts and labor, however, were more important than the blood he provided. Tall for a Marshallese man, with pockmarked cheeks from either acne or an illness in his youth, Thomas moved into Pinla's household, at which point he also started to work. He went fishing, ran errands, and pounded copra. Mature, hardened coconut flesh dried for hours in the sun or with a fire, copra is the main cash crop in the RMI (see Figure 1.5). In the late 1800s, the RMI was "the richest source of copra in Micronesia and the major trade intersection in the northern Pacific" (Hezel 1995, 45). Now, the global market for copra has plummeted, forcing the Marshallese government to subsidize copra production (Walsh 2003, 82–83). Nonetheless, copra remains the main source of cash for many outer island families. Through making copra, Thomas contributed to Pinla's house and family, producing the child as his own.

FIGURE 1.5 Making copra. The men are removing hard coconut meat from mature coconuts. They will eventually smoke the meat in the apparatus behind them. Photo by Elise Berman.

But Thomas had only minimal connections to the infant. First, according to rumors Thomas was disobedient, was a bad worker, and had a tendency to descend into vice. Thomas joined Pinla in Majuro for a couple of months toward the end of her pregnancy. Apparently in Majuro "he just drinks," a woman criticized, "and doesn't do anything else." "[Pinla's father says]," a second woman inserted, "Maybe [Thomas] hides his profits, to drink." These women implied that instead of working and giving his wages to his new parents as a good subordinate kinsperson should, Thomas hid his money and then used it to buy alcohol.

In these rumors, people painted Thomas as a model of another result of the U.S. colonial empire—idle and drunk Majuro youth. In the Japanese era between the two world wars, Micronesia was economically self-sufficient and had profitable city centers. World War II decimated the islands' economies as well as the Micronesians themselves. People died of starvation or were killed by bombs, others were forced off of their land or into labor by Japanese soldiers, and coconut groves were leveled. After the American military drove out the Japanese, they formed all of Micronesia into what they called the "Trust Territory." Since the United States mainly wanted Micronesia for its strategic location, the government invested not in roads, infrastructure, or the local economy but, rather, in military bases and nuclear weapons testing. Between 1946 and 1958, the U.S. military tested sixty-six bombs in the RMI, including the world's first and largest hydrogen bomb. These bombs had a total yield of 109 megatons. (In comparison, the total yield at the Nevada Test Site was one megaton.) The nuclear fallout that passed over the archipelago led to cancer, deaths, and stillbirths. But these health problems from nuclear testing are only some of the many negative consequences of American colonialism for the Marshallese people. Other consequences include dispossession and starvation, a loss of cultural practices and subsistence techniques, rapid cultural and social change, unemployment, and neglected health, education, and transportation infrastructure. The youthful vagrancy, alcohol abuse, and suicide problems that are widespread in Micronesia's urban centers are a direct result of America's simultaneous exploitation of the atolls, influx of monetary aid, and neglect of their economic and infrastructure needs (Barker 2013; Hezel 1987, 1995; Jenkins and McSwain 2005; Kiste 1974; Lowe 2003, 2016; Mahoney 1974; Marshall 1979; Opie 1991; Poyer, Falgout, and Carucci 2001; Rubinstein 1983; Yamada and Akiyama 2014).

But even if Thomas had been a perfect worker and model son-in-law, he simply had not been around long enough to make the infant his own. As is the case for many new fathers, he had joined the family only a couple of months before the infant was born. Although eventually women and men tend to settle down in permanent relationships, new *koba* arrangements are easily broken. In fact, right before the infant was born, Pinla's parents apparently threatened to break up the incipient partnership between Thomas and Pinla if Thomas "acts badly and wanders around [in search of bad deeds]." Although they did not immediately follow through with their threats, a year later Thomas was gone—whether through Pinla's parents' efforts or for some other reason. Fathers' connections to their children, unlike mothers' connections, seem to need years to accumulate (Pollock 2003). Thomas's few months of giving were not sufficient.

Grandparents and Siblings

Rather than Thomas, it was Pinla's parents—Deina and Kilin—who put a roof over her head, organized food-collecting and moneymaking enterprises, and cooked the food that she ate. It was also Deina and Kilin who decided that Pinla needed to go to the hospital and who called on their extensive kinship connections to find her a place in Majuro to stay.

Deina and Kilin were an established and highly respected Jajikonian couple. They both had Jajikonian ancestors who owned land, and Deina was closely related to a chief who controlled much of Jajikon. They had a large network of close kin who supported each other on Jajikon and numerous children whom they fed and cared for well. Several years ago, Deina and Kilin had been married in a ceremony in a church. Many couples eventually take this step of getting married (often years or decades after moving in together), positioning themselves as older and more respectable, as people worthy of power both in church and in the village as a whole.

Unlike Thomas, Deina and Kilin had fed Pinla since her childhood. For years they clothed her, educated her, and produced her as a woman able to have her own child. But they did not do so on their own. Rather, Deina's and Kilin's own parents and siblings, as well as Pinla's siblings, all helped. They all worked together for years producing food, eating together, and helping each other.

It was all of these interactions that produced Pinla as a person who gave birth to an infant girl. Therefore, even more so than Thomas, Pinla's parents, siblings, and grandparents were possessors of the infant. As was Terij—Pinla's grandmother.

But Terij was not the biological mother of any of Pinla's parents, be they adoptive or birth. The Marshallese kinship system is quite common around the world but, as Figure 1.6 shows, differs significantly from how many Americans and Europeans classify family members. In Jajikon, most people can be classified as a mother, father, child, grandchild, grandparent, or younger or older sibling. This is because, with some exceptions, Jajikonians call everyone in their own generation a younger or older sibling, everyone in their parents' generation a parent, everyone in their grandparents' generation a grandparent, and everyone in their offsprings' generation a child. For example, Pinla called her mother's sister not

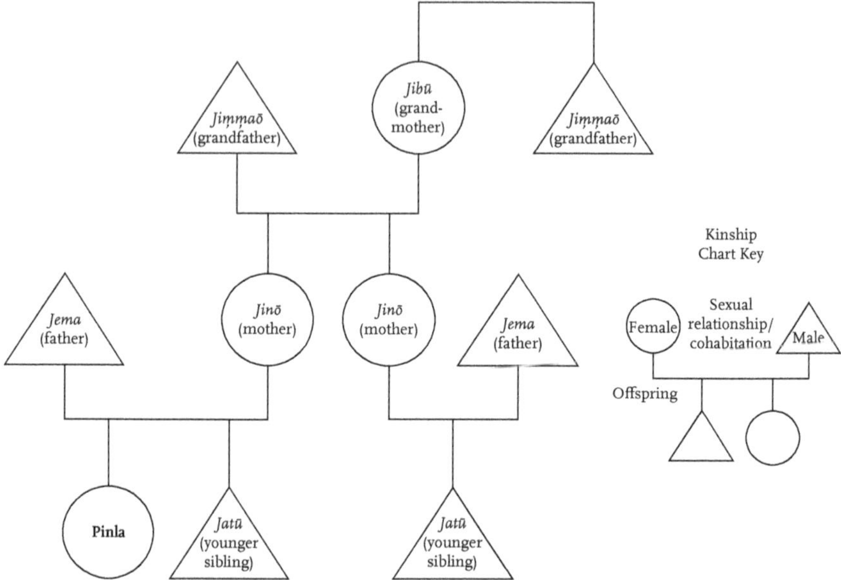

FIGURE 1.6 What Pinla called various family members. The English translation is in parentheses below the Marshallese kinship words.

her aunt but *jinō*, "mother." She called this "aunt's" son not her cousin but *jatū*, "younger sibling." And she called her grandmother's brother *jiṃṃa*, "grandfather." These relationships multiply outward indefinitely. Pinla's cousin's cousin (to use English kinship terms) was her sibling, and that sibling's child was also her child. In other words, Pinla had not just two mothers—birth and adoptive—but many, many more. She also had a constantly increasing number of offspring, innumerable siblings, many fathers, and many grandparents.[4]

One of those grandparents was Terij. Now, however, the situation gets a little murky. Pinla's adoptive grandmother Imon and Terij called each other siblings. But they did not share birth parents. Indeed, no one really seemed to know how Imon's and Terij's ancestors were connected (see Figure 1.7). When I pressed Imon on the subject she eventually resorted to the explanation that their ancestors were "relatives."

The sibling relationship between Imon and Terij—and the grandparent-grandchild relationship between Terij and Pinla—stemmed not from a strict genealogical accounting but from a long history of exchange between the two families. Terij and Pinla's parents helped each other out for years, making Terij a grandparent who could claim the infant. Terij's act of hospitality to Pinla made Terij even more heavily involved in the production of Pinla's daughter. It was Terij's roof over Pinla's head that allowed the infant to come to be, Terij's food

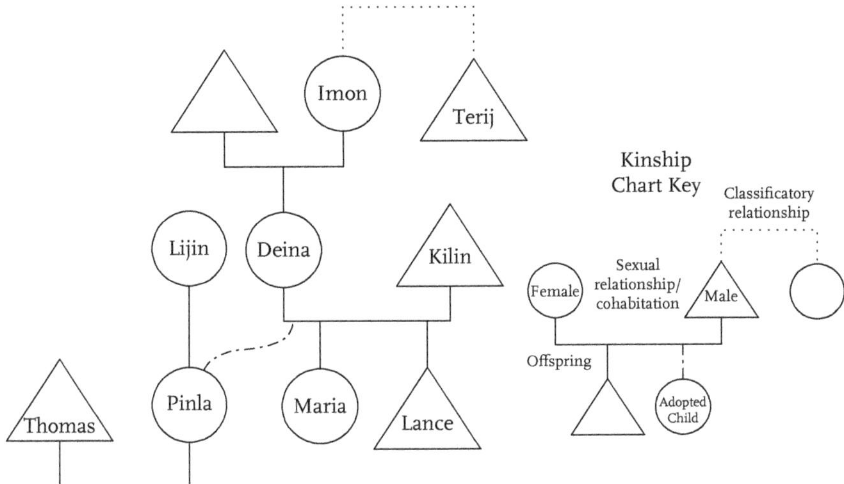

FIGURE 1.7 Imon and Terij's relationship.

that Pinla ate and channeled to the child. These actions helped make the child Terij's own.

Care: Creating Ties

This general premise that care, nurturing, and gifts create ties is an extension of (or the basis for) the bond formed in the womb between mother and child. Giving things, and specifically food, is central to kinship throughout the Pacific and beyond (Berman 2014a; Carsten 1995; Dickerson-Putnam and Schachter 2008; Mauss 1990; Sahlins 1972; Weismantel 1995). In the RMI, adults who care for elders and bring them food take those elders as their parents. People take each other as siblings if they live on each other's land and share food and labor. Infants who nurse together and have shared the same milk are siblings (Carucci 2008; Kiste and Rynkiewich 1976). As one woman who wet-nursed her kinswoman's child said, "I helped them" and then "they gave me my child." Indeed, people can only make sense of others if they incorporate them into their kin network. When I arrived and started living with a family, I became their daughter. They helped me, while I owed them monetary support and obedience. As a result, I also became connected as kin to everyone in the village, such that I had obligations to them and they had obligations to me. Another man, a friend of one of my new brothers, lived in our house for an extended period of time. My (host) mother eventually claimed him as her grandson.

Similar types of interactions connect people to other things that they say cannot or should not be taken away. Physically living and working on land, harvesting fruit, fishing, wearing clothes, or feeding pigs ties people to those material goods. The longer the physical connection, the stronger the bond. Several women told me that although people regularly ask for chicks and piglets, they do not ask for grown animals. As one woman explained, 'People have spent too much time feeding them.' Another woman differentiated pigs from chickens, stating that the pigs require more care and are more difficult to give. Many adults scoffed when I asked whether people request expensive things such as cars or boats. People 'will borrow them,' they said, but they will not take them (although they often forget to return them until pressed).

Finally, there is land. 'Can you ask for someone's land parcel?' I asked a man. 'No!' As another man explained, "I belong to that [*wāto*] land parcel, that *wāto* doesn't belong to me" (quoted in Walsh 2003, 122). Since attachment to land builds up over one's own lifetime and that of one's ancestors, many claim a deeper attachment to their ancestral land than their current place of residence. Two women from other atolls who had married into Jajikonian families told me that they were still *ruwamāejet*, a word defined in the dictionary as "stranger" but which has a deeper connotation of a person who intrudes into an ancestral space (Abo et al. 2018). "I love my island," the national anthem declares: "I will never go away from it, because here is my true place, my heritage forever."

As foreign powers have repeatedly removed Marshallese people from their land over the past two centuries of colonial rule, they have also violated people's identities and well-being. The Japanese relocated many Marshallese when they conscripted them into labor during World War II; Americans booted the residents of three atolls from their land to turn two atolls into nuclear testing grounds and one atoll into an army base; fallout from the nuclear tests made many other atolls uninhabitable; and the lack of infrastructure, schools, and economic opportunities has forced massive migrations to the United States. Finally, in the near future flooding and extreme weather patterns, the result of climate change, may force all Marshallese from their homeland (Rudiak-Gould 2013). There were severe droughts in both 2013 and 2016, and Bikinian refugees on Kili Island (where they were relocated after leaving Bikini atoll for nuclear testing) are already underwater and looking for another new home, potentially foreshadowing the future of the islands as a whole (Kaplan 2015).

Since ties between people (and between people and things) grow up through care, disputes between adoptive and birth parents often revolve around attempts to claim that the other parents' care was inadequate, thus invalidating their status as parents. As we have seen, Lijin tried to justify reclaiming Pinla by arguing that her sickness revealed that Deina and Kilin were poor parents. Adoptive parents are inevitably furious when birth parents reclaim a child, often citing their own labor and investment in the child as a reason why the child is theirs. 'I fed her and fed her,' Deina exclaimed when Pinla's birth mother took her away. 'And now that she is grown she takes her back?' Maria, Pinla's sister, agreed. 'She did not watch over her,' she said about Lijin, and so she should not take her.

Pinla herself seemed to agree that the labor and investment of her adoptive family tied her to them. A week or two after Pinla arrived in Majuro she ran away from Lijin and back to Terij and her adoptive family. Not all adoptive children do the same. Some choose to stay with their birth family; others run away from their adoptive parents of their own accord. But many adoptive children also feel too attached to their adoptive family to leave. "She is not my mother," one adopted ten-year-old said about her birth mother, claiming her adoptive parents as her own.

Labor, care, and the exchange of material possessions bind people to each other and make another's things one's own. Pinla and Terij were tied to each other, which means that Pinla's child was also Terij's. Moreover, if Terij took the infant in for long enough, the child might eventually refuse to leave.

Negotiations: Manipulating Speech and Space

Pinla's child was both hers and all of her kin's. Consequently, who would get the child was up for negotiation.

In this negotiation, Pinla did have some advantages. These stemmed not from her genetic connection to the infant but, rather, how the physical facts of pregnancy transform interaction (Berman 2014a).[5] Before birth Pinla carried the infant in her stomach; after birth, like most mothers, she nursed her for the first couple months (Gammino, Gittelsohn, and Langidrik 2007). During these times her infant was literally inalienable and under Pinla's physical control. If no one said anything, Pinla would keep the child. If anyone else wanted her, they would have to ask.

Asking and Shame

But in Jajikon, as in many other places around the world, asking is difficult (Brown and Levinson 1978). As one woman explained, and seventeen other adults whom I asked agreed, sometimes she was "ashamed [*āliklik*] to ask; it's like I am scared [*mijak*] to ask." This emotion, *āliklik*, is both similar to and different from the English emotion "shame." Like shame, *āliklik* is a public emotion and comes from the potential for external judgment (Addo and Besnier 2008; Fajans 1983; Lo and Fung 2012; Rosaldo 1983; Shweder 2003; Strathern 1975).[6] Unlike shame, *āliklik* refers not to one's subjective feelings but to people's actions (Besnier 1990; Irvine 1990; Lutz 1982, 1988).[7] When people say that they are *āliklik*, they do not mean that their hearts flutter or cheeks redden but, rather, that that they refrain from doing something wrong. *Āliklik* is what stops people from doing inappropriate things. Hence, one bilingual Marshallese-English speaker translated *āliklik* as "hesitate."

People sometimes view asking as inappropriate because asking is often the opposite of generosity (*jouj*). Asking serves to take rather than give; it represents a concern for one's own welfare rather than a concern for others. As one man explained, "If it were me and I had food, I say, 'Come and eat.' It's not you; you don't ask on your own, 'Ah, just give me this thing and that thing.' That is bad." Another woman pointed to the fact that she did not ask as an example of her moral superiority. "You see," she asserted, "even if it is for us, we don't ask." In contrast with these depictions of moral restraint, people often criticized those who ask too much as "lazy" or "insistent beggars" (*akweļap*) who lack "shame" (*āliklik*). In "Marshallese culture if you eat [at someone's house] and then you leave, the person with whom you were eating talks [about you]. If you hear [what they said], now you are scared to go and eat again and you are ashamed [*āliklik*]."

Quite reasonably, therefore, people hesitate to ask. Those who can get something without having to ask—like Pinla—have a clear interactional advantage in efforts to keep a child. All Pinla had to do to keep her infant was stay silent and hope that everyone else did the same.

Minimizing the Danger of Requests

But Pinla's claim to her child was transient, limited, and unreliable. It was her and others' silence that allowed her to keep her child, a silence that acted as an implicit agreement that the infant was hers. Terij broke that silence. She asked. By definition Terij was *not* ashamed.

Why not? There are several potential reasons. While all these reasons are specific to this situation, in different contexts these reasons help explain why, despite the dangers involved, people in Jajikon asked for things all the time. First, people could make requests less obvious, and less dangerous, by manipulating their form. Although I do not know the exact words Terij used, in chapter 3 I will show that adults frequently use various forms of indirect speech when asking for things.

People also often use the first-person possessive in requests, emphasizing their communal claims to infants and minimizing their *āliklik* (shame). "Give me my daughter [*nejū leddik*]," Siana reported she said when she asked to adopt her infant. "Go and say that Hukira should give me my gum [*kijō bwil*]," Imon said to a young man whom she commanded to ask for gum. "Give me my food [*kijō*]!"

a child demanded of his friend. This use of the first-person possessive is the only grammatically correct way to possess something in a Marshallese request. People would be confused if one were to say, as one would in English, "Give me some of your food." Nonetheless, the first-person possessive is still a choice since one could avoid marking possession at all. For example, a child running an errand said to a woman, "Give me the mosquito coil [*letok kōn̦am̧n̦am̧ eo*]." Consequently, people who choose to use the first-person possessive put linguistic pressure on others to give by indicating that the infant or good is already theirs.

Second, people often find it easier to ask things of those who are close to them. Explained a woman, "People who are your friends, your family, you are not ashamed [*āliklik*] to ask them for things . . . [but] with other people, you are ashamed [*āliklik*]."

Third, some people, such as Terij, are better at asking than others. Despite the above sentiment, some were still "ashamed" even "if they are really our relatives." But Terij was a particularly outspoken woman. During one meal with her family Terij teased me for lacking a Marshallese boyfriend, argued that I was not properly assimilating into Marshallese culture because I declined kimchi (a non-standard food in the RMI), and spent several minutes violating gender taboos by speaking about farting in front of male kin. The people in the room started laughing. 'She is bad!' Terij's partner exclaimed. Pinla and Deina called Terij a *bukarar*—a person who is willing to cajole other people into doing what she wants. Imon called her an *akwel̦ap*, an insistent beggar who does not take no for an answer.

Finally, some organizations of the physical environment can make it easier to ask. Specifically, when people see goods out in public that are clearly available, then they are more likely to ask for them. This is because things that are seen must be shared. Hence, the prototypical example of shame (*āliklik*), numerous people told me, is when people walk with food that they do not give: "If the rice is cooked, and you are carrying it on a plate, you are ashamed [*āliklik*] because you need to say, 'Eat!' " It is not the act of failing to share that creates shame but, rather, the act of being seen with things that one does not share. The public witnessing of signs of possession creates a profound affective responsibility to give while also diminishing people's hesitation to ask.

All of these different elements may have converged and influenced Terij's request. She may have asked indirectly and used the first-person possessive. Terij's inhibitions may have also been mitigated by her close relationship with Pinla as well as Terij's outspoken personality. Finally, the infant was in Terij's space, in her house. In a way, therefore, the child was already hers, giving Terij a claim over the infant and possibly removing the shame of asking.

The Danger of Refusing

But 'Pinla,' Imon told me, 'did not want to give.'

'So did she say no?'

'Of course not,' Imon scoffed.

Once a request is made, it is difficult to refuse. "Everybody in the world knows," a man told me, "that it is very hard to directly say no." Refusing embarrasses the asker and reflects negatively on the refuser. Adults feel "ashamed [*āliklik*] to say, 'Sorry, we have just enough food for our family,' " a woman explained, because such speech "embarrasses [*kajook*]" the other person. People also frequently criticized those whom they perceived as refusing to give. "That's how bad she is!" a woman exclaimed about a family member who apparently filled up her house with so many things that she had no space to give hospitality to her kin. "I say that woman is bad, is it true that she is a bad woman?"

"Yes," another person agreed. "Just think about the first birthday [*keemem*] of her oldest son." These first birthday parties are elaborate public feasts hosted by the child's family. During and before the feast people can also "claim" (*tōptōp*) goods from the family. When one little girl turned a year old, older children claimed all of the family's piglets, while women asked for the birthday girl's dress, shoes, and underwear. Their family was "wiped out," the birthday girl's mother told me with both exhaustion and pride.

In contrast, the "bad woman" was "really stingy with everything."

"That's right girl!"

"She hated it when people claimed things."

Through giving—or at least not refusing—people present themselves as good people who have the appropriate emotional reactions in a given social situation. These reactions include not only *āliklik* (shame) but also *būroṃōj* (sadness, grief, empathy). People often use the word *būroṃōj* to refer to people's grief when a kinsperson dies, their sadness when giving a child away, and the empathy that compels them to give.[8] For example, a storeowner said that he let people buy on credit because he was "empathetic" (*būroṃōj*) for them and their need for money. A woman whose child was adopted explained that she "was empathetic [*būroṃōj*] and gave because they want a child."

This need to portray oneself as empathetic makes it difficult for people such as Pinla to avoid acceding to a request. As with shame, people determine that others are empathetic from their actions. People who give when others ask or need something are empathetic. People who do not give are, by definition, not empathetic. It is impossible to refuse and be a good person: that is, someone appropriately filled with shame and empathy.

So once people like Terij make requests, those requests force a response. They change the status quo, transferring the balance of power away from people such as Pinla—those with physical control—and toward the person who asked. After Terij's request, Pinla had difficulty saying no.

The Power of Age

'Because,' Imon continued, explaining why Pinla could not refuse Terij, 'she is her mother.'

I paused for a moment. 'No,' I ventured, working through the relationships in my head, 'she is her grandmother.'

Imon looked at me. After a couple of seconds, she nodded. 'Her grandmother,' she affirmed.

Imon's movement between mother and grandmother was, I suspect, an example of how kinship relationships are not set in stone. It was clear that Terij and Pinla were kin and that Terij was in an older generation. But the specific name that people put to that relationship may change.

Regardless, Terij was Pinla's elder. This status as her elder made even an oblique and indirect refusal virtually impossible. For example, a woman explained her fear of asking an older relative to reciprocate for some cigarettes she had given him by stating, 'He is old[er].' As was the case for this woman, Pinla's youth made her speechless, albeit to varying degrees depending on whose story one believes. Pinla and Deina told me that Terij directed her request not to Pinla but to Pinla's mother Deina, who also lived with Terij during the last three months of Pinla's pregnancy. In doing so, Terij recognized Deina as the possessor of the infant, Deina as the person who had to speak, and Deina as the person responsible for holding onto the infant or giving her away. According to Imon, Terij did ask Pinla. But even in Imon's version, Pinla could not speak. She redirected the request to someone older, her mother.

But 'Deina could not say no either.' Imon threw a bundle of leaves into the pile behind her. Deina may have been older than Pinla, but she was still younger than Terij. Deina had no real ability to challenge Terij. Particularly 'because,' Imon continued in a resigned and accusatory tone of voice, 'Terij is an insistent beggar [*akweḷap*].'

'What did you say?' I asked Deina when I spoke to her about the interaction.

Deina shrugged. 'What was I supposed to say?' Lacking the power to oppose her elder, Deina sent the request further up the chain of command, to Imon, her own mother and Terij's older sister. 'Only I,' Imon declared expansively, 'can say no to Terij.'

I suspect that Pinla experienced her mother's and grandmother's protection as a relief rather than as a loss of voice.[9] In general, people prefer to delegate difficult speaking tasks to someone else. Parents and grandparents are supposed to fulfill such roles, just as children are supposed to defer. Such is the contract forged between the more and less powerful, a contract central to relationships of age.

Relationships of Power

Like everything else in the RMI, this contract is built on the mutual exchange of goods. Those with more power in the RMI supposedly have more things and an obligation to give generously. In turn, those with less power are supposed to defer to those with more, which entails obeying their commands and giving when asked.

Power in the RMI comes from five main sources: traditional lineage, church status, elected authority, material wealth, and age. These sources of power can be distinct. Some people are elders but not chiefs, while others are church leaders but not elected officials. In practice, however, powerful people often have multiple sources of authority. For example, many church leaders are also chiefs. People age into their roles as lineage leaders. Members of chiefly lineages have a disproportionate amount of political power in the RMI government. In the RMI's bicameral parliamentary government, elected officials supposedly hold the most power. The upper chamber is composed of twelve high chiefs but is supposed to be merely an advisory body. The senators elected to the lower chamber are the ones who actually make laws and decisions. But in practice, senators themselves also often are chiefs or chieftesses. Since the president of the RMI is elected by and selected from the legislature, chiefs and chieftesses have a significant amount of power in both the executive and legislative branches. The first Marshallese president was the son of a high chief and a chieftess from the two main atoll chains. Never voted out of office, he ran the country for twenty years, until his death in 1999 (Walsh 2003, 218–34).

Just as many elected leaders are chiefs or chieftesses, many of these leaders are also wealthy. Chiefs' numerous sources of wealth include tithes from the land that they control (in the form of copra taxes) and rent paid by those who live on their land. Among elected officials who are not chiefs or chieftesses themselves, many come from wealthy families who have historical connections to colonial powers or the church. For example, the current president is a member of an influential family elevated by foreign missionaries (Walsh 2003, 357; 2018). The first commoner president of the RMI was a resident of Bikini atoll, one of the sites of American nuclear testing.[10] In 1986, as part of a Compact of Free Association negotiated between the United States and the RMI, the United States agreed to pay some meager reparations for the harms caused by nuclear testing.[11] Under the agreement, some of this money goes only to the residents, and their descendants, of four atolls that the United States deemed affected by radiation. This restriction unfortunately means that many people negatively affected by radiation—including Marshallese workers sent in to clean up irradiated atolls, residents of additional atolls who experienced nuclear fallout, and people with land rights on the four specific atolls—have received no compensation (Barker 2013). The restriction of some funds to residents of four atolls also altered the balance of power in the archipelago by making members of those atolls wealthy relative to other Marshall Islanders, potentially leading to the election of a Bikinian commoner as president in 2003 (Barker 2013; Hezel 1995; Kiste 1974; Niedenthal 2001; Walsh 2003, 40, 342).

People with power, regardless of the source, have an obligation to be particularly generous and benevolent. It is much worse, several people told me, if chiefs and church leaders fail to give than if commoners fail to give. As a chieftess emphasized, "A true chief is very generous" (quoted in Walsh 2003, 118). People also regularly ask chiefs and chieftesses, elected leaders, and wealthy people for help with big expenses such as plane tickets or funerals. In turn, candidates for political office throw lavish feasts to try to get elected. "It was open season!" one candidate declared: "The day I announced my candidacy I came home to find people waiting for me by the backdoor, asking for money, food—you name it!" (quoted in Walsh 2003, 308).

While powerful people have an obligation to be particularly benevolent, less powerful people must defer to the more powerful through obedience, silence, and gifts. This means that opposition to elected leaders is often either subdued or indirect. For example, a senator once defended himself from another's criticism through discussing the fact that he, himself, did not criticize others. His statement both marked him as morally good for restraining himself from speaking against someone else and implicitly reprimanded the other person for speaking out. This response highlights how silence and obedience are valued while outspoken objections are not (Walsh 2003, 302–3).

In addition to obedience and silence, lower-status people defer to those of higher status through public displays of giving. Although people often greet foreign visitors, public officials, and traditional leaders with lavish gifts, the main venue of such public displays of giving is the church, while the main recipients are high-ranking church leaders. Marshallese identity today is virtually synonymous with Christianity. This process began in 1857, when two American Protestant missionaries arrived in the Marshalls (Hezel 1983, 201). Although historically most Marshallese have been Protestant or Catholic (but mainly Protestant), today dozens of different denominations and churches flourish within the nation.

While these denominations do differ slightly, they are also similar in many ways, including their emphasis on public giving. For example, in all denominations people greet newly arriving pastors with songs, dances, and huge baskets of food. Age-graded committees within a particular church—such as the youth group or the women's circle—regularly put on programs in which they sing, provide food for the whole congregation, and line the church with material wealth such as towels, soy sauce, rice, and handicrafts. This wealth goes to the hands of the pastors. The climax of these displays of public giving is Christmas (Carucci 1997b). On Jajikon, Christmas is a daylong series of performances in which group after group sings, dances, and gives money and goods. In 2009, the ministers of one Jajikonian church received $4,000, a stunning sum given by people who regularly lack two dollars to buy a can of tuna.

These displays of giving, as well as tithes to church leaders, reflect how Christianity has been transformed in the Marshallese context (Allen 2002; Rudiak-Gould 2010). Indeed, although people often see traditional Marshallese and Christian customs as in conflict with each other, on the subject of giving the two traditions supposedly converge. As a minister explained to me, "Our old customs and the gospel are the same . . . because [in both] there is a lot of watching over each other, loving each other, feeding each other, helping each other. If they build a house, everyone contributes." In many ways, church leaders have taken chiefs' place as emblems of benevolence and power. People give exorbitant amounts to church leaders, while they used to tithe to chiefs (Allen 2002, 105). Like chiefs, church leaders are supposed to be particularly benevolent, the caretakers of their people. At the same time, however, many church leaders are themselves chiefs, again demonstrating how different sources of power in the RMI converge and how all are based on the mutual exchange of goods.

Relationships of Age

Although any given interaction may or may not involve any of these power asymmetries, most interactions involve age hierarchies (Carucci 1997b, 70). Not only are no two people exactly the same in age, but most kin relationships directly mark relative age. For example, in Marshallese siblings are distinguished by not gender but birth order with the words *jei-* (older sibling) and *jat-* (younger sibling). Age also intersects with all the other forms of power, as people age into leadership roles in traditional lineages, the church, and politics.

As in other relationships of power, the more powerful—elders—are supposed to be both wealthier and more generous. "It is said, according to the beliefs of the Marshallese," a man told me, "that the oldest . . . is generous. He or she will be more generous than the people who are younger [younger siblings]." Good parents, many people told me, feed their children. A woman praised her father as "generous" because he gave her money and food when she asked for it. She contrasted her father with her mother, who failed her parental duties since she always said "wait" and did not give.

Youth must defer to their elders. Such youth control less wealth because, as one person said, "they are younger." Children and youth also work for their parents' households, their labor almost entirely under the control of elders until they move into their own household (which may or may not ever happen). Even then, elders can command labor and gifts. "She is old[er]," a woman said about her kinswoman, explaining why she was making handicrafts for her. Another woman did not want to give her son away to her mother but said she could not refuse. This elder-younger hierarchy prevails at all levels of difference, albeit to varying degrees. "Go and bring my backpack from over there," a ten-year-old boy commanded his six-year-old neighbor, who ran off with alacrity. "Younger sibling!" some children teased as a boy burst into tears, unhappy that the very kinship term *younger sibling* meant that he had to obey. When people grow old their children take care of them, look after them in the hospital, and eventually bury them. Some of the reasons people want children, many told me, is to have people to help in their work, as well as companionship and care in their old age.

Malleable Hierarchies and Negotiated Relationships

In theory, youth defer, obey, and give not only to repay a lifetime of care but also because elders really do know best. Many years ago, a famous Marshallese story goes, before canoes had sails, there lived Lōktañūr, a woman with many sons. The sons grew up and built canoes. They decided to race, agreeing that whoever reached the eastern island first would be chief. On the day of the race, Lōktañūr approached her sons with a large bundle in her arms.

"Take me aboard," she said to her eldest.

"Ride in Mājlep's canoe," he responded, fearing that her bundle and weight would slow him down.

"Take me aboard, Mājlep."

"Ride in Ļōbōl's canoe."

"Take me aboard, Ļōbōl."

"Ride in Jāpe's canoe."

Lōktañūr approached each of her sons in turn, and each rejected her. Finally, she came to her youngest. "Take me aboard, Jebrọ."

"Come, my mother," Jebrọ said. "Ride!"

Lōktañūr boarded her youngest son's canoe. Then, as her other sons paddled fiercely away, she unpacked her large bundle and showed Jebrọ how to build a sail. The wind at their backs, Jebro̧ and his mother quickly passed his older brothers. Jebro̧, the youngest son, became chief (story as told in Tobin 2002, 56–62).

This story reveals that power—should it come from age, noble status, or another source—is not only ascribed but also achieved (Sahlins 1963). Power entails responsibility. Anyone who shirks those responsibilities should no longer have power. Becoming a chieftess or chief used to depend not just on one's lineage but also on gaining the goodwill of one's people by generously providing for them (Rynkiewich 1972, 81–82). A chieftess claimed that a laywoman was really a chieftess because "many people recognized her selfless generosity" (Walsh 2003, 122). When Lōktañūr's eldest son disrespected his mother, he rejected hierarchy and duty, revealing that he should not actually be the chief or have the authority typically afforded to the eldest son.

According to this logic, it is not age that leads to generosity but, rather, generosity that leads to age and the authority associated with it. For example, one woman told me that God might punish selfish people by making them younger siblings. But generous people, a man told me, become older siblings: "God made him or her the oldest so that he or she will be generous and good to people." Parents who fail to appropriately care for their children may lose those children, either by others reclaiming them or by the children themselves running away (Berman 2014a). People who fail to be generous may lose their status as parents and the power entailed by that status.

Relationships between the United States and the RMI model this malleable nature of hierarchy and power (Walsh 2003, 192–217, 343–76). When the U.S. army captured the RMI during World War II, they handed the starving Marshallese crackers, canned food, and candy (Poyer, Falgout, and Carucci 2001). Since offering food is the prime mode of demonstrating *jouj* (generosity) and rightful power, these U.S. soldiers unintentionally positioned the United States as a benevolent elder or chief (Walsh 2003, 202). But although the United States took on the role of a benevolent provider and protector, ever since the nation took control of the archipelago it has betrayed its duty. As just a couple of examples of how the United States has failed, the nation moved numerous Marshallese populations off of their native land; ignored these populations as they starved on new atolls unsuitable to human habitation; contaminated many atolls with nuclear fallout, refused to give reparations to many affected residents and used Marshallese people in nuclear medical testing without consent; failed to invest in Marshallese education, health care, or transportation; and created a simultaneous malnutrition and obesity epidemic through providing packaged food as aid and transforming the Marshallese diet (Barker 2013; Gammino, Gittelsohn, and

Langidrik 2007; Gittelsohn et al. 1998; Gittelsohn et al. 2003; Hezel 1995, 272–73; Niedenthal 2001, 180–81; Yamada and Palafox 2001; Yamada and Palmer 2007). In addition, after providing all public services for forty years during the Trust Territory period, the U.S. government then completely withdrew all support, and the public infrastructure collapsed. Many in the RMI view the United States as an "ineffective coach, inattentive chief, and lazy and indulgent parent" (quoted in Walsh 2003, 373). "It's like we were asking the US if they could adopt us," one woman explained, "and like [they] have a baby and saying, 'ok, here's your milk, here's your bottle, now you take care of it.' And then not following up with it" (quoted in Walsh 2003, 370). Some argue that the United States, like other elders and chiefs who fail to provide, has lost its right to power and should step down (Walsh 2003).

If actions lead to power as opposed to the other way around, and age is power, then age is something not simply assigned by nature or the passing of time but, instead, achieved through action. In such a system, people's relative age relationships should be malleable, something produced through interaction. And, indeed, in some ways they are. For example, consider Deina and Terij. Who is older? One potential way to answer this question would be to compare their chronological ages. But people in Jajikon rarely invoke chronological age to explain relationships. Moreover, like many people Deina did not know her chronological age off the tip of her tongue. Another way of assessing Deina and Terij's relative age relationship would be to compare birth order. But anyone who was not present when both Deina and Terij were born would not necessarily know their birth order. Imon may remember, since she gave birth to Deina. Most other people, however, have to rely on Imon's authority. A third way of evaluating their relationship would be to consider generational age—Whose mother was older? Here again, we must rely on Imon's authority. Imon claimed that she was Terij's older sister, but no one, Imon included, could detail the exact relationship between Imon's and Terij's ancestors. Finally, although Imon seems to be the main authority on Terij and Deina's relative age relationship, Imon herself discussed Terij's relationship with the family in several different ways (see Figure 1.8). Imon told me once that Terij was her younger sister, which would make Terij Pinla's grandmother and Deina's mother. But Imon also told me that Terij was Pinla's mother, a claim that would put Terij and Deina into the same generation. From a generational standpoint, moreover, if Deina and Terij are members of the same generation, then Deina could be older than Terij since Deina's mother, Imon, is supposedly older than Terij's parents.

Until this negotiation for Pinla's child, I myself always assumed that Terij was a member of Deina's generation as opposed to Imon's. Like Deina (and

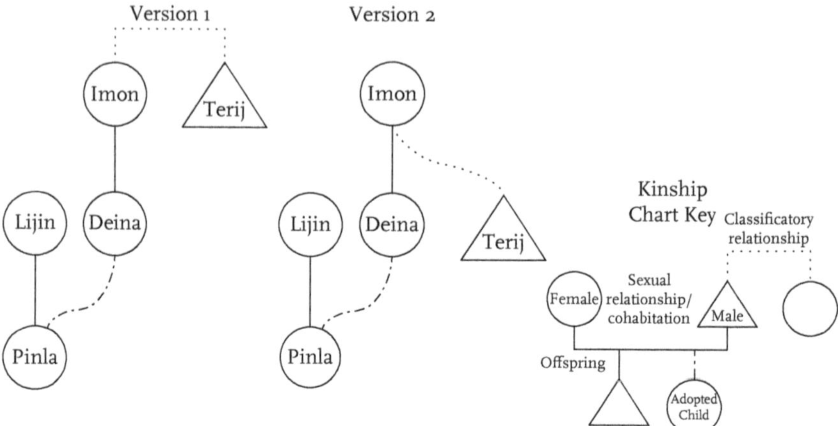

FIGURE 1.8 Different potential kinship connections between Imon and Terij.

unlike Imon), Terij had a young child and no grandchildren. In addition, when Terij asked to adopt Pinla's infant, she asked to adopt the infant as her daughter as opposed to her granddaughter. That said, during this negotiation Terij positioned herself as older than Deina. Deina was unable to say no to Terij's request for a child; Deina had to send the request up to a higher authority.

But while sometimes relative age is malleable, it is also structurally entrenched in people's histories and their bodies. Here a comparison with gender may be helpful. What it means to be a member of a particular gender, such as a woman, is culturally produced (Butler 1999; West and Zimmerman 1987). At the same time, a person's position as a woman in a given society stems from many different factors over which individuals have little control: the structure of society that positions people with certain attributes into the social identity "woman," how others react to them, their life history of being perceived as female, and even a personal history of feeling like a woman. Similarly, relative age relationships in the RMI are often structurally entrenched, built up through so much history that they cannot be easily erased. For example, Pinla was never going to be older than Deina. Deina had changed Pinla's clothes, bathed her, ordered her, and fed her since she was young. Their younger-elder roles were firmly established.

Pinla was also never going to be older than Terij. When Terij provided a house for Pinla, Terij reproduced herself as Pinla's older kin. Terij reinforced her status as an elder who had the responsibility to be benevolent and the power to command obedience.

The Infant's Fate

'What did you say?' I asked Imon. According to Imon, she and Terij talked on the radio. In 2010 many villages on the outer islands lacked phone service and relied on shortwave radios for communication.

'I said no!'

I was suspicious. People never say no. But they do say things that they interpret as no after the fact, even though the word *no* may never have crossed their lips. That said, if anyone actually did say no to Terij, it would have been Imon.

'But Terij said that she was going to take her. [So] I said,' Imon continued, 'the baby needs to come here to be washed.'

This frequent washing during an infant's early months is ritually required. I watched one baby squirm in a tub as her mother and grandmother carefully scrubbed her clean. Then her mother took out a small cloth ball. Earlier she had collected special herbs—part of what people call "Marshallese medicine"—from plants on their land. The cloth ball was packed tightly with these leaves. The mother dipped the cloth in water and then held it over her baby's body, squeezing gently to let drops of the medicine-infused water fall against the baby's chin, stomach, and legs and finally into her open mouth.

"And if we don't bathe them . . . ," I began.

"She will smell like pee," the baby's grandmother interjected, referring to what happens when the baby gets older.

"Will she get sick?"

Joash (2004) writes that Marshallese medicinal practices after birth protect the baby spiritually and ward off disease. But people's ideas of the purpose of rituals are not always uniform.

"No," the baby's mother said. "But people will say, 'Ugh! She smells like. . . !' "

Imon's excuse had some coherent logic to it. This bathing is significantly easier in Jajikon than in Majuro because the necessary plants are more readily available. Nonetheless, her words were clearly an excuse. It would have been relatively easy for Imon, as she so often did for other grandchildren living in the capital, to pick the necessary plants and send them to Terij.

Despite the obvious nature of Imon's excuse, it did what she wanted. It clearly communicated to Terij that Imon wanted the infant back in her physical space.

But Terij, as Imon complained, was an incessant beggar who has no shame (*akweḷap*). 'The baby can be washed on Majuro,' Terij apparently declared.

Imon had no more moves left. So she did the only thing she could. She agreed.

It is tempting to try to explain this infant's fate by discussing Marshallese social structures. Gifts such as hospitality incur debts, including Pinla's debt to Terij. Age commands deference, making both Pinla and Deina defer to Terij's wishes. Close kinship relationships mean that children belong to everyone, including Terij.

Ultimately, however, none of these social facts in and of themselves explain why Terij got the infant and Pinla, Deina, and Imon did not or why Pinla's many other kin did not take her. Imon was Terij's elder; shouldn't her words have prevailed? Terij had her own duty to care for Pinla, which included respecting Pinla's needs and making sure that Pinla had children in her household. Pinla had several other grandmothers, parents, and siblings who had claims. Pinla's birth mother had her own rights—I know of several cases in which birth mothers adopted a child born to a child whom they had given away decades earlier.

Understanding this adoption incident requires recognizing how Terij's very request, as well as her ultimately successful effort to claim the infant as her own, were subject to both the contingencies of interaction and the power of age. The former includes not only people's idiosyncratic personalities and desires but also what people say and the organization of space.[12] Pinla felt the subjective pressure that compelled her to give only after the infant, or Pinla's pregnancy, became visible. Pinla was also only involved in the negotiations at all, even silently, because she grew the infant in her belly, giving her a certain amount of physical control. Terij's physical closeness to Pinla and the infant is what gave Terij the opportunity to ask. Had Pinla given birth on Jajikon, Terij may well have never had such an opportunity. Had Terij lived farther away or in a different house, it also would have been more difficult to insist. Finally, Pinla, Deina, and the baby all lived in Terij's space and were subject to her commands. Imon claimed that she was the only one with sufficient authority to reject Terij's request. But she was on Jajikon, a physical distance that limited the power her age would otherwise have afforded her. Consequently, she was unable to employ the standard delaying tactic, "wait" (Berman 2014a). Imon claimed that she tried. She said that Terij should wait until after the ritual bathing to take the infant. But, as Imon tells the story, her statement had no force because she did not actually have the infant with her at that moment. It was Terij, and not Imon, who was content with the status quo.

These contingencies of interaction both influenced and were influenced by people's ages. First, it was the infant's young age that made this negotiation possible at all. As children grow they take on agency and age out of their ability to be given. For example, one mother put off giving her child for so long that he grew so old that the mother could not give him away (or so she claimed). He "might go and sleep there [at the adoptive family's house] one night and then come back. Two or three nights, and then come back. Because he was this age [she gestured with her hand], and I didn't give him when he was small." In contrast, newly born infants lack agency. Like food and other goods, babies cannot choose where to live; they cannot walk or talk and so cannot indicate their preferences. People note this good-like characteristic of infants both grammatically and in their discussions of adoption and exchange. Grammatically, in Marshallese both offspring and food are alienable and possessed by a possessive classifier—a word similar to *my* but which one can only use with certain types of things. For example, the classifier *kij-* possesses food. *Kijō ek* means "my food fish" or "my fish." The classifier *nej-* possesses a whole class of important things, including, but not limited to, radios, jewelry, pets, and children. *Nejū ļaddik* means "my important thing boy" or "my son." But although people must use a classifier for offspring, they possess all other family members through a suffix attached to the root word that refers to the kinship relationship itself. *Jinō* means "my mother." This grammatical difference may be tied to the pragmatic fact that people do regularly ask each other for both children and food but not for other kin such as mothers. Recall how Deina described adopting Pinla: "It's like if [I] fill a plate of food and give you your food. . . . They shared her with us just like food."

While the infant's age positioned her as givable, Terij's relative age gave her control over her house and speech. Terij's wealth, land, and capital are partly what helped her succeed in claiming the child. Consequently, one could argue that this story reveals the importance in negotiations for children of not age but power. But in the RMI, age is power. The two cannot be separated. First, age leads to power. Terij grew into her control over her house and ability to offer hospitality. Second, power is age—powerful people are seen, treated, and interpreted as older. It was not only Terij's land and wealth but also her elder status—which cannot be entirely separated from her land—that made it more difficult for Pinla and Deina to refuse. It was partly through this interaction that Terij reestablished herself as an older person and re-created her age relative to others and their age relative to her.

And so, Pinla had to give. Unlike her elders, she did not have the social power or sufficient control of her space to be able to avoid that responsibility. Like all young people in the RMI she lived in someone else's house. Those people also controlled the things that she produced, including the infant whom she birthed.

Leaving Majuro

The two-month-old girl smiled and burped, squirming in Pinla's lap. We sat in Terij's house.

'What is her name?' I asked. Before the birth Pinla had asked me for suggestions. Whimsically, I had proposed my sister's name, Jessica. Immediately, Pinla declared "Jessica" the future name of her unborn child. I did and do not know whether she was serious.

Regardless, Pinla clearly viewed that name with affection. Years later Pinla and I found ourselves again at Terij's house watching the now older girl. Pinla's parents continued to stay with Terij when they visited Majuro, the exchange of a child perhaps cementing a relationship that had already been close. 'She should have been Jessica,' Pinla lamented. In other words, she should have been hers.

Three years earlier, however, Pinla sighed. 'I do not know her name, because they took her.' In giving away physical possession Pinla also gave away the right to name the infant. At the same time, Pinla's gift drew Terij and Terij's family closer, building the extensive Marshallese kinship relationships that ensure that everyone has a home, food, companionship, and love. But just as marriage can be bittersweet, involving both loss and gain, sharing children in the RMI reinforces family ties while also creating feelings of sadness. 'It was hard,' Pinla said, referring to her effort to keep her daughter. 'I am staying in their house.'

Pinla soon returned to Jajikon. The baby stayed in Majuro, with Terij.

Notes

1. I counted all people who lived in Jajikon for more than three months during the year that I was there.
2. Unlike most adoptions in the United States in which authority is entirely transferred to the adoptive parents (Modell 1999).
3. Basso (1970) describes a similar role of silence in introductions among some Apache groups in Arizona. Basso argues that people stay silent in unpredictable situations. One example of such a situation is when strangers meet each other.
4. Spoehr (1949, 182) explains the Marshallese kinship system, a variant of a Hawaiian kinship system, in more detail. This system is very flexible, so kinship terms may change depending on the specific circumstance. In addition, there are some exceptions to what I have described above. First, cross-cousins—children of opposite-sex siblings—may be either siblings or potential marriage partners (*riliki*). A special term distinguishes the mother's brother, although this term may be an older word as I rarely heard it used in practice. Spoehr states that people sometimes called spouses of siblings *inō* (sister) or *manō* (brother), but I was more likely to hear people use the English words *sister* and *brother*. In addition, people do also sometimes use the English loanword *auntie*, although I heard "auntie" much less often than *jinō* (my mother). Finally, while everyone has many mothers (*jineir*), they do not use the vocative *mama* with all of them. The people they call "mama" depend on who raised them and with whom they feel close. But everyone in a mother kinship position (or grandparent or sibling) has a theoretical right to claim an infant, as well as the obligation to care for all their children regardless of whether those children call them "mama" or not.

5. For how the physical environment constrains interaction, see also Duranti 1992; Goodwin 2000; and Hanks 1990.
6. Scholars have often contrasted "shame," an emotion that reacts to external judgment, with "guilt," which supposedly comes not from public embarrassment but, rather, inner turmoil.
7. *Āliklik* is also different from the shaming routines many language socialization scholars discuss in which parents socialize children into cultural values through negatively assessing their behavior (Lo and Fung 2012). Such routines are also common in Jajikon and have their own name, *kajjookok*. *Kajjookok* literally means "to cause *jook*," an emotion that I translate as "embarrassment" in order to distinguish it from *āliklik*. In reaction to such routines people say that children feel *jook* (embarrassment) but not *āliklik*.
8. Similar emotion words that combine sadness and empathy exist in other Micronesian languages (Lutz 1988; Rauchholz 2009).
9. Parents are not always protectors. If they live elsewhere, they too may be trying to gain control over a child. In this particular case, however, Deina's and Pinla's interests aligned. They lived in the same house, so keeping the baby with Pinla also meant keeping her with Deina.
10. Bikini atoll is the namesake of the bikini bathing suit. Louis Reard invented the bathing suit in 1946 during the first round of nuclear testing (Teaiwa 1994).
11. A U.S. attorney general himself concluded that the sum of money the United States offered was vastly inadequate. A tribunal established to adjudicate claims ran out of money in 2009 (Barker 2013, 35).
12. It is possible, even likely, that the negotiations did not occur exactly as people reported them. Nevertheless, ultimately Terij did get the child, while Pinla did not. Moreover, it is clear that Pinla, Deina, and Imon all tried to retain the child. All three talked about the negotiations in a way that emphasized the importance of speech and space. Finally, their stories support other evidence—to be provided in chapter 3—that speech and space both interact to influence negotiations for goods and people.

2 WHAT IS AGE AND WHERE DOES IT COME FROM?

A THEORETICAL ANALYSIS OF AGE AND LANGUAGE SOCIALIZATION

This book analyzes the sociolinguistic significance, use, and production of age differences in the RMI. Here I discuss the theoretical basis for the most counterintuitive part of my argument—that people produce age differences through interaction.

What Is Age? Age and Ideology

I define "age" as a characteristic that distinguishes people from each other according to their position in the life course. The "life course," in turn, refers to people's maturation, socialization, and change as they grow and move from birth to death. Within the life course people may be in different "stages," which I define as culturally recognized periods or age groups.

For many in the modern and globalized world, "age" means chronological age.[1] "How old are you?" people ask. The answer is a number, such as "five." This number comes from another number, one's date of birth. In everyday life in many places today, these numbers influence how one spends one's day (day care, school, work, or a retirement home), how much money one makes (salaries, child support, social security payments), how much power one has (to drive, drink, or vote), and whether one is likely to go to prison for a crime. Researchers working with children regularly record the age of their subjects not only in years but in months, and sociologists and epidemiologists often use chronological age as an independent variable for comparison with other aspects of social life (e.g., Schieffelin 1990; Soley and Sebastian-Galles 2015; Tamis-LeMonda et al. 2017; Yang and Land 2008). "Age," an anthropologist writes, "has to do with the chronological passing of time" (Lamb 2015, 855), and according to a historian, age "is a direct, objective measure of the duration that someone has lived" (Chudacoff 1986, 4). Although we can deceive others about our age, the historian continues, "ultimately we cannot change or manipulate it" (Chudacoff 1986, 4). This view of age as not only chronological but also immutable is common: a sociologist concerned with age as a sociological variable writes, "Age may perhaps alter one's propensity to drink alcohol or form close relationships, but not the other way around" (Finch 1986, 20). These examples support Eckert's argument that "to the Western social scientist, chronological age *is* age" (1998, 154).

But age is not chronological—at least not in many times and places. In parts of West Africa, women measure age not by counting time but, rather, by the wear and tear on their bodies caused by childbirth. A twenty-five-year-old woman with four children is older than a forty-five-year-old woman with one child. Moreover, age can be reversed. When women stop giving birth, they grow younger (Bledsoe 2002). Some people in the RMI, like many other people in the world, do not know their chronological age (e.g., Cleveland 1989; Rogoff 2003, 152–57). Even in Europe and the United States, the concern with chronology is historically new (LaRossa and Reitzes 2001). Before the middle of the nineteenth century, the United States had "no uniform age of entry into, or departure from, . . . schools, and it was not uncommon to see very young children in the same classroom as teenagers" (Chudacoff 1986, 15).[2] In England in the early nineteenth century, *child* denoted a period of independence as opposed to a specific chronological status. Since laborers in factories were dependent on their managers, many of them were not yet independent adults but, rather, "might be described as infants" (Steedman 1995, 7).

The various ways that people around the world evaluate age show that chronological accounts of age are culturally specific *ideologies*. Throughout this book I use the word *ideologies* to refer to "shared bodies of commonsense notions about the nature of" age, childhood, gender, race, or language (Rumsey 1990, 346). Although chronological ideologies of age are widespread today, they are historically new and cross-culturally rare (Fortes 1984; Neugarten 1996a; Steedman 1995). There are many alternative ideologies of age. For example, age could be relative. Thus, the answer to the question "How old are you?" would be "Older than John." Age could be based on ability. A Marshallese woman described her son's age by putting her hand at a certain height above the ground and saying, "Able to talk." If developmental researchers adopted this ability-based approach, they might separate children according to what they can do instead of how many months they have lived—a drastic change in research design. One could also evaluate age according to major life course events and the statuses associated with them. Tallensi men, for example, become autonomous adults not at the age of eighteen but when their father dies (Fortes 1984, 103). Some biologists evaluate age like the women in West Africa, by focusing on specific organs, which all mature on their own timescale: from the perspective of their heart people may be mature, but from the perspective of their hands they may still be immature (Beall 1984). Alternatively, age could be chronological, but the relevant span of time could be different. For example, in many East African societies people group others in classes spanning six or ten years, what anthropologists have called "age-sets" (Baxter and Almagor 1978; Meiu 2015).

Ideologies of life stages also vary across cultures. Adolescence is a relatively new phenomenon in Europe and the United States and does not exist everywhere (Bucholtz 2002; Kehily 2007). Lesko (2012) argues that modern views of adolescence as a specific chronological period characterized by raging hormones, peer pressure, and liminality arose in the late 1800s as a way of thinking about and confronting social change. Many in Japan, India, and Samoa do not recognize "middle age" as a life stage (Shweder 1998). People also have different ideas about what aging in later life entails: in parts of Japan and India (and in the RMI), aging is a process of advancing through the social hierarchy, but in the United States, many see aging as a period of decline (Lamb 2000, 2017; Lock 1998). While most people recognize a period of life that can be translated as "childhood," the timing of this period and the characteristics of children differ dramatically (Heywood 2001; Lancy 2015; LeVine et al. 1994; Montgomery 2009). For example, whereas in international law people are "children" between the ages of zero and eighteen (United Nations 1990 Convention on the Rights of the Child), many Navajo divide the life course into eight stages that are based on competence, with no real chronological counterparts. People do not become fully mature until the last stage, which often does not start until they are at least thirty years old (Chisolm 1996). Even the ideology that children are immature is not universal. In a number of societies people believe that children are ancestors reborn (Gottlieb 2004; Gupta 2002).

Such ideologies are not mutually exclusive and often coexist. In the RMI, as we will see, people switch between various notions of age, including chronological ones, depending on the context. Even in the United States, statements such as "He is young for his age" or "She does not look like she is thirty" reveal that people who often rely on chronology may simultaneously view it as an inadequate measure of development or a person's status. When people try a seventeen-year-old as an adult or have children skip a grade in school, they use nonchronological evaluations of development. At the same time, however, the fact that it is possible to say "He is young for his age" shows the overwhelming influence of chronology. In places and times where chronology is less relevant, people are less likely to compare other markers of age with chronological ones or to structure key social institutions around chronology. Thus, in different societies people have a tendency to place a greater weight on some ideologies than others. Moreover, all ideologies do not exist everywhere or in the same form. Many people do not believe that it is possible for a woman who has finished childbearing to grow younger.

The Cultural Life Course

Life experiences, development, and maturation also shift across contexts (Eberhart 2006). First, children develop in different ways and at different rates depending on their cultural and social environment (Rogoff 2003; Vygotsky 1978, 1998). Most American children cannot swim until they are in middle childhood, but Margaret Mead (1930) observed the Manus children of Papua New Guinea swimming as soon as they started to walk. Middle-class American children are often precocious verbally but unable to deal with household responsibilities, whereas Kwara'ae children as young as three care for infants and Fore infants in Papua New Guinea handle fire by the time they can walk (Brown and Gaskins 2014; Harkness and Super 1992; Sorenson 1979; Watson-Gegeo 1990). Wogeo children do not walk until they are two, because parents do not let them learn (Hogbin 1943). In societies where people believe that children are reborn ancestors, children may display mature abilities—they talk about their past lives, take on personalities that relate to the people they used to be, and display adult behaviors such as criticizing children or even adults (Gottlieb 1998; Gupta 2002). In some societies children are imaginative, and in others, rational (Clark 1995; Mead 1930); in some childhood is a time for learning, and in others, a time for working (Zelizer 1985). Childhood is a cultural category (James and Prout 1997b), and children's capabilities often reflect social expectations.

Second, the timing and order of life events change historically, across cultures, and between individuals within a society. The chronological age at which American men marry differed between men born in the 1920s and men born after 1937 (Hogan 1978). At the end of the twentieth century a new distinction arose between the "young-old" and the "old-old," that is, people of similar chronological ages that are either healthy and vigorous or sick and frail, respectively (Neugarten 1996b). Individuals who violate the expected timing of events within their own society—such as women who have children before they finish school—suffer psychological harm. A woman of the same chronological age who has a child in a society where motherhood is expected would not suffer such harm (Neugarten 1996b). Both Andrew Jackson and Ishmael Beah went to war at the chronological age of thirteen. Andrew Jackson was the seventh president of the United States, and Ishmael Beah is a survivor of the 1990s civil war in Sierra Leone. But Jackson's contemporaries saw him as "on time" and a war hero, whereas late twentieth-century international human rights organizations call Beah a victim (Rosen 2015). Even within a society, vital life course events—such as the birth of a child or marriage—do not take place at a single chronological age or even in the same chronological order. For example, Johnson-Hanks (2002, 870) has shown that the chronological ages and sequences in which contemporary Beti women in Cameroon have their first child, get married, go to school, and get their first job vary widely. Although Giudice, Angeleri, and Manera (2009) argue for five biologically determined human life stages, they also argue that such stages do not occur at fixed chronological ages, may not occur at all, and are plastic and sensitive to environmental influences.

Finally, culture affects the biological expression and chronological timing of aging during adulthood. Women of higher socioeconomic statuses start menstruating chronologically earlier than their poorer peers (Beall 1984). In the United States, puberty is arriving earlier and earlier (Neugarten 1996b). Blood pressure rises after young adulthood in industrial populations but stays steady in many nonindustrial populations (James and Baker 1995). People of lower socioeconomic status tend to die chronologically earlier (Davey-Smith et al. 1997). Other cultural differences also affect the chronological timing of mortality. For example, a switch from hunting and gathering to agriculture in the Mississippi Basin led to earlier mortality and greater arthritis, two supposed biological markers of chronological age (Goodman and Armelagos 1985). All of this evidence reveals that the social, psychological, and biological characteristics that distinguish people of different ages vary across contexts and are influenced by culture.

Age is not completely malleable. Like gender, it is highly constrained, partly by biology and partly by society. Newborn infants cannot walk or talk.[3] One distinctive feature of the human life course is our extended period of rapid brain growth in early life. This period is associated with greater plasticity and high rates of learning, enculturation, and language socialization (Bjorklund 1997; Rogoff 2003, 67–71; Trevarthen 1988). Someone who has spent ten years as a younger sibling may be unable to reimagine themselves as an elder sibling; someone who looks like a child may be unable to present themselves as (or feel like) an adult. But just as the environment can affect gene expression (Thayer and Non 2015), cultural and environmental influences transform the way in which age constraints express themselves. This is particularly true for most of the characters in this book who are what Marshallese call *ajri* (children), as opposed to *niñniñ* (infants).[4]

But it is also true in the beginning of the life course since enculturation begins in infancy (LeVine and Norman 2001). During the first year of life infants' crying is culturally conditioned: Inuit and Zinacantan infants rarely cry, while Bielefield infants in Germany are comfortable being left alone (Crago 1988; LeVine and Norman 2001; Rogoff 2003). Although no newborn infants can speak their parents' language, by six months their babblings start to be culturally conditioned, reflecting the phonemes of their language (Brown and Gaskins 2014; Kuhl 2009). Sesotho and Inuktitut children use passives early, but children who speak English find passives difficult (Allen and Crago 1996). Samoan parents believe that young children are naturally cheeky and that they curse. As a result, Samoan parents interpret their children's first word as a curse word: "eat shit" (*tae*). Lo and behold, the children's first words are curse words: "Eventually the child becomes the curser she or he is 'expected by nature' to be" (Ochs 1993, 293–94).

Producing Difference

Where do all these differences come from? Answering this question requires first distinguishing between types of life course variation. Consider Kori and his mother from the introduction. First, we might ask how Kori differs from what his mother was like when she was a child or how Kori will be different from his mother when he grows up. These concerns relate to cohort or generational differences and include questions such as, Was Kori's mother also willing to walk with food as a child, even though she is not now? When Kori grows up, will he gain *āliklik* (shame), and will it be the same type of shame as the emotion that currently prevents his mother from carrying food in public? Second, we might ask how Kori's interactions with his mother compare with interactions between children and adults elsewhere. This concern relates to how children take on culturally particular developmental trajectories, becoming different from other children in other cultures. It includes questions such as, Why do Marshallese children such as Kori run errands for their parents daily but many middle-class American children do not? and Why do Marshallese children largely lack *āliklik* until they are almost teenagers, whereas children elsewhere seem to feel similar emotions earlier (Fung 1999; Lo and Fung 2012)? Finally, we might ask what made Kori different from his mother at that very moment in time. This concern relates to what I call "age differences" and includes questions such as, Why did Kori lack *āliklik* (shame) in contrast to his mother?

I will discuss each of these differences in turn.

Cohort Differences

A cohort is a group of people who move through life and encounter events together. For example, members of the freshman and sophomore classes in college are members of two different cohorts. Life course theorists argue that differences between cohorts arise partly through differences in the developmental timing of historical events (Mayer 2009). For example, Elder (1974, 1998) analyzed how two different cohorts—people born in Oakland in 1920–21 and people born in Berkeley in 1928–29—had different experiences of the Great Depression and, as a result, different life course trajectories. While the Oakland Cohort encountered the Great Depression during adolescence, the Berkeley Cohort encountered it during childhood. This encounter with economic hardship left members of the Berkeley Cohort at a disadvantage for the rest of their life, leading to later high school graduation, lower earnings, poorer health, and disadvantages for their children. Elder's work shows how disadvantage accumulates over the life course and how the developmental timing of events creates differences between cohorts of people.

Life course theorists view these different life course trajectories as partly the result of an interaction among cohort, period, and age. "Period" refers to a historical time period, such as the Great Depression. "Age" often goes undefined (e.g., Elder and George 2016), but in theory it is culturally specific and malleable: Elder and Rockwell differentiate between "chronological age," which marks development time, and "social age," which they refer to as "social roles and timetables" (1979, 2). Several scholars in the life course tradition analyze how the meaning and nature of age varies across cultures (Neugarten 1996a, 1996b; Riley 1987; Riley, Johnson, and Foner 1972); Elder, Shanahan, and Jennings argue that "a sociocultural perspective gives emphasis to the social meanings of age" (2015, 9).

In practice, however, such work is the exception: "age" in life course studies usually means chronological age and tends to operate as an independent variable (Eckert 1998; Laz 1998, 2003; Llamas 2007). For example, Elder and George discuss how "cohort" in the social sciences typically means birth cohort and state that "members of birth cohorts are the same or approximately the same age" (2016, 60). Here, they treat age as chronological, assuming that people will interpret the word *age* as "chronological age" and treating it as an unmarked and naturalized category (for other examples, see Yang 2007; Yang and Land 2008).

Whereas life course theorists often focus on the interaction among cohort, period, and age to explain cohort differences, Cole analyzes people's "representations of generations" (2010, 15)—their cultural perspectives on their future. She builds on structure theorists who argue that social change occurs as people act within social structures and then, through their actions, change those structures (Sahlins 1985; Sewell 1992, 2005). Cole claims that all social structures contain inherent variation with respect to people's place in the life course and their representations of the future. These views of the future are both a part of social structure that shapes action and a form of variation within the system that allows for change. Cole provides the example of youth in a city in Madagascar who start to imagine futures for themselves that differ from those of their ancestors. As a result, they take different paths through life, joining Pentecostal churches or the sexual economy rather than getting married and joining a Protestant or Catholic church. How people imagine the future and their place within it shapes "choices and trajectories," making "certain paths, certain social trajectories, easier to imagine than others" (Cole 2010, 16).

Different Children

Analyses of cohort variation focus on generational differences, but anthropological accounts of childhood and socialization focus on how children in one place become different from children elsewhere. These differences arise, scholars argue, because development is itself a culturally mediated and culturally variable process. Influences on children include, but are not limited to, parental ethnotheories, the material environment, social structures and social institutions, and children's interactions with relatives and peers. The interaction among all of these different influences (and more) creates what is sometimes called children's "developmental" or "ecological" niche and results in culture-specific developmental outcomes (Bronfenbrenner 1979; Harkness and Super 1992; Rogoff 2003; Super and Harkness 1986, 1997; Whiting and Whiting 1975).

For example, children in a Sri Lankan village and middle-class American children have tantrums in early childhood—what Americans call the "terrible twos." Their parents, however, have different ideas about how best to deal with such tantrums. Many upper-middle-class American parents think that they have to set limits and avoid giving in; many Sri Lankan parents think that they should give in because their children are too young to know any better. Contrary to middle-class American beliefs about how such indulgence will affect children, older Sri Lankan children are largely well behaved and obedient. Chapin (2014) argues that this transformation is due partly to how Sri Lankan parents signal displeasure by frowning, wincing, and turning away even as they give in. Through these signs, parents make children's tantrums uncomfortable, eventually leading the children to "disavow" their desires and subsume their needs to those of their elders. This developmental trajectory is culturally specific. On the one hand, not all children have tantrums—many Aka children in early childhood do not (Hewlett 1992). On the other hand, although both Sri Lankan and middle-class American children have tantrums, they grow out of those tantrums differently. Sri Lankan children become (often) very deferent to elder kin; middle-class American children, less so (Chapin 2014).

Chapin's account here is an analysis of how people take on culturally specific practices, beliefs, and subjectivities: the process of "socialization." Many socialized practices and beliefs are so ingrained in our everyday behavior that they appear to us as natural (Bourdieu 1984). For example, whereas most Marshallese adults automatically avoid carrying food in public, American adults do not think twice about drinking a cup of coffee or eating a sandwich at the bus stop. These adults have different subjective reactions to similar situations: some feel shame, while the others do not.

Some of these different beliefs, practices, and subjectivities are produced by the use of language and other signs in interaction, a phenomenon known as "language socialization" (Duranti, Ochs, and Schieffelin 2012; Garrett and Baquedano-Lopez 2002; Kulick and Schieffelin 2004, 349; Schieffelin and Ochs 1986). For example, while studying an agoraphobic woman and her family, Capps and Ochs (1995) discovered that the woman regularly retold her daughter's stories as dangerous experiences. They argue that through such speech the woman (unconsciously) taught her daughter to be afraid; she socialized her daughter into fear and agoraphobia.

Not only do language socialization practices produce children in one place as different from children elsewhere, but they also influence gender, racial, and ethnic differences (e.g., Fader 2009). Consider, for example, gender categories among the Kaluli of Papua New Guinea. Many Kaluli say that men are emotional, disobedient, and aggressive, whereas women are restrained, obedient, and passive. Bambi Schieffelin shows that such differences are socialized through interaction beginning in infancy. Kaluli mothers stop infant girls who bite from nursing but smile at biting boys and allow them to continue. Mothers also criticize angry girls but appease angry boys by giving them food, objects, or attention. As a result of these manipulations of different types of signs including speech, gestures, facial expressions, breasts, food, and the children's own bodies, by the time children are two and a half years old, Kaluli girls offer to take care of younger infants and help out around the house, whereas boys merely eat the food that they are offered and enjoy playing with fish traps and knives (Schieffelin 1990).[5]

People also learn to associate categories such as boy and girl with different characteristics—such as emotional or nonemotional—by observing and using signs in interaction. When Kaluli boys explode in anger they perform their identities through both actions and speech (Butler 1999; Schieffelin 1990). As Goffman (1959) argues, they put on an unconscious performance, taking on a social identity and reproducing it. In so doing they also instill gendered senses of themselves and create links in people's minds between maleness and angry emotions (West and Zimmerman 1987). Just as smoke points to fire, among many Kaluli maleness points to emotionality.

Linguistic anthropologists call these links "indices" (Silverstein 1976). Indices are signs that people see as having some sort of causal connection to that which they represent. Just as clouds point to rain because rain is causally linked to clouds, many forms of speech point back to social identities. For example, not smiling in the United States is often seen as a sign of masculinity (McElhinny 1995). This does not mean that men never smile or that women always smile. It simply means that men are more likely to avoid smiling or that when they do smile, they are interpreted as less masculine. This relationship between signs and identity is often indirect (Ochs 1992). For example, police officers in the United States smile relatively infrequently, and police officers are often male. As a result, more men than women find themselves in situations in which not smiling is appropriate. As men continue to be police officers more often than women, and hence continue to smile less often than women, associations between not smiling and masculinity are produced. Both observers and performers learn to link signs, such as not smiling, to particular types of people, such as men. But they often misinterpret these cultural links as innate and view not smiling as an inherent aspect of masculinity as opposed to the result of a social system that sees both masculinity and not smiling as appropriate for police officers (Irvine and Gal 2000; McElhinny 1994). Through their actions and speech people reproduce such connections between signs and identity, creating both beliefs in differences and the experience of difference itself.

Age Differences

Research into cohort differences focuses on how social and generational change takes place. Research into socialization has shown that development is culturally contingent and linguistically mediated, that children in one place are different from children elsewhere, and that children are socialized into different gendered or racialized subject positions within a society. But what makes children different from those elders with whom they interact every day? What made Kori different from his mother at the very moment they interacted?

Like concerns with the production of gender and racial differences, this concern with age differences is a question about variation within a particular society. But whereas cultural and linguistic scholars now regularly analyze gender and race as socially produced forms of variation and personhood, scholars are less likely to talk that way about age differences (Coupland 2004; Eckert 1998, 2014; Laz 1998, 2003).[6] In linguistic anthropology and sociolinguistics, this gap exists in the study of both language variation and language socialization. With respect to variation, Llamas argues that "age is perhaps the least examined and the least understood in sociolinguistic terms. Unlike gender, ethnicity or social class, age is often approached uncritically and treated as a biological fact with which to categorize speakers, and against which other facets of our identity are played out" (2007, 69; see also Eckert 1998). Sociolinguists do distinguish between apparent time (age differences in language use as measured at a specific moment in time) and real time (actual linguistic change in a population over generations) (Cukor-Avila and Bailey 2013). Although this approach reveals age-correlated linguistic variation, it does not theorize age itself as a sociolinguistic construction. Likewise, as I have argued elsewhere, much language socialization research is focused on "the production of something else—linguistic forms and genres, gender or racial identities, power structures and social organization, relationships, language shift or bilingualism, even peer cultures—rather than, ironically, age itself" (Berman 2014b, 112–13).

But work on language variation and socialization nonetheless shows, if only implicitly, that age is socialized through language. First, although work on adolescents' and children's interactions may not always explicitly address the construction of age, this work nonetheless reveals that such interactions are tied to child or youth identities that are often constructed in opposition to other identities (Bucholtz 2011; Eckert 1987; Goodwin 1990, 2006; Kyratzis 2007; Mendoza-Denton 2008). Language socialization research shows that children often take on forms of speech not because they are easier or more common in their language but because they are seen as appropriate to their social position. For example, Samoan children say *'aumai* (to bring/give) earlier than they say *sau* (come), despite the fact that *sau* is semantically less complex, because *'aumai* is something appropriate for children to say to older and higher-status individuals (Platt 1986). Recent work on language shift reveals that entire language varieties (i.e., codes) are often associated with different age groups. In both a First Nations community in Canada and villages on the Caribbean islands of Dominica and St. Lucia, English is the language of youth and people's indigenous or creole heritage languages are the languages of the elders (Garrett 2007; Meek 2007, 2011; Paugh 2012b). This differential association between code and life stage stems partly from ideologies about how the codes embody maturity or immaturity. For example, in the First Nations community people view their indigenous language, Kaska, as a form of specialized knowledge. People who speak Kaska mark themselves as knowledgeable and authoritative, qualities that are supposed to accrue with age. Consequently, only elders are "socially sanctioned, capable speakers of Kaska," and children must speak not Kaska but English (Meek 2007, 34; 2011). Similarly, in the village in Dominica people associate Patwa (their heritage language) with boldness and English with accommodation. Since children are supposed to accommodate their elders, Patwa is seen as more appropriate for adults (Paugh 2012b).

In cases of language shift it is easy to see how age differences are produced through children's socialization into specific codes. It is obvious that children do not naturally speak English instead of Patwa or Kaska. Nor is there any inherent link between Kaska and respect or between English and accommodation. Children in these societies speak English not because they are immature but, rather, because of how ideologies of immaturity and/or childhood produce certain types of speech as appropriate and natural for children.

It is somewhat harder to see how age differences are socialized when the form in question is not an entire code but "immature" behaviors or speech patterns such as lacking shame, walking naked, or directly refusing to give. I argue, however, that the process through which Marshallese children come to lack shame and speak directly, in contrast to their elders, who usually speak indirectly, is similar to the process through which children become speakers of English, in contrast to their elders, who speak Patwa. In both cases, specific modes of speaking, acting, and feeling are associated with different ages and with ideas of maturity or immaturity.

Conclusion

Just as Kaluli ideas of men as emotional make men more emotional and Patwa ideas of English as an accommodating language lead children to use English, children become immature partly because people expect them to be immature and treat them as such. I define immaturity as a trait attributed to people seen as not yet fully social—typically but not exclusively children (Berman 2014b). In the RMI, general expectations that children are people who do not hide or feel shame interact with social practices to produce children as people who are willing to do things that adults will not. Producing children as immature means producing them as people who are different from their elders; it is involved in the interactional production of age differences and with age itself.

My analysis of the production of age weaves together several threads that are only loosely connected in the literature. First, combining both language socialization research and childhood studies, I focus explicitly on the linguistic and social production of age. A great deal of research examines childhood as a social construction, but much of it is nonlinguistic and cannot address the minute interactions through which childhood is produced, whereas language socialization research does not usually treat the production of age and childhood (Berman

2014b; as examples, see Bluebond-Langner and Korbin 2007; James and Prout 1997a; Stephens 1995). Second, building on studies of language and gender, I examine the interactive construction of not only aged people—such as children or youth—but also their characteristics—such as "immature" or "mature." Just like terms such as *masculine* and *feminine*, immaturity and maturity are neither stable nor reliably linked to the people whom they supposedly describe. Understanding why labels of immaturity or maturity vary as well as how they get attached to people is vital to our understanding of the production of difference.

Finally, building on recent scholarship, instead of studying the construction of either childhood or old age in isolation, I investigate age and age differences in general, taking "age [itself] as an analytic" (Cole and Durham 2007, 2; see also Danely and Lynch 2013; Sobo 2015; Toren 1993). Although a switch from analyzing children to analyzing age differences may seem insignificant, I argue that this change allows us to think differently about cultural practices. For example, consider one central focus of anthropological research, gender. Sarah Lamb (2000) argues that gender not only differs across cultures but also changes across the life course—as Indian women grow older they become more masculine. Here, a concern for age differences helps Lamb analyze how gender intersects with other forms of identity and reveals that gender is not static but constantly changing (see also Gardiner 2002; Krekula 2007). With respect to socialization, then, children and other novices are not merely socialized into gender categories but move through these categories as they age. But it is not only gender that changes across the life course; everything changes across the life course. Subjectivities, personhood, identities, economic practices, social relationships, ideologies, agency, racial identities—all of these aspects of society (and more) are aged. Taking age as an analytic makes culture dynamic: culture changes not only as society changes but also as individuals change, moving through aged subject positions.

This dynamic view of culture also leads to new ways of thinking about socialization and cultural reproduction. Classic and current models of language socialization present it as the result of interactions between novices and experts. Socialization is the process by which "children and other novices in society acquire tacit knowledge of principles of social order and systems of belief" (Ochs 1986, 2) or the study of "how children and other novices apprehend and enact the 'context of situation' in relation to the 'context of culture'" (Kulick and Schieffelin 2004, 351). It focuses on how "particular culturally meaningful practices become acquired (or not) by children and other novices" (Ochs and Schieffelin 2012, 1). The phrase "children and other novices" has been fruitful, allowing scholars to argue that socialization is not child-specific but a lifelong process, that adults are also socialized through interaction, that children play an agentive role in their own socialization, and that all interactions are potentially socializing contexts. For example, language socialization research has shown how African American cosmetology students become professional stylists and how interaction between women and children socializes the adults as mothers and the children into cultural practices (Jacobs-Huey 2006, 2007; Kulick and Schieffelin 2004, 350; Ochs 1992).

But this effort to theorize socialization as a lifelong, fluid, and multidimensional process is hampered by the novice/expert frame. First, the novice/expert model does not fit many accounts of peer language socialization in which children take on culturally specific forms of being and speaking through interacting with other children (Kyratzis 2004).[7] Some "peers" may be in novice/expert relationships—multiage sibling and kin groups are common around the world (De Leon 2007; Goodwin and Kyratzis 2012, 366; Howard 2007; Rogoff 1981). But peers also influence each other outside of the novice/expert frame (Nguyen and Kellogg 2010; Sawchuk 2003). Second, the novice/expert framework does not theorize how novices become novices. Although one could argue that novices socialize future novices to be novices, or that experts produce novices as novices before turning them into experts, the language here is cumbersome. Finally, the words *novice* and *expert* implicitly present socialization (and cultural reproduction) as a linear process. Although much language socialization work already speaks against such a linear model—showing the influence of peers, children's own agency, the differences between types of immaturity around the world, and the unexpected turns that socialization can take—retaining the words *novice* and *expert* inadvertently undermines this work.

Rather than viewing socialization as the result of interactions between novices and experts, therefore, I suggest that we see it as the constant and continuous production of difference—including age differences. This model accounts for peer socialization interactions in which children influence each other and produce peer identities distinct both from those they used to have and those they are yet to acquire. The model also explains how novices become novices: they are socialized to be different from experts and to be immature. It can even account for social change. If people are learning to be not only similar to some but also different from others, these differences can take many forms. Socialization takes place as people—babies, children, youth, adults, and elders—constantly try on, modify, and discard age-specific modes of being, thinking, and speaking.

Before children learn to be adults they learn to be different from adults—they learn to be children. They take on child-specific forms of acting, giving, speaking, and feeling. The chapters that follow analyze what these differences are in the RMI and how they are produced.

Notes

1. For more discussions of ideologies of age as chronology, see Bledsoe 2002; Chudacoff 1986; Fortes 1984; Gupta 2002; Heywood 2001; Huijsmans et al. 2014; James and Prout 1997c; Laz 1998; Kertzer and Keith 1984; LaRossa and Reitzes 2001; and Shweder 1998.
2. Chudacoff drops the word *chronological* in front of "age," revealing how the word *age*, to many, simply implies chronological age.
3. Beng parents (in Côte d'Ivoire), however, believe that their infants are reborn ancestors. The infants spend their time between lives in the *wrugbe*, the afterlife, where they understand all of the languages of the world. Infants emerge speaking the language of *wrugbe* and continuing to understand all languages. As infants grow, they forget *wrugbe* and other languages, starting to speak only Beng (Gottlieb 2004). Interestingly, modern developmental science has a similar perspective. Infants start out able to distinguish between all phonemes but eventually lose the ability to hear phonemic differences that are not salient in their own language (Kuhl 2009).
4. There are relatively few cross-cultural data on many aspects of later childhood, and often the data that do exist are poor. Consider the proposed "five to seven year shift," a supposed universal shift from being relatively helpless to people with some responsibilities (Rogoff et al. 1975; Sameroff and Haith 1996; Weisner 1996). The problems with this argument are multiple. First, the observed chronological ages of this change vary enough across cultures that the shift is "fuzzy and highly variable . . . and its descriptive usefulness could be easily questioned" (Giudice, Angeleri, and Manera 2009, 3; see also Rogoff 2003, 169–70). Second, since many people around the world do not measure age chronologically, often ethnographers guess at children's chronological ages based on the ethnographers' own preconceived notions of development, rather than the other way around (Rogoff 2003, 169; Rogoff et al. 1975, 366). Third, there are many examples of societies whose children take on "responsible" behaviors outside of this chronological age range, showing that even if the shift does exist in general, it is nonetheless cross-culturally variable (Rogoff et al. 1975). Fourth, it is not clear what would constitute evidence of a shift as opposed to simply a gradual change in behavior over time. Finally, while some proposed universals of development are controversial, others are either culturally mediated or culturally variable. For example, if indeed there is a shift toward more responsibility in later childhood, the specific responsibilities that children take on vary dramatically: some children become independent caregivers of younger children, while many middle-upper-class children in the United States are seen as incapable of such an activity (Weisner and Gallimore 1977). Similarly, children's memories and planning strategies (something else that is supposed to increase in later childhood) differ across cultures (Lightfoot, Cole, and Cole 2013). Some Navajo children take longer to plan their route through a maze than some American children. The Navajo children also, however, make fewer mistakes once they start through the maze,

a difference in line with a cultural preference for thoughtfulness over speed (Ellis and Seigler 1997). Other proposed universals of development in later childhood include bigger and more physically capable bodies, some changes in brain organization, and increased interaction with the peer group (Lightfoot, Cole, and Cole 2013, 389–501).

5. There are also drastic differences in how middle-class parents in the United States treat their children. Such parents tend to describe day-old infant girls as soft but day-old infant boys as strong. They are more likely to criticize girls who engage in large motor activities but praise girls who play with dolls. They are also more likely to verbally stimulate girls than boys and to handle male infants younger than three months more roughly than female infants (Cherry and Lewis 1976; Fagot 1978; Lewis and Weinraub 1979; Meredith 2015).
6. As Lamb has argued, studies of social life "commonly list (in a now almost obligatory practice) race, class, gender, ethnicity . . . [and] sexual orientation . . . as crucial distinctions that cut across all groups, but age is mentioned only rarely" (2000, 8). Lamb wrote that sentence eighteen years ago. Since that time, both the anthropology of aging and the anthropology of childhood have blossomed as fields (e.g., Bluebond-Langner and Korbin 2007; Danely and Lynch 2013). Nonetheless, the following examples drawn from simple searches of Anthrosource and the *Annual Review of Anthropology* show that the phenomenon she mentions is still present: "current interest in identities—especially the conventional threesome of race, class, and gender" (Brodkin 2000, 240); "race, class, and gendered disparities" (Thomas and Clarke 2013, 307); "intersecting oppressions of race, class, and gender" (Maddox 2015, 96); "intersectionality that works across class, race, sexuality, and gender" (Weis and Fine 2013, 222). As these examples reveal, in recent as well as older works people often leave age out of discussions of social and linguistic differences and inequalities.
7. Kulick and Schieffelin (2004, 351), who assert that language socialization studies must be longitudinal in perspective and demonstrate the acquisition (or not) of practices over time, might argue that many of these works are studies not of language socialization but of language and social interaction. In support of their argument, many of the studies referenced in Goodwin and Kyratzis's "Peer Language Socialization" (2012) chapter do not discuss change over time (measured either longitudinally or latitudinally). For example, Goodwin's (1980, 1990) work on gossip analyzes children's interactions but does not discuss either how children's gossip changes as they grow or differences in patterns of gossip between children of different life stages. Similarly, Evaldsson's (2005) analysis of boys' insults examines how they use insults and the effect of the insults, as opposed to change over time or differences between life stages. But even if some peer socialization work does not fit Kulick and Schieffelin's paradigm, it is clear that children—older, younger, and similar age—affect each other and that any model of socialization must take this mutual influence into account.

3 ON THE ROAD

HOW TO GET OUT OF GIVING TO ADULTS

Karlin leaned toward me with anticipation. 'There is soda in Liklob.'

A village slightly smaller than Jajikon, Liklob was only a few miles away. I often ran there at dusk, past the coconut trees that reached high into the sky on either side of the two tire tracks that forged a single path through the jungle, enjoying the view of the lagoon and the ocean. Jajikon and Liklob both rest on fairly wide stretches of land. Wideness is relative; it takes five minutes to walk across Jajikon. But the untamed coconut forest that runs between the villages is narrower, a place where at times the lagoon almost meets the open sea (see Figure 3.1).

The thought of soda made my mouth water. I had not had a sugary drink for weeks. Nor, of course, had Karlin, unless you count the spoonfuls of sugar that people sometimes added to cups of water. Our typical diet was plain white rice and fresh fish or canned tuna—occasionally spiced up by salt fish, breadfruit, coconuts, soy sauce, or spam. Depending on the season, we also snacked on papaya, pandanus, limes, pumpkins, and a small tart red fruit that people call "apples." But soda? That was a treat normally reserved for when someone returned from the capital, Majuro.

Apparently, however, an enterprising store owner in Liklob had brought some in.

It went without saying that if I walked with Karlin to Liklob, the soda would be my treat. I could not buy a soda for myself without buying one for her. And I was known as a person with money, whereas Karlin, like most young women, did not have an independent source of income.

Despite my desire for soda, I hesitated. It was still early in my fieldwork, but I already unconsciously knew that there was a difference between everyone knowing that I had money and people actually seeing me buy things. Up to that point in time I had not bought anything from a store in Jajikon. On numerous occasions I craved lollipops,

FIGURE 3.1 Road next to the lagoon heading into the coconut forest between villages. Photo by Elise Berman.

but I could not figure out how to buy them without children seeing me and demanding their share. I paid my research assistants privately, something in their interest as much as my own. If anyone saw the money, they too would be immediately obligated to give it away.

My mouth watered. I wanted some soda. And I did not want to refuse Karlin, who—in her indirect way—was asking me for a gift. Buying her soda and going with her to Liklob would bring us together; it would make us friends.

So I said yes.

In hindsight, I should have listened to my inhibitions. Buying and drinking soda turned out to be an enormously complex enterprise, one that required deeper knowledge of Marshallese communicative norms than I had at the time. My main predicament was that since there were 250 people in Jajikon I could not buy sodas for everyone. But adults in Jajikon expect each other to share the things that they have. Therefore, somehow I needed to avoid giving (Berman 2012).

Unfortunately for me, I did not yet know the appropriate ways to avoid giving in Jajikon. Or, rather, I did not yet know how to appropriately avoid giving to adults. Adults and children in Jajikon have different communicative patterns.

I had learned a bit, by this trip, about the child-child methods of avoiding giving, which I will discuss in chapter 4. But my journey to Liklob with Karlin abruptly exposed my ignorance about adult-adult interactive norms. In this regard, I was both similar to and different from Jajikonian children.[1] On the one hand, like children I frequently did and said things that adults should not. In fact, throughout this trip Karlin tried to use me like a child, to say and do the things that she preferred to avoid. On the other hand, often Jajikonian children do things that adults avoid not out of ignorance, like me, but because they inhabit a different social status with different social requirements. In contrast, I saw myself as having many of the same responsibilities as adults. Therefore, I became uncomfortable with the positions in which I found myself.

This trip quickly socialized me into the numerous forms of indirection that adults employ to avoid giving to each other. Their use of indirection, moreover, is not limited to avoiding giving; adults also often ask for things, criticize each other, and even gossip indirectly. Adults are not always indirect. Some elders and other more powerful people—like Terij and Imon, as we saw in chapter 1—are more willing to speak. Other speech acts, such as asking for a piece of fish during a communal meal, are not difficult and do not require indirection. But often speaking directly is dangerous: it can mean laying claim to a lie, a request, a refusal, a criticism, gossip, or knowledge. It can also mean taking responsibility for goods and marking oneself as a possessor who has an obligation to give. In such difficult situations, adults often use indirection to separate themselves from dangerous words and acts.

These uses of indirection are in no way unique. People around the world use various types of indirection and deception to save "face"—the positive social value that people can claim for themselves through their actions (Goffman 1967, 5). Requests, refusals, lies, gossip, criticisms, and assertions are all acts that, in the RMI and elsewhere, often put one's face at risk. Brown and Levinson (1978, 70–71) argue that asking is intrinsically face-threatening because it indicates that the speaker is willing to impose on another's freedom of action. Deception is the main method of saying no among Japanese adults (Clancy 1986); while anthropologists have discussed widespread indirection about possessions in many sharing-intensive societies (Altman and Peterson 1988; Berman Forthcoming; Firth 1936, 83; Hansen and Hansen 1974, 13–14; Marlowe 2004, 190; Peterson 1993).[2] In Jajikon as elsewhere, avoiding giving and negotiating other potentially dangerous situations often requires careful manipulations of speech and other signs.

My difficulty was *not* that Marshallese adults lied or evaded more than my friends at home but, rather, that they did so differently. While I found the Marshallese need to hide food restricting, Karlin told me that she found

American culture constraining because it is impolite to blow your nose without a tissue.[3] In both Jajikon and Chicago (where I lived prior to Jajikon), it is rude to wave a hundred-dollar bill in the air or eat birthday cake in front of guests who have none themselves. But before going to Jajikon I rarely consciously thought about how I kept my money out of sight (instead of carrying a transparent purse) or how I waited until guests were gone to eat the extra cake in the fridge. Such acts of concealing were invisible to me, until I encountered similar acts of concealing in unfamiliar contexts.

Despite these similarities, the hegemonic power of U.S. colonialism has produced negative views of Marshallese communication, views that further marginalize a people whose economy and culture have been battered for hundreds of years by colonialism, nuclear testing, and now climate change. I frequently heard people at the hotel bar in Majuro complaining about how Marshallese never follow through with their promises or plans. Such beliefs have even influenced some Marshallese people's understanding of themselves. Several friends in Jajikon told me that Marshallese people lie more than Americans. 'Marshallese people lie a lot,' one friend told me. 'American culture is good,' she continued, 'Marshallese culture is bad.' These criticisms of their own communicative practices is an example of "linguistic insecurity," something common in many indigenous and marginalized communities (Macaulay 1975). Briggs (1986, 90–92, 121–24) would also say that the criticisms are a result of "communicative hegemony," in which the interactive norms associated with people out of power, often indigenous people, are marginalized or pathologized in comparison with the norms associated with people in power, which appear normal or even invisible. The visibility of Marshallese patterns of concealing and simultaneous invisibility of similar (but different) patterns of concealing among many non-Marshallese visitors to the Marshall Islands is an example of this communicative hegemony. Negative views of Marshallese communicative practices reflect how the inequalities created by colonialism affect all aspects of Marshallese life, including views of their language.

In this chapter, I introduce such patterns of communication, showing how they are reasonable and often tied to adults' concerns for others' well-being and needs. I begin by analyzing methods of avoiding giving between adults. I then discuss the role of language, and specifically the concept of *riab* (lying), in adults' efforts to construct themselves as people who have given all they can. Finally, I discuss how, in a small village on a small strip of land, it is hard to hide. In fact, it is so hard to hide that avoiding giving usually requires other people's help. People frequently ignore the glimpse of a dollar bill, act as if they did not hear their friend mention a catch of fish, or look away as people transport goods. This help that they provide is another form of generosity, of allowing people to keep the things that they have.

But, of course, although people often do help, sometimes they do not. And I did not know whether they would choose to help me—whether they would allow me to keep my soda or put pressure on me to give it away.

Avoiding Giving

When I first moved to Jajikon, I unpacked all of my belongings and stacked them neatly in my room. This room was a small rickety wooden structure with a tin roof that my new family generously loaned me. (My stay temporarily displaced several of the boys in the household who had slept on the floor.) The rest of the family slept in the larger, also rickety, wooden structure just across the coral pebble yard. Marshallese households consist, minimally, of a sleeping house and a cookhouse. Others, like mine, may have additional living buildings and an enclosed fireplace for smoking coconut meat so that it can be sold to the copra processing plant (see Figure 3.2).

It took a couple of weeks for people to become more comfortable with me. Then, friends and family members who came by took one look at my huge

FIGURE 3.2 Marshallese household compound. Photo by Elise Berman.

container of ibuprofen, pile of mosquito coils, and box of blank DVDs and asked me to share. As my supplies for future days diminished rapidly, I realized that I needed to change my ways. I needed to do what people call *ņōņooj*—hiding.

Hiding

Polite, appropriate behavior in Jajikon requires keeping things out of sight. People keep goods in a corner or a separate room of their house, often in a chest or covered with blankets. A man who bought a small can of kerosene at a store stuffed it in his pocket for the walk home. Another man carried a bag of rice home on the lagoon beach, avoiding the more populated road. Several women told me that they liked to buy things from stores at night under the cover of darkness. After a couple of months I learned, upon returning to Jajikon from Majuro, to wait until night to produce the treats that I had bought for my family. 'Now,' my host mother said smiling, 'you know.'

By concealing their goods from the view of others, people construct themselves as not responsible for giving. As we have seen, it is public signs of possession—that is, carrying food in front of others—that create the subjective feeling of shame (*āliklik*). One way to be a good person and avoid this shame is to give. The other way is to hide the signs themselves. As a woman explained, "I will not carry food by your house on the road, because if I take food from my house and walk toward your house, I will pass the people in Jujan's house. Then I will say, 'Eat.'" In other words, if she walked with food, her shame would force her to give. She avoided that shame by hiding the food rather than carrying it in public.

How much one needs to hide depends on the nature of the good in question and the person asked. All adults agreed that it was against Marshallese custom to eat while walking or to carry a ready-to-eat meal—like cooked fish or rice—in public. For example, I was chatting with a neighbor by the side of the road when we saw a young woman dart between houses with a plate of food in her hand.

'Hey, what is that?' my neighbor called out.

The woman did not slow down. Instead she produced a small piece of a pancake, as if to indicate that the piece was all that was left. 'It is all gone!'

The man scowled. 'She is bad,' he muttered under his breath.

I grinned. I frequently heard the same words spoken about him, well known as one of the lazier souls in town. People described him as someone who constantly asked for things but never did any work to acquire them himself. Regardless, however, everyone would agree that the woman should not have carried food in public. 'Is it bad to walk with food?' I asked.

'Yes.'

Many people argued that this prohibition applies to all types of food. In 'Marshallese culture, we don't walk with food, all food, apples, candy, all of it,' a woman told me. Others limited the ban to either (1) what some people called "real food," which typically meant cooked food that people eat for meals such as rice, fish, bread, or pancakes; (2) "Marshallese food," which referred not only to fish and breadfruit but also to things such as rice and pancakes that are everyday staples; or (3) ready-to-eat food, which I define as food that people can immediately consume, such as cooked rice. In contrast, uncooked rice cannot be immediately consumed and is less necessary to share. Some people said that carrying snacks such as candy and Marshallese apples or a very small amount of food is fine. Claimed one woman, 'I walk while eating a lollipop all the time!' Others disagreed about the candy or the apples but said that carrying uncooked food, such as bags of uncooked rice or unopened cans of tuna, was OK.

But while people may disagree in theory about whether walking with snacks such as lollipops is taboo, in practice adults often avoided carrying any ready-to-eat food where someone might see them. I did see two women eat some Marshallese apples on the road, but one was a teenager and others criticized the second—Lacy—as "crazy" and a "person who is always looking for food."[4] On another occasion Lacy munched on some bread that she managed to commandeer from some women as she left their house. I happened to be walking past the house at the same time. Upon seeing me, rather than offering me some of her bread Lacy loudly suggested that I get some of the bread the women had cooked. Basically, Lacy forced those women to give. As the women gave me some bread they implicitly criticized Lacy when they asked, 'Are you not ashamed?' I responded, 'I am, but look at Lacy!' The women instructed me to put the bread in my pocket and not do as Lacy did. A young woman told me that people avoid carrying things such as soda or lollipops not because it is explicitly against Marshallese custom but because carrying them means that 'people will ask for [them].' If she had a lollipop, she continued, she would get rid of the stick so no one could see it. In fact, I once saw a young man walking with a lollipop. As he drew close to a crowd of people he pulled the stick out of the lollipop and tossed it into the woods, concealing the candy in his mouth. Similarly, although it is not necessarily explicitly wrong to carry unopened cans of tuna, bags of rice, or nonfood items such as soap, if people see such things they may very well ask for them. Since it is better to avoid such requests than refuse them, people often make an effort to keep things concealed if they can.

Commodities

There are, however, some things that need not be hidden. Land, cars, old toothbrushes or pillowcases, grown animals, and grown children are so associated with people that it is inappropriate to ask for them. This category also includes goods so unattached to people that, rather than given, they must be sold: commodities. Turning goods into commodities is an effective strategy to avoid giving without having to hide.

Commodities are "things to be sold" (*men in wia*). Identifying a commodity is not as easy as it might seem. An unopened bag of rice is not, by definition, a commodity that people need not give. People have to transform goods from potential gifts into commodities through the use of signs. The typical way of doing this involves starting a store in one's house. People bring in numerous goods, tell others that the goods belong to "the store," and then proceed to sell the goods. The more established stores had a faded piece of paper—a business permit from the capital—taped to a wall. But families without stores also sometimes sold goods simply by labeling them as things to sell.

One day a lovely smell of cooked bananas floated out of my family's cookhouse. My host mother was making a common Marshallese treat: banana bread. Made from small bananas that were much sweeter than any I had ever bought in an American grocery store, everybody loved it. When my host grandmother had made some a few weeks earlier, everybody had asked for it; within a day, the banana bread was gone. But this time my host mother sold the bread that she made. There was banana bread at our house for several days.

As this example reveals, the line between gifts and commodities is fuzzy at best. In Jajikon people typically pay for goods not only with money but also with copra. Bags of copra are heavy and half the size of a person. Consequently, people do not regularly carry them around. Thus, accepting copra as currency means selling on credit, something that people feel pressure to do. For example, one woman found running a store difficult because she felt ashamed (*āliklik*) to refuse to give things to kin on credit. Another store owner said that if someone really needs something, they give. Such stores may or may not produce profit.[5] One three-month period of receipts indicates that the copra people eventually gave to settle their debt rarely equaled the cost of the goods they had bought on credit. One man had a debt of $88.45.[6] He brought in copra that was only worth $31.22. The next month he bought at least $50.00 more on credit. As one store owner said, "People don't pay, from now until tomorrow."

Nevertheless, selling things allows people to do something that is otherwise impossible: to accumulate goods. Typically, surpluses are "impossible," as one man told me, to hide. "How can you hide ten bags of rice?" he asked rhetorically. But while people do criticize store owners who fail to sell on credit, they do not criticize store owners who maintain surpluses. Things to be sold do not count as real possessions. They belong to the store, not to the people, meaning that people do not ask for them unless they are asking to buy on credit. Moreover, many people told me that they are more "ashamed" to buy things on credit than to ask for gifts. This ability to display without hiding, to buy without immediately having to give, may be one reason why people start stores in the first place.

Speech and Transferred Responsibility

But although the soda in the store in Liklob was a commodity, after Karlin and I bought it the soda would become ours, something we had an obligation to give and needed to hide. And beyond hiding the soda itself we also needed, it turned out, to hide any words that pointed to the soda.

Although Karlin and I had originally planned to go get soda the next day, I realized that I was free earlier than expected. It was a boat day. Men gathered on the dock hauling packages. Children ran around everywhere, jumping in the water, staring into the boat, inspecting the packages as if they could see what was inside. A couple of older grandmothers sat on the edge of the dock joined by newly returned kin. Karlin and the younger women stayed farther away, not yet bold enough to enter men's space.

I joined them. 'Let's go today,' I blurted out.

The women pounced on my words. 'Where are you going?'

I hesitated, belatedly realizing my mistake. If I told them that we were going to Liklob, they would want to know why. If I told them why, I would have to tell them that we were going to get soda.

One's obligations to give depend on how one manipulates not only goods but also words. Adults often try to avoid talking about anything that they would prefer not to give. "Eat rice!" my Marshallese mother regularly called out, inviting passersby to share the rice that she had cooked. Strategically, she avoided mentioning the fish or meat that she had also prepared, increasing the possibility that people would politely decline her offer. In contrast to meat or fish, rice was boring and bland.

So when the women asked me where we were going I did not answer. Perhaps, I naively hoped, they would forget about the conversation.

Of course, they did not. 'Where are you going?'

I peeked at Karlin out of the corner of my eye, silently appealing for help.

Unfortunately, she spoke. 'Elise, they are asking you a question.'

I hesitated.

'They are asking you a question,' she insisted.

I glared at Karlin. Unfailingly kind, Karlin eventually became one of my best friends on the island. She never got tired of my questions and generously offered up her time so that I could understand her way of life. Her reflections on

Marshallese culture were both insightful—she helped me negotiate a tense situation between two families—and occasionally humorous. She also never tired of caring for her many younger siblings and relatives. "Hurry!" she commanded her brother when a little girl was crying, determined to give the girl food as good Marshallese adults do. To the chagrin of her younger relatives, however, Karlin often enacted her duty to both care for and command them more vigorously than some. "Kyle, don't you hear!" "Ah, give it to me." "Why aren't you giving it to me?"

I quickly fell into the category of another younger sibling, someone whom she cared for, fed, and commanded. For the rest of that day she continued to command that I speak in her place, just as she had near the dock. Eventually, I grew frustrated by her constant efforts to make me respond to people's questions instead of answering them herself. I asked, 'Why do you tell them to ask me?'

Karlin hesitated. 'If I say I am going to Liklob, they will ask me to bring things back. So, I tell them to ask you.' By telling people that we were going to Liklob, we also opened ourselves up to requests for goods. Karlin's strategy to avoid those requests, and the responsibility to give that they would create, was to remain silent and force me to speak. If I spoke, I would take responsibility not only for my words but for any goods to which they could point.

This tactic has been described in linguistic anthropology as manipulating the footing or the participant structure of an interaction. Goffman (1981) argued that the act of speaking actually involves multiple roles that can be concentrated in one person or distributed over many (see also Goodwin and Goodwin 2004; Hill and Irvine 1993b). First there is the "animator," the person who literally opens their mouth and speaks. Then there is the "author," the person who wrote the text or told the animator what to say. Finally, there is the "principal," the person whose social status is embedded in the utterance. For example, the president's press secretary is the animator of words that may have been authored—i.e., written—by another member of the staff. Those words reflect most on the social status of neither the press secretary nor the writer but the president. Hence, it is ultimately the president—the principal—whom people take as responsible for the contents of the speech.

In the RMI, we can extend such insights to possessors of material goods—such as soda—who have an obligation or responsibility to share. The "animator" physically holds the soda, the "author" tells the animator what to do with the soda, and the "principal" is the person who has the actual social power to control where that soda goes. For example, a landowner is the principal in control of the coconuts on his land. He may, however, have his son act as author and instruct other children to collect those coconuts. Those children are then the animators. In the case of material goods, therefore, we should call principals "possessors": people who have power over goods and also the responsibility to give them away.

As I have shown, in Jajikon people tend to see those who are carrying a good not only as animators but also as principals—that is, as possessors with a responsibility to give. But it is possible for people to try to change such an impression: to present themselves as mere animators who, like the children in the example above, are not in control of the good in question.

At one point during my stay I sat in the Majuro hospital hallway with some other people from Jajikon. One of them, a teenager, listened to an iPod.

'Whose is it?' I asked.

"It belongs to people."

'Which person?'

'People,' she vaguely replied.

'She is saying,' an older woman interrupted, 'that you are lying.' I was not, actually, but apparently that is how the woman interpreted my questions. Indeed, later in private the teenager admitted that the iPod was indeed hers. But, she explained, if she claimed it as her own, people would say, 'Give it to me so that I can listen for a little while.' By stating that it belonged to "people," she established herself as an animator but not a possessor—as someone who did not control the iPod and could not give it away.

The teenager was manipulating the participant structure, but she was also lying, a typical way to get out of giving. Indeed, people see "lying" (*riab*) about goods, exemplified by the phrase "it is all gone" (*emaat*), as a part of hiding. "Adults say it is all gone . . . they hide it," a woman explained to me. 'Do you have any tuna?' one man asked a second man. 'It is all gone,' the second man said about the four cans of tuna that I could see in the next room. My research assistants told me that they regularly "lied" in response to requests for money by saying that I had not yet paid them or that they had already spent their money. One scolded me for answering truthfully when people asked when I paid her, explaining that I should not even reveal what days she worked.

I too eventually resorted to lying.

'Where are you going?' the women insisted.

I put off the inevitable as long as possible. 'To Liklob.'

'To do what?'

I hesitated. Then I lied. 'Just a trip with no specific purpose [*jam̧bo*].'

The women fell silent. Karlin and I walked away.

All of these different ways of avoiding giving—hiding, turning goods into commodities, presenting oneself as an animator, lying—are manipulations of signs. Through these manipulations, one can conceal the link between people and material goods that marks possession and a responsibility to give.

Language as Social Action

Such transformations work, when they do, partly because language is not simply a reflection of the world but also a way of shaping it. By manipulating speech people engage in social action—action that affects what truth and lies are and whether people have an obligation to give.

Lies and Truths (Riab and M̧ool)

The Marshallese words *riab* and *m̧ool* have two meanings. First, *riab* can simply mean "false." For example, the phrase *riab in naan* literally means "false words" and often refers to children's nonsense speech. Second, people can also use the words *riab* and *m̧ool* as moral evaluations of whether utterances are good or bad. Good speech is *m̧ool* (true/right), while bad speech is *riab* (false/lie/wrong).

Some utterances are both false and immoral and obviously *riab*. Others, however, may be accurate but immoral or inaccurate but moral (see also Coleman and Kay 1981). In such situations, people move back and forth between calling these utterances *riab* or *m̧ool*. For example, a research assistant and I reviewed a video in which a boy, Carl, ate some fish. When he finished eating, there were still fish in the pot. He walked to his neighbor's house, where he saw his friend Nick.

"Carl!" Nick said. Apparently, Nick could smell the fish on Carl's hands. "Ah, you didn't bring me my fish dude? Carl, go and bring me my fish dude."

"The fish is all gone," Carl responded.

My research assistant evaluated Carl's statement as *m̧ool* (true/right). When I protested that the video showed that there were still a couple of fish in the pot, my assistant responded that maybe the fish were "the food of others." The boy could not give the fish away, so his words were right and *m̧ool*.

My assistant's comments reveal how Jajikonians, like many other people, often evaluate speech according to not whether it is sincere but, rather, its effects (Carr 2010; Du Bois 1993; Rosaldo 1982). I never saw an adult discipline a child for lying itself. Adults did discipline children for the effects of their lies—such as for going swimming after saying that they would not swim. Here, however, the main problem was not the child's false words but, rather, the action of swimming. Marshallese parents and older siblings frequently lie to small children to get them to behave. 'Look there is chocolate over there!' a mother cried, successfully getting her small son (not yet talking) to go where she wanted him to go (there was no chocolate). Adults also typically do not tell their children that they are adopted (Berman 2014a). People with whom I spoke saw such speech as creating a negative linguistic separation between parent and child, making children feel rejected even though they are loved. Finally, many said that people who knew damaging gossip should say "I don't know" in response to a request for information rather than speaking. Such a statement may be "*riab* [a lie]," one man said, but it is also "good."[7]

If we evaluate speech according to its effects rather than its referential accuracy, there are several reasons why lying about goods may be appropriate or good. First, people sometimes thought that requests indexed greediness and laziness. During interviews I presented adults with a hypothetical story: 'There are two fish left, and your husband hasn't eaten,' I said. 'Someone says, "Is there any fish?" '

Raina instantly interrupted me, explaining what she would say in such a situation. 'None.'

'Is it a lie or the truth?'

'I lie. Because why are they asking for fish, why don't they go fishing?'

Second, lying may be necessary for the well-being of other family members. As one woman commented while sympathizing with a friend who gave all of her coconut oil away, "And then when you give it to them so that they can oil themselves, there is no oil left for your daughter." Another woman explained that sometimes people have to "lie" (*riab*) because others have not yet eaten.

Finally, as we saw in chapter 1, directly refusing someone, or even saying something like 'I need that one fish for my husband,' embarrasses (*kajjookok*) the asker and negatively affects one's relationship with that individual. As one person explained, saying " 'I am sorry, I can't go' . . . will make the other person sad." Rather than making people sad and embarrassed, it is often better to lie and say that there is no food. Alternatively, if the request is for something in the future, it is often better to say yes even if one is not going to give. Such responses make people comfortable and reaffirm their status as kin.

My statement "just a *jam̧bo*" maintained harmonious relationships between everyone, relationships that would have been jeopardized had I admitted to buying soda for Karlin but not the others. I caused no one embarrassment, and I avoided my own shame. Therefore, I did not need to give.

Requesting and Joking

Or so I thought.

Upon leaving the women I followed Karlin's lead. But instead of departing for Liklob as I had expected, we ended up back at Karlin's house. We walked across the yard, our broken, patched-up flip-flops crunching loudly against the coral pebbles.

Pulling her muumuu conservatively over her knees, Karlin sat down near her father Ronji and her brother Nick (see Figure 3.3). I joined her a little more

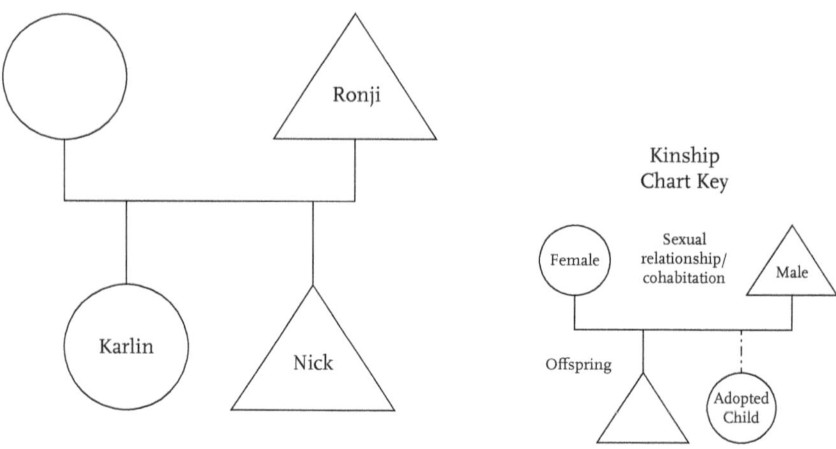

FIGURE 3.3 Karlin's family.

awkwardly. We sat in silence for a few moments. Eventually Karlin turned to me. 'Maybe we should go on Sunday.'

I stared at her, surprised. Our latest interaction had made it clear that Karlin had no desire to talk about our trip to Liklob. Moreover, while I was socially incompetent, she was not. Why did she mention the trip?

In hindsight, Karlin was a skilled user of speech to achieve her goals and to shape society to her desires. It turns out that she wanted some bicycles. Karlin's father controlled two, just the number that we needed.

But Karlin could not ask for the bikes. People, as we have seen, feel ashamed to make requests, particularly of someone higher in rank. Saying something such as "Give me the bicycles" implies that one has the right to those bicycles. Karlin was a youth in her father's house with no right to demand that he give. Even more polite requests such as "Could I use the bicycle?" would clearly position Karlin as responsible for making a request, creating embarrassment for Karlin if Ronji should refuse her.

So Karlin used indirect speech to disguise her request. By suggesting that we put our trip off until Sunday, she implied that we wanted to go today. Ronji could infer that we would like some bikes for the trip and choose whether or not to offer them to us. Karlin made a request while leaving the power where it belonged: in her father's hands.

Karlin's speech was particularly oblique but nonetheless not that unusual. When asking for things that adults are not sure other adults are willing to give, they tend to use various forms of indirect speech. People say things such as 'Is there any tuna?' 'Is there any meat?' 'What is that?' "Did you have good fortune (a good catch)?" or "Oh Mariana! Are there not any limes?" These questions about the existence of goods are necessary since people often really do not know what others have. But such questions also serve as indirect requests, since if people admit to having something, they immediately have to offer to give it away.

Adults may also joke. Indeed, adults in Jajikon joked constantly. "How old are you?" I asked one of my adult friends. "Two," she said, clearly false. A woman said that her granddaughter was not going on a trip. When I mentioned this to the granddaughter later, she exclaimed exasperatedly, "She is joking!" A friend called out to her grandfather that the boat had arrived (it hadn't). 'She is pregnant,' a woman teased her daughter (she wasn't).

This joking, when refusing to give or making a request, works like other forms of indirection: it allows people to avoid responsibility. Consider the following example: An older woman yelled to her kinsman walking across the street, "Go and tell Hukira that she should give me my gum!"

"Ask for gum with so many people on the dock?!" her kinsman called back in a loud tone of voice. Since people rarely have enough to share with all, asking in public is rude because it forces a person to give to everyone. Hence the man's question, combined with his loud and comical voice, suggested that people should interpret the woman's original request as so ludicrous that it must be a joke. Joke requests are not real requests and do not compel a gift.

"Okay," the woman said, following her kinsman's suggestion to frame her request as a joke, "you should say [to your mother], 'Give me my food disrespectful girl [*luweo*] because I am broke from supporting my in-laws!' " The two burst into laughter. *Luweo* is a disrespectful female vocative, something a son would not typically say to his mother. The woman's additional off-color reference to annoying in-laws who ask for things established her request, and his refusal, as jokes. Consequently, the man had no responsibility to give, and the woman had no reason to be ashamed of being refused.

Leaking Signs

Through indirection, Karlin managed to imply that we wanted bicycles without taking responsibility for having asked for them. But her speech had an unfortunate side effect: it exposed the trip we were going to take and pointed to the soda that we were to buy.

Ronji voiced the inevitable question, 'Where are you going?'

I groaned silently. Then I said nothing. This particular situation was Karlin's mess.

Of course, Karlin had other ideas. 'Show it,' she commanded, meaning that I should explain what we were doing.

If I had been Marshallese I probably would have found a way to force the responsibility for speech back onto Karlin. At the time, however, my political skills were limited, and I could see no way out. Reluctantly, I spoke. 'To Liklob.' Then, anticipating Ronji's follow-up question, I bit the bullet. 'Just for an aimless trip [*jaṃbo*].'

'Lie [*riab*]!' Nick declared.

My heart jumped, and I started to panic. Our secret, it seemed, was out.

Of course, our secret had never really been secret. It is possible that Nick overheard us planning our trip. Even if he had not, however, we gave off so many signs that one would have to be dense to not know what we were doing. Our request for bicycles pointed to a trip to Liklob. At that moment in time, a trip to Liklob pointed to soda. Everyone knew that there was soda in Liklob. I have also since realized that many would have interpreted my phrase "just a *jaṃbo*" as a lie. For example, when I took walks I frequently told people that I was just on a *jaṃbo*. Since I actually was going nowhere, I viewed *jaṃbo* as the most accurate description of my actions. But no one believed me, so they repeated their question until they got a more specific answer. This general expectation that people use *jaṃbo* to hide actions or intentions reflects adults' larger expectations that other adults' words are opaque, they often serve to hide and misdirect.[8]

Finally, our trip was never a secret because in Jajikon there is nowhere to hide. The single road that runs the length of the islet runs right past everybody's front doors. Most activity takes place under a tree in the yard, particularly because modern houses sport tin roofs that, unlike the older thatched roofs, magnify the sun. Consequently, people walking past spy the soda that people drink or the can of tuna unfortunately peeking out from behind the door, smell the fish that men have caught, see people making fermented breadfruit or gathering up a bag of copra. In turn, all goods and people that move through the village pass under the watchful eye of someone. Most people transport things along the single road. Others, trying to avoid the public eye, take the more secluded lagoon beach, but this option is imperfect. Even on the beach I often passed children playing, men fishing, or other people also trying to be inconspicuous. Moreover, the beach is not always available. At high tide the lagoon comes all the way up to the vegetation line. The ocean beach is a craggy land of large sharp coral boulders. Beyond the lagoon beach and road, there are no real ways to travel lengthwise across the village.

Our soda revealed itself through our words, our actions, the bicycles we asked for, and the road we had to travel on. These signs expose all people's lies just as they exposed mine.

Lying and Avoiding Giving

So what? Telling untruths is not in and of itself bad.

But *riab* has two meanings—it can mean false, or it can refer to immoral speech. Accusations of *riab*, therefore, are essentially accusations of immoral speech. Specifically, *riab* is associated with three very bad things: negative gossip, stealing, and not giving.

First, people criticized those who spread negative gossip as liars (even if the gossip was accurate) and praised those who refrained from spreading gossip as truthful (even if they had to say false things to keep the gossip to themselves). A Marshallese saying, "the mouths of women" (*lo̧ñin kōrā*), reflects a criticism of gossip that ruins relationships and reputations, speech largely seen as the domain of women (Berman 2012, 163). A woman said that claiming "I don't know" about gossip that one has merely heard but not seen is "true [*m̧ool*]" because one's source of information—hearsay—is not sufficient. Indeed, even if one has information on good authority, "it is not lying [*riab*]" to say "I don't know," "because it is not a good thing [to talk about]."

Second, many said that lying leads to stealing.[9] "In Marshallese culture, if we lie a lot, then we steal." Another person said, "Stealing is the friend of lies." Children should not lie, because if they do, an adult told me, they will "grow up and steal." This deep negative evaluation of theft makes sense considering the overriding importance of giving and sharing in Jajikon.

Finally, people who *riab* (lie/speak immorally) also fail to give. The word for thank you in Marshallese, *kom̧m̧ool*, combines *kwe* (you) with *m̧ool* (true) to mean, literally, "you are true." It is more than a metaphor; every adult I asked repeated a saying: people who are "stingy . . . lie," while those who give "are true" (Walsh 2003, 118). In Jajikon the moral character trait of kindness and generosity (*jouj*)—which people demonstrate largely through giving—is also connected to speaking the truth. Seven other adults said something similar to one woman, who explained, 'People who are generous do not lie.' Another woman said that if people are not generous, they say that they will give but then "run away." People often distinguish between jokes (*kōjak*) and lies (*riab*) based on whether or not a person ultimately gave. Numerous adults called a hypothetical man who said that he had no rice "joking" if he eventually gave the rice but "lying" if he did not give. "Because if he says that it is all gone and the other person leaves and he does not give to him, he is greedy. But if he says that it is all gone and gives, he is joking."

Accusations of lying are often accusations of not only immorality, therefore, but also stinginess. Those who avoid giving to help their family may view their statements as good and not necessarily lies at all. But those who do not get that for which they ask can, if they choose, interpret acts of not giving as markers of lying and also as indications of immorality and social distance. In other words, truth comes not from speaking but from the act of establishing positive social relationships—that is, giving (Robbins 2001, 2007). Although it is not bad in and of itself to speak untruths, it is bad to get caught.

Depending on Others

Nick caught me. 'You are going to get soda!' he continued. 'And if more people go with you, you won't buy it; if I came, you would not buy soda!'

I think that in my situation other adults would have simply denied Nick's accusation. Language shapes social relationships, after all, and the best way to shape social relationships is to deny anything that could be harmful. Just like what philosophers call "bald-faced lies" (Stokke 2013)—statements that everyone knows are lies but cannot be proved as such—such statements force the outcome into what one wants it to be. For example, I once asked a young woman who had been traveling on a boat that rescued a capsized vessel to tell me what happened.

'I don't know,' she said. Perhaps she did not want to be seen as gossiping.

Frustrated, I burst out, 'But you were on the boat!'

'I was on [the other boat].'

'But it picked up the passengers from the overturned boat!'

'Well,' she reconsidered, 'I was sleeping.'

'She is lying,' a woman broke in. 'She just does not want to share.'

'Are you saying you don't know even though you were there?' I asked.

The young woman paused. 'It's a joke.'

I frequently said similar things back in the United States. I told people that I would love to go to a party but was sick, that I was feeling great when I was not, or that the food was delicious when it was horrible. But while the basic principle—a concern for relationships and the situation rather than reference—was similar, the situations in which such a concern is necessary differed and I was not yet quick enough on my feet.

Karlin's past behavior gave me little hope that she would help, but I still looked appealingly at her.

Of course, she did not speak.

Surprisingly, neither did Ronji.

In fact, Ronji acted as if he never heard Nick's accusation. Instead, he silently stood up. He walked over to the shed, his slow and measured pace the norm on an island where time means little and the weather is hot. Then he gave us two bicycles and, without a word, sent us on our way.

Cooperation

Ronji helped us hide. He ignored the signs of not giving and actively worked to create an illusion that we were not responsible for giving him soda. Why? One possible explanation is that he—a mature adult, unlike Nick—was like many adults uncomfortable with the possibility of overtly challenging us. As with requests, lies, and possessions, adults often avoided accusations, criticisms, or disagreements due to shame (*āliklik*) or fear (*mijak*). For example, a woman's laughter led me to interpret her husband's command to do something that I clearly did not want to do as a joke. But the man was serious. His wife was laughing because she was uncomfortable with our relatively direct confrontation. As Karlin explained when I consulted her for help understanding this incident, "In Marshallese culture . . . we do not say it."

Adults' emotional discomfort with interpersonal conflict, as well as their shame or fear of accusing others, certainly explains why many adults refrain from challenging each other. But I wonder if such a reason explains why Ronji did not challenge Karlin and me. With younger and less powerful individuals Ronji did not mince words. He terrified everyone younger than him, ruling them with sharp, commanding speech. His children, who regularly ignored their mothers' orders, obeyed him without question. Ronji once openly accused a younger man who was in a son-father relationship with him of stealing cigarettes, upbraiding the man in public in front of others. Because he was both Karlin's father and in a father relationship with me, Ronji had the authority and personality to speak.

Thus, Ronji may have acted as if he did not know that Karlin and I were getting soda not because he was afraid to speak but because, as our father, it was his job not only to command us but also to care for us. *Jouj*, care for others, includes respecting others' autonomy of movement and control over material wealth, whereas shame (*āliklik*) inhibits people from neglecting their duties as an elder to be *jouj*. For example, one man, the oldest sibling in his family, told me that he would not ask his younger siblings for things because his greater power would compel them to give. "If it were me," he said, "and I go and ask for something from my younger siblings, it might be something that they really need, but if I say give, they will give."

"Oh, because they are your younger siblings?" I asked.

"Yes, because they say that he is the oldest. . . . So I myself need to think, my younger brother or my younger sister, they also want this thing and they also need it."

"Because you are ashamed [*āliklik*]?"

"The reason that I am ashamed [*āliklik*] is because I know that he or she needs it."

Just as the elder brother was ashamed to ask for things from his younger siblings, Karlin's father might have been ashamed to force us away from our desires, to use his greater power to compel a gift. Or perhaps he was concerned for our feelings and the embarrassment that we would surely feel if he forced our deceptions into the spotlight, where we could no longer pretend that they did not exist.

Successfully avoiding giving depended not just on Karlin and me but also on everyone else. While Nick chose to force our soda into the open, Ronji let us go. As did many others. Our trip was filled with moments in which our obligation to share hung in the balance and depended on how others interpreted and manipulated signs. As Karlin and I rode our borrowed bicycles out of town, the calls and questions followed. "Where are you coming from?" "Where are you going?" "What are you doing?"

'Ask Elise!' Karlin inevitably yelled.

I resigned myself to speaking. 'To Liklob, just for a *jam̧bo* [trip]!'

But like Ronji, no one said anything. They let us go; they cooperated to create the illusion that we were not going to get soda, that we were not possessors and had no need to give.

Uncertainty

The problem with depending on others is that one does not know what they are going to do. People like Ronji could ignore our amazingly obvious journey to buy soda. Or, like Nick, they could call us out. As the older brother said, although he himself avoided forcing his younger siblings to give, "some people are not [ashamed]." Since others' actions are always unpredictable, it is dangerous to be close to any signs of possession.

Which is why, an hour or so later, two young women and I stood huddled in the woods between Liklob and Jajikon unable to return home. One of the women was Karlin. The other woman was her kinswoman Siana, who had asked Karlin and me to wait when she saw us riding out of town. She eventually joined us on her own bike. Since no one said anything about soda or Liklob, I had no idea why she was riding with us and I wondered whether I would end up having to buy a soda for Siana as well. It turned out, however, that Karlin's and my goal was so obvious that—without anyone saying anything—Siana apparently knew what we were up to and joined us for the same reason. She also bought two sodas at the store in Liklob.

We stopped in the woods because neither Karlin nor Siana was willing to carry the soda into Jajikon. But the two women disagreed about how to deal with the problem. Siana proposed that we drink our soda immediately, hidden by the trees from the eyes of others.

I thought that this was an excellent idea.

Karlin did not. 'We are going back,' Karlin told Siana.

'But there are so many people in my house!' Siana protested.

'I need to get back to cook rice,' Karlin said. In private, she told me that she actually wanted to return home so that she could drink her soda with ice—which her family had brought that day in a cooler from Majuro.

Siana thought for a couple of minutes. Then, she found her way out. She told me that she would come over in the evening to drink the sodas (I had a private room). She then neatly solved the other part of her problem—getting the sodas to her house—by handing her sodas to me.

And so—still learning Marshallese cultural norms—I did something that all Marshallese adults would have felt too much shame (*āliklik*) to do. I hung the partly transparent plastic bag of sodas on my handlebars and biked home.

I felt the weight of eyes staring at me as I rode sweating down the road. "Where did you come from?" "Where are you going?" "What are you doing?"

I had almost reached the safety of my house. But first, I had to pass the church. Several older women were clearing weeds in the yard.

'Come here!' one of them called.

I groaned. 'Just a minute!' Rudely turning my back to her, I hurried to my house. I stashed the sodas inside, stowing them in a plastic container hidden from prying eyes. Then I returned to the church.

'Give me a dollar,' the woman said.

My heart jumped. Sodas cost a dollar. 'Why?'

'For the church! It is just a dollar!'

I relaxed. She was talking about a fundraiser for the church. I gave her a dollar, happy not only to give but also that my adventure had gone unnoticed. I walked away, convinced that I had succeeded, that no one knew what I had done.

Adults, Interaction, and Shame

Of course, I was wrong. A couple of months later a friend and I somehow got onto the topic of soda. 'Why didn't you give me any?' she asked, referring to this time when I rode through town. She knew about the soda, she told me, because she could see it. My flimsy plastic bag, like so many forms of speech, inadequately hid its contents.

Which meant that the old women in the churchyard also saw the soda, as did everyone else. But the women—like Karlin's father and my friend—silently agreed to act as if they did not know. As I suspect they did countless times every day, they swallowed their words and hid their understanding, allowing avoiding giving to take place by outwardly accepting the illusion that we did not need to share.

But an illusion is just that, an illusion. People may choose not to buy into it. Nor do illusions stop the gossip and behind-the-scenes critique of those who do not give. Responsibility for goods and to give almost always "leaks" out, typically onto the animator, the person speaking the words or carrying the goods (Hill and Irvine 1993). Consequently, adults are almost always responsible for that which they hold or that which they say. If they hold something, they should have shared it. If they say something, they were the ones who lied, gossiped, asked, or criticized.

If signs inevitably leak, then it is best to stay as far away from them as possible. Karlin and Siana refused to carry the soda through town. Despite the plastic bag, they were ashamed (*āliklik*).

As I should have been myself. But in the beginning of the trip, I was not. My lack of shame made me similar to a child. Karlin used me, just as adults often use shameless children, to animate her words (where we were going) and the soda itself (I carried the soda). Through me, she separated herself from responsibility for these dangerous actions and possessions.

But I was not secure in my childlike status. Unlike children, after all, I did in fact control quite a bit of material wealth. I began to feel obligated to share this wealth or, at the very least, conceal it more effectively. I found carrying the soda extremely uncomfortable; I disliked talking to Ronji and others about the trip; I worried that people criticized me or gossiped about me behind my back. Although Karlin viewed me as able to transport and talk about soda without feeling a need to give it, I did not feel that way myself.

In future similar situations I avoided speaking, walked along the beach instead of the road, brought along an opaque backpack that more adequately hid its contents, or avoided such trips entirely. I became *āliklik*, appropriately ashamed.

Drinking Soda

Karlin, Siana, and her friend waited until dark to sneak over to my house. I am sure that people saw them—if not the women still sitting across in front of the church, then the many men gathered in my family's yard. People in Jajikon have an uncanny ability to identify each other by their silhouettes.

Imagining dozens of eyes staring at my house, I closed my curtains. Loose pieces of cloth that blew open in a breeze, they did little to help me hide. I drew the sodas from underneath the table; my responsibility to give weighing heavily on me as I guiltily imagined the people outside. The other women seemed to have no regrets. This was my house, after all, and so all of the consequences would fall on me. I think, in fact, that they were delighted. Not only did they get to drink soda, but our secret tryst had an enjoyable element of danger to it. Karlin filled our cups with ice.

We drank the soda. It was refreshing.

Notes

1. This similarity between the ethnographer and children has been noted by many anthropologists (e.g., Briggs 1971, 27, 252; Gay y Blasco and Wardle 2007, 146–47). Ethnographers who are new to an environment often feel like children and may be treated as such.
2. Numerous scholars have criticized Brown and Levinson for presenting an ethnocentric analysis of face based on Western presumptions of a rational actor strategically manipulating social interaction (e.g., Bargiela-Chiappini 2003; Mao 1994). Others argue that politeness changes with context, meaning that we should study how people conform to or break the norms associated with different speaking genres (Blitvich 2010, 2013). Considering the fact that many Marshallese discuss their own seemingly face-saving actions as the result of emotions as opposed to reason, and that their use of indirection changes with context (and age), such criticisms are likely well founded. The basic point that asking and refusing are often face-threatening, however, fits with Marshallese communicative norms.
3. In Jajikon people would hold one nostril closed with one finger and then blow out of the other nostril onto the ground.
4. These women's actions may also have been due to the fact that since it was apple season everyone was constantly eating apples. Their abundance may have made hiding them both less important and more difficult.
5. For a discussion of different methods of understanding and producing profit, see Chayanov 1966; Mayer and Glave 1999.
6. The currency in the RMI is the U.S. dollar.
7. Many forms of Christianity as well as many Western philosophers and linguists, in contrast, often have a very different language ideology in which they prize sincerity (Grice 1989; Keane 2007; Searle 1969). This importance of sincerity is often tied to a view of speech as mainly referential. In such ideologies, the purpose of speech is to refer to things or people's inner states. Consequently, good speech is speech that either accurately describes the world or sincerely reflects people's inner states (Grice 1989; Keane 2007; Robbins 2007; Silverstein 1979). This influence of evangelical Christian views of

language and sincerity is evident in Jajikon and specifically in the evangelical churches. "Don't lie [*riab*]," a man warned me once when I said that I was out of mosquito coils. "If you are lying [*riab*] you will go to hell." "God is truthful and his promises are not lies [*riab*]!" an evangelical pastor proclaimed: "The words of God are true [*m̧ool*]." Lying is particularly bad if one is in church, a woman claimed, criticizing some men who said in church that they would bring meat but then never did. But while in theory lying is bad, in practice, outside of church people approached speech with much more concern for its effects than its sincerity.

8. An additional example of this general idea that words are opaque is the prohibition against swearing to the truth of one's statements by saying, "on the face of God [*mejān Anij*]!" Such swears are bad partly because they involve taking the name of God in vain. "Have you seen God?" a woman demanded when I declared "on the face of God" to convince her of my truthfulness. "Then you should not use his name!" But they are also bad because the very unreliability of speech means that such swears are inevitably lies (*riab*). As a woman explained, since people "lie a lot" it is wrong to swear because it is unlikely that one is telling the truth. She found a hypothetical situation that I proposed—in which someone swears on God but is speaking the truth—counterintuitive and impossible to imagine. Adults, she continued, are scared to swear on God because they may not follow through with their words. Moreover, if one swears on God and lies, numerous people told me, something bad will happen: an accident, a broken finger, or death.
9. While negative gossip is associated with women, stealing is often associated with young men. A woman who stayed home from a feast to protect her house from theft said that she was protecting it from young men, specifically teenage boys.

4 "GIVE ME MY FOOD"

HOW TO AVOID GIVING TO ANOTHER CHILD AND PRODUCE RELATIVE AGE

Rōka sat alone. His dark black hair barely peeked above the top of the white church bench, his orange shirt hidden by the rows in front of him. Silently, he watched other children talk, play, and run around the church as they waited for rehearsal to begin.[1]

Perhaps he was shy (*jook*). Although his mother was from Jajikon, Roka's family had been living on his father's home island. They had arrived in Jajikon only a couple of weeks earlier.

Perhaps Rōka was scared (*mijak*). Rōka was tall enough that he seemed almost ready to start school. But he was still shorter and younger than most of the other children in the church.

Or perhaps he was simply trying to minimize the negative consequences of his behavior. Rōka was doing something that adults, at least, would say was bad: eating a lollipop in broad daylight while surrounded by people.

The lollipop was eminently shareable. Marshallese children (and adults) constantly took candy or gum out of their mouths and gave it to others. Licked or untouched, if seen, a lollipop had to be shared.

Unlike the adults we encountered in the last chapter, Rōka did not go out of his way to hide his lollipop from others. He did not throw the stick in the bushes and conceal the candy in his mouth or wait until night to consume the lollipop. Nor did other children. I frequently saw children who, like Rōka, deliberately exposed their goods to others and engaged in forms of conspicuous consumption, indicating that they lacked *āliklik*, cultural shame.

In this chapter I follow Rōka and his lollipop along with the children who attempted to take the lollipop from him and analyze these children's forms of speech. As we will see, in addition to conspicuous consumption children also do many other things that adults tend to avoid in front of their peers. Children constantly and publicly demand that others give. They explicitly insult and criticize each other. They also directly refuse to give.

These modes of communication are not the only way that children interact with one another. Children are often generous or, like adults, may hide goods or lie about them to get out of giving. But in the children's world, power is often gained through explicit (as opposed to implicit) acts of control—through conspicuous consumption, demands, refusals, and criticisms. Such methods parallel accounts of insults, shaming, and confrontations in children's peer groups elsewhere, interactions through which children negotiate identities and construct hierarchical power relationships (Blum-Kulka and Snow 2004; Cook-Gumperz and Corsaro 1986; Evaldsson 2005, 2007; Goodwin 2006; Goodwin and Alim 2010; Goodwin and Kyratzis 2007, 2012; Kyratzis 2004; Tetreault 2010). Such methods explicitly contrast with the way adults in Jajikon often negotiate control over possessions with each other. Ultimately, as future chapters will reveal, these differences between adult-adult and child-child speech patterns allocate children a central role in familial economic transactions and social relationships.

Our particular story has four main characters: Rōka and his kin Kinta, Lari, and Kyle (see Figure 4.1). All four children used various forms of explicit and direct speech to try to control Rōka's food. Through these various direct forms

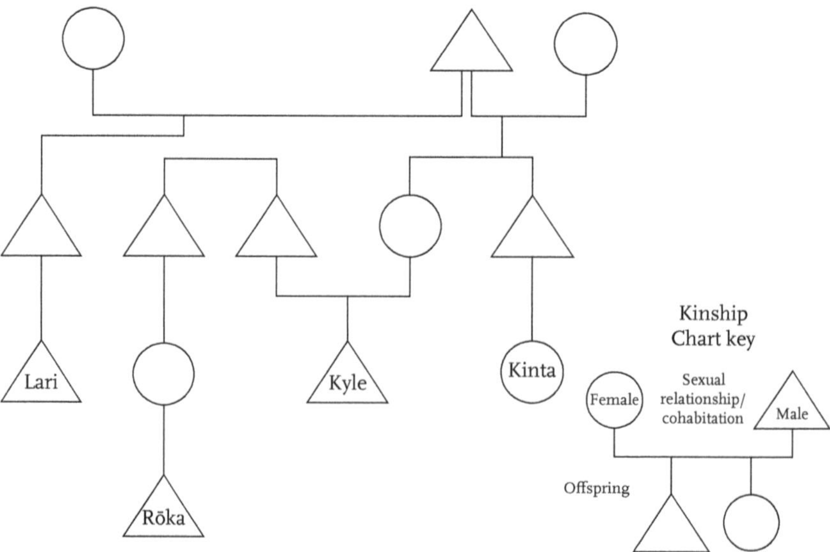

FIGURE 4.1 Rōka's relationship with Kinta, Kyle, and Lari.

of speech and behavior, Rōka, Kinta, Lari, and Kyle negotiated their hierarchical status relationships—who has power over whom.

The children also negotiated their relative ages—who is older than whom. In Jajikon, age is power. Power negotiations, therefore, are also age negotiations, and vice versa. The children's negotiation for the lollipop was an interaction in which they produced themselves as older or younger than each other—in which they produced age.

Who would get the lollipop? Could Rōka keep it, or would he have to give? And what would that tell us about his age?

Conspicuous Consumption

Among children in Jajikon conspicuous consumption is a presentation of the self (Goffman 1959).[2] Specifically, it is a presentation of a powerful self, someone who is able to control material wealth and has the ability to either share that wealth or withhold it from others.

Past events reveal that Rōka was clearly on a mission to distinguish himself—to establish his status among the other children. A month prior to the rehearsal in the church, and a mere five days after arriving on Jajikon, Rōka wandered across his yard while nibbling on a pancake.

Pancakes were a breakfast staple in Jajikon. My host mother made them virtually every morning by mixing flour, copious amounts of sugar, and water in a bowl and then frying the cakes in a dented, well-used frying pan over a fire. Known as "pancake" in Marshallese, hers were always perfect circles, a testament to her skill and experience. Like everyone, she served them without maple syrup, butter, powdered sugar, or berries. Yet, somehow, they were always delicious.

As a breakfast food, pancakes fall into the "real food" category, something that—among adults at least—it is explicitly bad to eat while walking around. But Rōka held the barely eaten circle in his hand as he approached three older boys gathered around an upside-down wheelchair in his yard. Missing the seat and a wheel, the wheelchair gleamed as sunlight reflected off a thick red coating of rust. It had not been used for years.

One of the boys held his hand out, releasing the single working wheel. It spun in the breeze. "Rōka, a little."

Rōka turned his back. "No."

"Hey Rōka!" a different boy—Kyle—called.

Kyle's father was Rōka's grandfather's brother. This meant that technically Kyle was Rōka's father (see Figure 4.2). Such genealogical distinctions often seemed to matter less to many children than relative age. But Kyle was also a

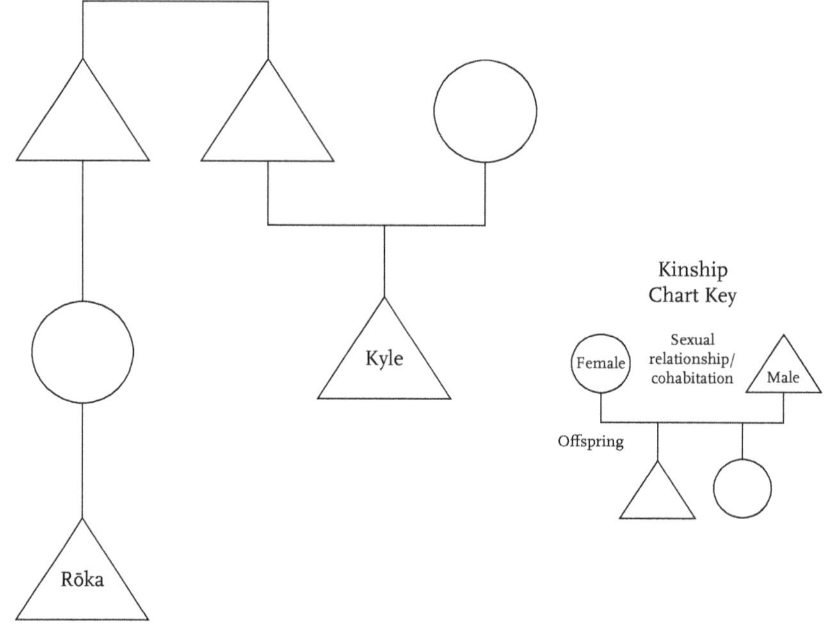

FIGURE 4.2 Rōka's relationship with Kyle.

foot taller than Rōka. He had been going to school for several years and was old enough to run regular errands for his parents. Moreover, Rōka was temporarily living in Kyle's house. Kyle should have had the authority to make Rōka behave appropriately.

"Give me a little of my food," Kyle demanded.

"Hey, you didn't give me my food," Rōka objected. Perhaps Kyle had refused to give the day before.

"I won't give you your toy, a shell."

"What's this, what's this?" Rōka taunted. He walked away. His statement made little sense—he was not holding anything in his hand. But his implication was clear. Rōka did not need Kyle's shell; Kyle had no power over him.

It is tempting to interpret Rōka's behavior as pure absentmindedness. He was young; perhaps he simply did not know what he was doing. Perhaps, overrun by a desire to join the boys, he did not think about the consequences of walking with a pancake.

But ninety seconds later Rōka returned. Planting himself directly in front of Kyle, Rōka stopped only a couple of inches from his face. His pancake in his hand, Rōka blatantly flouted the general principle that once seen things must be shared.

"Give me a little of my food; why are you so greedy dude!?"

"Hey," Rōka protested again, "why didn't you give me my food?!"

This second display of his pancake, at least, was not an accident but an apparently deliberate attempt to show off to Kyle and punish Kyle for previous transgressions. Such an interpretation is consistent with children's self-understanding. Many explicitly discussed their conspicuous consumption as part of a child-child battle for status and regularly evaluated children like Rōka who displayed their possessions as "show-offs." As one girl complained about another, "She always shows off [*kakōl*] and doesn't give me my food."

Hence, Rōka's tactics were not unique (see Figure 4.3). A girl roughly the same height as Kyle munched on a pandanus fruit as she joined a group of children. A younger girl around Rōka's age ate food in front of her cousin. She taunted, "I said, Is your mouth watering?"

Unlike this girl and Rōka, older children often avoid explicitly showing off with their speech. These older children depend on physical displays of their possession, so much so that those who consume food completely out of sight often find themselves in a predicament: they want to communicate to others their good fortune but have no way to do so.

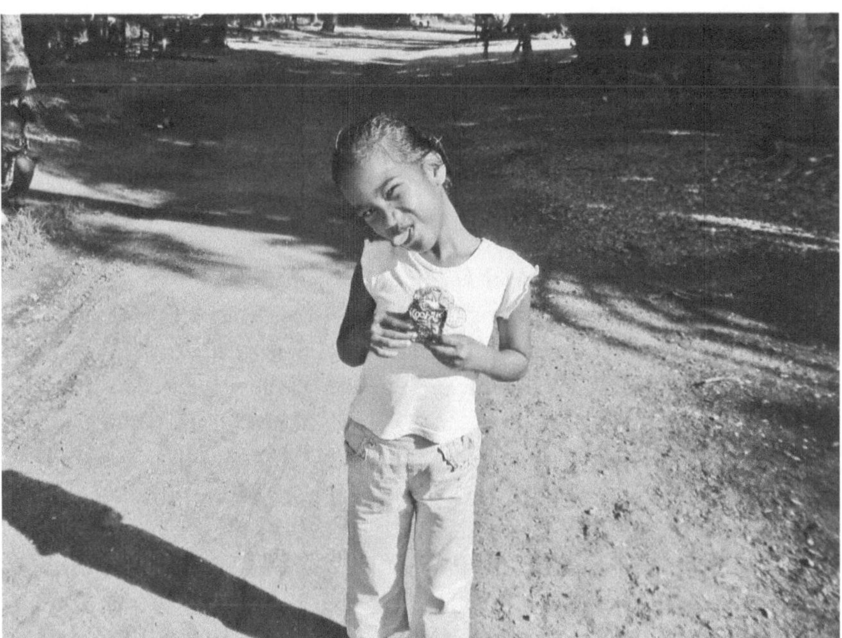

FIGURE 4.3 Child displaying a packet of Kool-Aid. Photo by Elise Berman.

Liti—slightly younger than Kyle—found an ingenious solution to this problem. She leaned casually back against the wooden wall. "What did you eat?"

"Rice," her friend Angela replied.

Liti initiated, and Angela obligingly participated in, a typical Marshallese greeting. Similar to saying "How are you?" people regularly ask each other what they ate and typically do not necessarily expect interesting responses. Analogous to "Fine," the response "Rice" is vague, uninformative, and appropriate. People eat rice at every meal.

Liti grinned broadly. "Cheese balls," she burst out, preemptively jumping ahead in the ritual instead of waiting for Angela to ask, "And you?"

"And what else . . . ah!" Angela yelled as Liti's words registered. Angela's response, "Rice," is standard because it hides food and forces people to say "And what else?" if they want the details about the more interesting things that a household has. Now, however, Angela realized that Liti had begun the ritual to provide an opportunity for conspicuous consumption—to reveal her control over valued wealth. "Girl, it wasn't rice!"

"Yeah?" Liti laughed. Her smile threatened to jump off her face onto the wall behind her.

"Ah, bananas and salt fish."

Among children as well as adults, control over wealth affords status. But people see explicit acts of conspicuous consumption such as Liti's or Rōka's as child-typical forms of interaction. One of my research assistants who watched the video of Rōka in church called his behavior *kōmmejāje*, showing off with food. *Kōmmejāje*, she told me, was unique to children.

Demands

"Hey Roka, give us our food [*letok kijed*]," Kinta demanded.

With thick, tight curls and bright, intelligent eyes, Kinta often walked with her head held high, a refreshing display of self-confidence that came from a secure home, a strong family, many friends, and a history of success. Exceedingly smart, Kinta had the highest grades in her class. When I asked who was popular, several other girls pointed her out. During interviews, five girls drew her as one of their friends. Articulate and talkative when among her peers, Kinta provided much of my understanding of childhood in the RMI.

Like Kyle, Kinta was Rōka's elder kin (see Figure 4.1). She lived with her grandparents but often slept over at Kyle and Rōka's house. Thus Kinta—quite reasonably—also expected that Rōka should defer to her. And so, Kinta demanded that he give.

As did Rōka's many other elder kin who were also in the church. "Hey Rōka," Kyle pressed, when Rōka did not respond to Kinta. "Give Kinta her food."

"Hey Rōka," a third child, Lari, commanded. A sharp-eyed, mischievous, loudmouthed child, Lari was also Rōka's elder kin, although he spent much less time at Rōka's house than either Kyle or Kinta (see Figure 4.1). "Give me my food [*tok kijō*]!"

This command, "Give me my food"—literally "Toward me my food"—was a constant refrain among children. Like Lari, children in my recordings often shortened *letok* (give me) to the deictic *tok* (toward me) and rarely included in their demands politeness markers such as "can you" or "please." "Give me my food," Kinta commanded another younger child just a minute before commanding Rōka. "Give me my food!" Kyle said to Rōka. "Give me my food," a girl said to a boy a minute before Kinta's demand to Rōka. "Give me my food!" a girl declared to an older boy three minutes later. "Give me my food dude!" another boy demanded. "Give me my pandanus fruit," a girl said to Kinta when they were playing outside the church later in the year. "My lollipop!" a boy called out to Kinta several months later as she passed by on the road. In all of these utterances, the children also used the first-person possessive *kijō*, "my food." As we have seen, among adults this first-person possessive is both the grammatically correct way of possessing things during requests in Marshallese and a way of claiming possession—of stating that the food is already theirs.

Such explicit demands stand in stark contrast to the oblique requests, detailed in chapter 2, that adults make when asking for things that they know others do not want to give (Berman Forthcoming). The children were perfectly capable of speaking differently and frequently did, particularly when speaking with adults. In fact, Kinta once explicitly rejected my hypothesis that if sent on an errand by her grandparents to ask for salt from an elder kinswoman, she would directly demand a gift.

"And you would go to Sōkol and say, 'Give me a little salt,' isn't that right?" I asked.

Kinta shook her head.

"But what?"

"We don't say, 'Give me a little salt.'"

"What do you say?"

"Could you give me a little salt?" Kinta explained as she included the politeness marker *komaroñ* (can/could you).

A boy younger than Rōka (he had begun to talk only in the past year) asked his older sibling for a glass not with the child-typical "Bring me the glass" but a more polite negative form, "Are you not going to bring my glass?" This boy may have been trying to ask indirectly, although the fact that he repeated this demand incessantly for ten minutes (with the same grammatical structure) suggests that he had not learned the situational appropriateness of different grammatical forms. Regardless, his speech reveals that children much younger than Kinta are capable of making various forms of indirect requests.[3]

The children's demands reflect not immature linguistic development but, rather, their social situation. Like all children, they were capable of speaking indirectly. They chose, instead, to demand Rōka's food, marking themselves as people either close enough or powerful enough to compel Rōka to give.

Giving and the Stages of Life

Lari, on his part, was partly successful. Rōka handed him the lollipop, granting him a brief taste.

Perhaps Rōka was willing to share a lick with Lari because he liked Lari better than he apparently liked Kyle or Kinta. Rōka lived with Kyle and Kinta, positioning them as elder siblings whom Rōka may have wanted to challenge or defy. Or perhaps, a month after the pancake incident, Rōka realized that if he was to survive in Jajikon, he had to be accepted by at least some of the other children as one of them.

Among children as among adults, this requires gifts. Unanimously children, like adults, praise people who are generous and criticize those who are stingy. "It is bad to be greedy," a girl said. "They go to church and they say, 'To whom does greediness belong?' And they say, 'It belongs to the devil.'" Kyle called a friend "really greedy" because he hid food to avoid sharing it.

Although children have little wealth, that which they have they often generously share with others. "Eat," a boy just starting puberty exclaimed to his slightly younger friend; a girl and a boy shared a drink on the way to school; a girl took gum out of her mouth and gave it to her friend, who put it in her own mouth. When a plastic bracelet fad hit the village for a couple of months, children constantly passed the bracelets around between them. George wore Carl's bracelet, Jaki wore Jilaba's bracelet, and Jilaba wore Kyle's bracelet.

Sometimes, of course, children do not want to share. Then, like adults, they often hide things and lie about them. For example, I asked a boy roughly Kyle's age how he would hold onto a bracelet that I gave him as a prize. He said that he would "lie" and say that the bracelet belonged to someone else. Indeed, on another day when Kinta asked for this boy's yo-yo he responded that it was not his. I once gave a girl Kinta's age a balloon and cautioned her not to tell the other children because I did not have enough to give to all. 'What will you say when they ask where you got it?' I asked. 'I found it by the lagoon,' she replied instantly, showing an ability to creatively and convincingly lie on the spot. When I gave a slightly younger girl a balloon she stuffed it in her pocket. 'Are you hiding it?' I asked.

'Yes,' she said.

'Why?'

'So that people don't take it.'

Later on, her mother asked her where her balloon was. 'There is no balloon,' the girl lied.

The need to both give and, if they do not give, hide and lie stems partly from the solidarity that children owe to each other, an even greater solidarity than they owe to people in other stages of life. The Marshallese word *ajri*, "child," has both a definite and a relative meaning. As a definite term it refers to people in a particular stage of life who are older than babies (*niñniñ*) but younger than youth (*jodrikdrik*) and adults (*rūtto*) (Carucci 1985). These stages, along with elders who are called old men or women (*l̗al̗l̗ap* or *lōl̗l̗ap*), constitute the five verbally distinguished stages of life in Jajikon. Various comments from both children and adults reveal that they do see childhood as a real stage. For example, I asked a girl Kinta's age when they were going to play a game. She responded "never" because "the children [*ajri*] in this town have rejected it." Some people also divided children into little children (*ajri jidikdik*) and either children (*ajri*) or older children (*ajri rūtto*).

These stages, however, have no clear boundaries. The biggest rite of passage, a child's first birthday (*keemem*), does not formally mark a different status but merely begins a gradual passage from babyhood to childhood (Carucci 1985). Some people said that after the first birthday people were children (*ajri*), while others said that people were still babies (*niñniñ*). In turn, although several adults called children who had already had their first birthday either babies (*niñniñ*) or little children (*ajri jidikdik*), a boy older than Rōka claimed that he himself was a little child (*ajri jidikdik*). Similarly, although puberty may mark the difference between children and youth, there were people past puberty who stood in the children's lines and hung out with children, and there were people not past puberty who danced with adults and did adult-type work. Some people claimed that having a partner or having a child is what makes people adults (*rūtto*), although others with such attributes continued to call themselves youth. Partners such as Pinla and Thomas casually move in together and, just as casually, separate. Many partners eventually get married, but others never do. One young woman explained about the difference between children and youth, 'Those who want to be older are older, and those who don't are still children [*ajri*].' The boundaries of all of these stages of life are fuzzy, and classifications of people shift depending on the situation.

But although people's statuses are fuzzy on the borders, there are some people who are clearly children and others who are clearly not. Children do a number of things that mark them as a social group. They stand together in the children's line for food at parties, separated both from adults (*rūtto*), who stand in a separate line, and from babies (*niñniñ*), who do not stand in line at all (Figure 4.4). Postpubescent youth stand in either of the lines as they choose. Children also tend to socialize with other children, rather than with adults, and spend much of their time in play with each other without the supervision of either adults or older children (Berman 2012). Time away from elder supervision increases slowly as babies turn into children, just as the relative amount of time spent in play versus work diminishes gradually as children grow. Children also sing with the Sunday school group at church and go to school during the week. Since school in Jajikon ends at eighth grade, people past eighth grade either do not go to school or go live in the capital, marking themselves as no longer completely children.

Finally, children expect their peers to share. This expectation, and the constant acts of giving, are typical of relationships between children around the world. Just as exchange is the prototypical prosocial act that binds society together (Mauss 1990), relationships between children in Israel, Papua New Guinea, Korea, the

FIGURE 4.4 Children's line for food. Note the tall boy standing next to a small child. Photo by Elise Berman.

United States, and elsewhere are made and broken through acts of sharing (Chin 2001; Ferguson 2001; Katriel 1987; Nukaga 2008; Schieffelin 1990; Thorne 2005). Of course, children in Jajikon give not only to other children but also to many others: to elders because they owe them deference, to babies because they need to care for them, and to everyone else because they are kin. But while gifts to adults and babies inevitably also serve as either deference to authority or care for the dependent young, gifts to other children have a different quality: they bring children together in solidarity with one another (Berman 2014b). As one child said when explaining why she gave, 'Children share with children.'

Negotiating Status Between Children: Producing Relative Power and Age

"Hey Rōka!" Kinta complained. She still wanted her food.

Rōka ignored her.

Kinta was not happy. "Hey Rōka!"

Fed up, Rōka brandished his lollipop in the air, in an explicit act of conspicuous consumption. "Here it is with me!"

Rōka did not seem particularly concerned with becoming friends with Kinta. Nor should he have been. Children sometimes give to each other due to their shared status as children, but children also often selectively give more to people whom they consider, or want to be, their "friends." As a boy said when I asked whether he got tired of giving things to others, "But they are my friends!" A girl explained that if she did not share with a friend, the friend would "talk to everyone. And I will hate her, and [then] my friend will be no more." A boy agreed, stating that if he did not give children "won't be my friends." Sharing with friends is obligatory; sharing with nonfriends is not.

And Kinta and Rōka were not friends.

One obstacle was gender. Kinta drew a picture of four friends for me, all of whom were other girls.[4]

The second obstacle was age. In some ways Kinta and Rōka were both children (*ajri*)—they both stood in the children's line for food at festivals. But in other ways Rōka was immature (*ajri*) relative to Kinta, who was mature (*rūtto*). The word *ajri* has a relative as well as definite meaning and can translate as not only "child" but also "immature person." Who is an "immature person" (*ajri*) shifts with context (Carucci 1985). A grown man called his younger siblings—most of whom already had their own offspring—"children (*ajri*)." As he said, "If I were to go and ask something from the children [*ajri*] who are my younger siblings. . . ." A woman with young children referred to herself as an "immature person [*ajri*]" in comparison with an older kinsman in his forties who was "really old/mature [*rūtto*]". A woman justified sending her young son (he had just begun to talk) on an errand by saying, 'Because you are mature/a big boy [*rūtto*].' Kinta herself once chastised someone who hit her much younger kin by saying, 'Do not hit immature people [*ajri*].' Here, she clearly viewed herself as older (*rūtto*) in comparison with her kin.

Evaluating Age

But what is it that made Kinta older and Rōka younger?

One might think that the answer would be that Kinta was chronologically older than Rōka. Since the RMI is and has been a member of an increasingly globalized world for more than a century, it has long had things such as canned meat, monetary currency, formal education, and chronological age. Sometimes, when I asked people their age, they responded with a chronological number. On the capital people organize meetings and festivals for specific days and times. For example, Christmas falls on December 25. In Jajikon both church and school supposedly begin at specific times, and children are supposed to enter kindergarten at the age of five or six. At birth the hospital issues children yellow immunization cards that record their birth date and family information.

According to her yellow card, Kinta was ten years old. But Rōka did not have his yellow card; his mother told me that she left it behind on the capital. Nor did she know Rōka's chronological age. When I asked her, she told me that she thought he was five or six.

Some people, like Rōka's mother, knew neither their own nor their children's chronological age. Consider what happened when a minister tried to record children's birth dates for a church camp. The central office of his church—the Salvation Army—was in the United States, which I presume is why the forms for the camp asked for birth dates at all.

"Okay, Carl," the minister said.

"June eight, ninety-seven," Carl responded.

"What day were you born Carl?" the minister asked for clarification.

"Day eight. Oh, eight, ninety-seven."

"Oh eight ninety-seven?"

"The eighth day of . . . ," Carl trailed off.

The minister recognized the problem. "Month?" he asked.

"Ninety-seven," Carl said.

The minister looked at him. "But year?"

Carl paused. He and the minister started laughing.

The minister asked Carl and some of the other boys some more questions and eventually turned to a younger boy, Simon.

"Simon, come," the minister commanded.

"Huh?"

"Do you know what month and year you were born in?" Carl asked Simon.

"Dude!" Simon exclaimed. "I have no idea."

Some of the birth dates the minister ultimately recorded were probably wrong. I checked as many immunization cards as I could. Carl was close. Although the minister seems to have written down June 8, 1997, Carl was supposedly born on June 19, 1997. (He would have been twelve at the time of the conversation.) As for the rest of the children, I would not be surprised if the minister recorded at least some birth dates that were off by one or two years (or potentially more). Simon knew nothing about his birth date (which I discovered by asking his mother to find his yellow card); a mother told me her son was thirteen, while his yellow card said that he was twelve; a boy claimed that he was ten, but he had just turned nine according to his yellow card; a mother shrugged when I asked about her daughter's birthday, expressing ignorance. Some parents did not have their children's yellow cards at all.[5]

Finally, children also adjusted their chronological age to suit their purposes. When I first went to Jajikon, I planned to study children between the chronological ages of seven and twelve. This is because I was interested in the psychological stage of "middle childhood" and when I began my research I held a chronological ideology of age. So, I told the children that I was only interviewing children between those chronological ages. Unsurprisingly, the children's response was, if they were younger, to simply declare that they were seven or, if they were older, to declare that they were twelve, so that they could participate. One little girl came up to me and asked to be interviewed, claiming that she was seven. I told her that her mother had told me that she was six. "Mama is lying," the girl responded. Then she further inflated her age, "I am in the eighth grade!"

In addition to manipulating chronological measurements of age, people also frequently employed nonchronological evaluations. For example, I once asked a friend to define different life stages. She did so by pointing out different people whom we knew. She described some as "girls [*leddik*]", others as "young women [*jiroñ*]" because they had "boyfriends," people like herself with children as "women [*kōrā*]", and people who did not have children anymore as "old women [*lōḷḷap*]". A woman told me that "babies [*niññiñ*]" were people who did not walk yet. Another woman put her hand at a specific height above the ground, explaining that children at that age (height) were too old to be adopted. People also marked age relationally. When I asked a grandmother about her granddaughter's age, the grandmother responded, 'Older than Lionel' (another grandchild); when I asked a woman about a boy's age, the woman responded, "Older than James."

'How old are you?' I asked Asuin, a small boy who was not yet in school.

One of his friends responded instead, 'I am older than Asuin!'

A third child disagreed. 'You are younger than Korina!' she declared.

These different measurements of age—chronological, relative, ability—can be linked. People who are born earlier may take care of a baby and mark themselves as older; people who experience similar life events together—a cohort—may feel themselves to be similar in age. Most children in Jajikon go to school, something else that affects evaluations and experiences of age. Chudacoff (1986, 29–48) argues that chronological age became important in the United States partly through the rise of chronologically age-graded education. In the RMI as well, school reinforces chronological evaluations of age. In theory, children are supposed to start kindergarten at the chronological age of five or six and advance a grade for each year of their life. These school classes shape children's friend groups. I had the children draw pictures of their friends during interviews. The friends who were the furthest away in chronological age were typically neighbors, while the closest were children in the same class.

But although cohort experience—and particularly formal schooling—may create rough correlations between chronological age and life course experiences, older-younger relationships are still quite malleable. First, Johnson-Hanks (2002) argues that the order of life course events themselves varies dramatically and does not proceed in a regular chronological fashion. In Jajikon, although in theory children start school at a uniform chronological age, in practice some children start later. For example, Rōka did not start school because, his mother told me, he did not want to. Moreover, children do not move through the grades in a uniform manner—some never pass first grade, others repeat grades multiple times. Second, friend groups often span relatively broad chronological age ranges. For example, Lari, who was ten according to his yellow card, drew six boys as friends all between the chronological ages of nine and twelve. Third, within these friend groups people care deeply about relative age. Since they do not know the chronological answer to this question, they produce their relative age relationships in other ways. Fourth, although children often drew only a limited number of other children as their friends, they generally played in extended age groups that mix children of different heights, abilities, and grades in school. Finally, although birth order often helps establish people's relative age relationships with each other, many people do not grow up together. People in the RMI are very mobile: they move regularly between villages and atolls as well as between the RMI and the United States (Hess, Nero, and Burton 2001). When I returned to Jajikon three years after I first went, many people were in the United States or Majuro, while others had come to live in Jajikon. These moves mean that many people do not have a lived experience of their birth order.

Since Rōka had just arrived on Jajikon, people had no experience caring for him. Rōka's place in society, and his age relative to others, had to be created through interaction.

Threats, Insults, and Criticisms

One way that children mark and create themselves as older is through verbal and physical signs of power and status—threats, insults, and criticisms.

Consider Lari. A sharp-eyed, mischievous, loudmouthed child, Lari was in the same class at school as Kinta, but Lari was more intimidating and regularly cowed younger children into submission. 'He is very bossy,' one child criticized.

Lari lived up to his reputation. "Ah," he yelled at five other children gathered at the front of the church. "Sit down!"

The children did not sit. Menacingly wielding a large stick, Lari advanced on the children. "I am going to hit you," he threatened.

Four of the children—all smaller than Lari and only a little bigger than Rōka—scampered quickly back toward the benches. 'All the little children are scared of him,' one of my assistants commented as we watched the video. 'They listen because they are scared of his stick.'

Signs of Force

In the above interaction, Lari made use of one way that children create relative age relationships—threats of physical force. In Jajikon force, fear, and age are closely intertwined (Berman 2018). This is partly because adults believe that the main way to get children to obey is through fear (*mijak*). For example, a woman explained that one child was naughty at his grandparents' house but behaved at her house because he "feared" her partner. Since obedience marks fear, and a defining feature of hierarchical age relationships in Jajikon is that youth obey their elders, fear also marks younger status. Conversely, instilling fear marks elder status. Children regularly explained their fear of others by citing relative age. One girl was "afraid of Lance because he is older than me." She also feared her cousin "because she is old." Kyle was surprised when I asked whether he was scared of two boys who were on the verge of being youth. "But they are old!" he exclaimed, indicating that fear of elders is a given. Finally, children and adults alike present this fear as a physical fear of elders' ability to reinforce their commands through force (Berman 2018). Children fear their parents, one girl told me, "because they are fierce, they will hit them." Claims of "fear" (*mijak*) mark both physical power and elder status.[6]

Since children supposedly obey mainly because of their fear of force, elders discipline children partly through threats of force and, occasionally, physical punishment.[7] Consider how a small boy's elders responded to him when he scrambled on top of some boxes.

"If you sit there and lean back, you will fall," the boy's mother warned.

"Rubin ah!" the boy's grandmother scolded. "Don't play with that thing. I am going to hit you. I am going to hit you. Get down! Get down! Get down because you are going to fall. I am going to hit you."

Like this grandmother, older children try to compel youth through signs of force (Berman 2018). Actual physical punishment is relatively rare. People severely condemned those who hit too hard or too often, while children frequently got into trouble if they hit younger children. But indices of force are ever present (Berman 2018). These signs may be physical, such as wielding a stick. Or they may be verbal. "Are you going to play in the building?" Lari scolded. "I don't care, you'll get beaten here." "Watch out because I am going to beat you here, sit sit. Because I am going to beat you. Sit." Other older children also threatened those whom they saw as younger, including Lari himself. Annoyed at Lari for whistling, his older sister threatened, "Lari, I could hit you." "Ah," she yelled to another child. "Don't talk harshly over there dude, I will really punch your mouth in." Such signs mark people as strong and able to reinforce their commands through force—that is, as elders.

Although elder-younger relationships in Jajikon are built partly through signs of power and fear, these signs may or may not correspond to chronology or even size. One boy justified his fear of Kyle, whom he drew as one of his friends, by stating that the latter was older. But according to their yellow cards the two boys were the same chronological age. Lari threatened five children with his stick. Four of them, all smaller than Lari, ran away and sat down. One child was slightly taller than Lari and, according to their yellow cards, two years older. This particular child did not obey.

Lari pulled his bat back, faking a swing.

The other boy flinched and moved back toward the benches.

Despite the boy's greater size and chronological years, this interaction produced him as younger that Lari. Lari commanded the boy and threatened corporal discipline, all markers of greater power and elder status. The boy obeyed, a marker of fear and youthful status. The boys created their age relative to each other.

Signs of Social Control

Perhaps, therefore, Rōka let Lari have some of his lollipop because Lari was particularly scary. But he did not extend the same courtesy to Kinta. His lack of deference frustrated both Kinta and Kyle.

"Ah," Kinta threatened. "If you take it, your grandfather will hit you."

"We hate you," Kyle added.

Direct and explicit criticisms and insults such as this are common between children. Like Lari, children regularly declared, "I hate you," "You are so stingy," or "Don't be greedy" when another child did not give. "I hate you because you aren't giving me my food," a little girl around Rōka's age said to another girl. "You are stingy."

As with signs of force, however, these criticisms and insults are asymmetrically distributed. Younger children do not criticize older children. Consider the following conversation between Kyle and a girl about to go to high school.

"My food," Kyle demanded of his older kinswoman.

"Ah man," the girl responded, "that thing [the food] will be too small. It is for the two of us [her and a different friend] to fry." In other words, while she did not have enough food to share with Kyle, she did have enough to share with her preferred friend.

"Just a little," Kyle pleaded.

The older girl ignored him.

"Hey, just a little!" Kyle demanded again.

The girl continued to ignore him.

Kyle let it go. He did not declare, "I hate you" or "You are stingy." By failing to threaten and criticize he implicitly accepted her claim to rank—her assertion that she was older than him and could get away with keeping things to herself.

In contrast, children regularly scold and criticize younger children who fail to give to them. "Why are you so greedy dude!?" Kyle berated Rōka when the younger boy did not share his pancake. "Ah Lena, you are greedy Lena. You are greedy Lena," Lena's classmate criticized when she did not share a toy. A girl close to puberty was furious when her significantly younger kinswoman refused to give her a magnet. "She doesn't know," taunted the older girl. "She's worse at spelling than Trint" (Trint won the spelling bee for the younger girls' grade). "Wow, so shameful. It's shameful, she is older [than Trint] but can't spell as well as Trint.... You are trying to be so sexy, but your gums are too big.... Hey, the big-gummed girl... hey the sexy girl... you smell like poop."

Producing Peers

On the one hand, the asymmetry of threats and criticisms between Rōka and the other children marked Rōka as younger than them. On the other hand, Kinta's and Lari's repeated demands and criticisms, combined with Rōka's resistance to those demands, also produced all the children as people relatively equal to one another—as peers.

First, demanding food marks interlocutors as peers. The control afforded by greater age comes with responsibility. This responsibility includes an expectation that those who are older should give to those who are younger and should not take things from them. One should not take food from the mouths of babes. For example, a girl in the beginning of puberty tried to get a cookie from a baby who had not yet had her first birthday. When the baby did not let go, the older girl gave up; she did not declare, like Lari, "I hate you!" Kinta once protected a small child from an older girl who demanded gum. "It's your food because you chewed it," Kinta interjected maternally. When children refrain from demanding things, they mark people as not "children" (*ajri*) but "babies" (*niññiñ*) who are too young to need to give. In contrast, when Kinta, Kyle, and Lari tried to force Rōka to give through demands, threats, and criticisms, they marked Rōka as not a baby (*niññiñ*) but a child (*ajri*) old enough to have an obligation to share.

Second, just as demanding creates addressees as people old enough to give, refusing creates addressees as children young enough to be resisted. Children fear elders. Consequently, although they may ignore commands, they typically do not explicitly refuse to obey them (Berman 2012, 222–23). But Rōka taunted Kinta and Lari, waving his lollipop in their faces. Rōka rejected their authority, producing them as not adults but fellow children—his peers.

Children who produce threats, criticisms, and insults mark themselves as older by presenting themselves as wielding physical and verbal power over others. Simultaneously, children like Kinta and Lari who incessantly demand, and children like Rōka who object and refuse, present themselves as equal enough to engage in a battle for status, as fellow children. As relationships of power and solidarity emerge, so do relationships of age. Age, like power, is emergent and interactionally achieved (Boggs 1985; Goodwin and Kyratzis 2007; Howard 2012).

Refusals: Indexing Childhood

Kinta stretched her hand out toward Rōka. *My food.*

"Ah I won't!" Rōka declared.

Kinta said something else, annoyed.

But Rōka refused to give. "I won't!"

Rōka here did something that adults avoid among their peers: he explicitly refused to give. Again, Rōka was not the only child to act in this way. "I won't," a girl said to her older sibling when the latter demanded her bracelet. Even older children often said things that, although perhaps more polite, were nonetheless obviously refusals. "Ah," Lari exclaimed when several younger children in the church demanded his own food, "everybody has had some!"

"Lari!" a child complained.

"I haven't gotten any dude!"

"Ugh it is too small," Lari declared. "Us two [he and another friend] are going to eat outside; this stuff is only for the two of us."

Lari justified his refusal (there was not enough food), but he made no attempt to hide it. Like Rōka, but unlike adults, during an interaction with peers he went on record as someone who does not give. Through these refusals, Rōka and Lari indexed themselves as children.

In addition to directly refusing to give, Rōka, Kyle, Kinta, and Lari said and did many other things that adults typically avoid among their peers. Rōka paraded around with food. Kyle, Kinta, and Lari directly and insistently demanded that he give. And the older children criticized Rōka.

Most of these strategies are neither unique to children nor necessary. Adults also sometimes ask directly and criticize each other. Nor, moreover, do children always use such strategies. For example, explicit refusals are not children's first line of defense. Many preferred instead to get out of giving by staying silent and ignoring demands. Kinta once walked past one of her friends playing marbles in the street. 'Give me one!' Kinta yelled. Her friend ignored her. Similarly, when the children first demanded that Rōka give, rather than explicitly refusing he ignored them. This use of silence is similar to some adult methods of avoiding difficult interactions.

But although children and adults sometimes act and speak similarly, children also often create situations that adults go out of their way to avoid. Adults might very well say to another adult, "Give me my food" if that adult was parading around in front of them with lollipops. But since adults typically do not parade around with lollipops, others do not have an opportunity for such a demand. Children's conspicuous consumption and demands also make many indirect modes of getting out of giving impossible. It is pragmatically difficult to say, "It is all gone," while eating a lollipop. It is also difficult to remain silent in the face of repeated and insistent demands to give. In Rōka's case, the presence of his lollipop meant that his silence was no longer sustainable and he had to refuse.

Thus, although not strictly limited to children, many of the things that happened in this interaction are linked to children and child-specific social environments. As already mentioned, an adult said that showing off with food is something that only children do. As another example, surrounded by children who constantly said, "Give me my food," I initially assumed that such forms of speech were the appropriate way to ask. Upon arriving at my friend's house one day I saw her taking cinnamon buns off of the fire. I said, "Give me my food." My friend immediately scolded me, shocked at my impoliteness. When I protested that children speak in such a manner all the time, she responded that they were children but I was an adult and must speak differently. When children speak and act in these ways they not only negotiate their relationships with other children but also create an indexical connection between such forms of speech and childhood.

This relationship between directness and childhood is historical rather than natural (Berman 2014b). It comes about not because Kinta, Lari, Kyle, and Rōka were unable to act differently but, rather, because of the environments in which they found themselves and a general expectation that children should speak in these ways. Interactions such as the ones discussed here both reflect and reproduce age and speech differences. But as Irvine and Gal (2000) have shown, people often misinterpret indexical relationships between speech and social status as natural—as reflections of people's inner nature. Similarly, as we will see in chapter 5, Marshallese adults see children's actions as a reflection of their natural immaturity.

Lari's Last Word

Rōka ignored Kinta, turning back to Lari. Either Lari took the lollipop, or Rōka offered it; regardless Rōka did not complain.

Kinta stretched her arm out. "My food!"

"What's the name of this thing again?" Lari commented. "I am only biting off a little."

"Rōka dude," Kyle complained, "give me my food dude."

Lari strode off to discipline some other children. When he returned, Rōka, Kinta, and Kyle were gathered together close to the window. Someone, potentially Lari, asked again for some food. This time, however, Rōka rebuffed him or her.

"Man," Lari said, "you are really stingy."

Notes

1. An earlier analysis of this interaction appears in Berman 2014b. Another child in church recorded this interaction while wearing the small camera that attached to a headband he wore on his head. Occasionally, in this chapter, I note that I am not sure exactly what happened at a specific point in the interaction. This is usually because the child recording the incident looked away at that moment.
2. The term *conspicuous consumption* comes from Veblen 1953. According to Veblen, people engage in conspicuous consumption when they consume luxury goods in public and use the display of wealth to increase their social status. Campbell (1995) argues that Veblen's theory of conspicuous consumption has many problems. Veblen

does not specify whether the consumption is conscious or unconscious or whether the effects of the consumption are to display wealth, enhance one's prestige, or widen the wealth gap between people. These different effects may or may not be linked. Veblen also focused his arguments on the leisure class, a focus that obviously does not apply to Jajikon. The children are not members of, nor are they trying to join, a specifically wealthy class of people. Despite this confusion, I use the term *conspicuous consumption* because children "conspicuously" display their wealth by "consuming" it in public. Children also explicitly see such forms of consumption as acts of showing off and as tied in some manner to their status.

3. Many other language socialization studies have also shown that young children are often able to produce forms of speech associated with maturity, although they may not regularly do so. Tzotzil Maya children in early childhood use adult request forms, Kwara'ae children put on "child mode" and "adult mode" performances, young Thai children take on adult personae in conflicts with peers, and Nicaraguan children take on adult genres during pretend play (De Leon 2007; Howard 2009; Kyratzis 2007; Minkley and Legassick 2000; Watson-Gegeo 2001).
4. I interviewed children and had them draw their friends. Although most of the time children drew only other children of the same gender, 35 percent of the children included at least one child of the opposite gender in their drawing.
5. Several people told me that the yellow cards themselves might be wrong. Kinta's older relative claimed that her yellow immunization card was not filled out at birth. Rather, the authorities went to Kinta's grandmother for the information after the fact, and (according to the relative) the grandmother gave the wrong answer. I was unable to check on the accuracy of the birth dates on the cards, but I did find that several people's names were incorrect. For example, one child had a different last name on his card, while another child had his father's first name written down as his own. These different names may reflect the fact that many new parents did not decide on a name for their child until several months after birth, while other children's names changed when they were adopted.
6. I suspect that the prominence of physical power, threats of force, and fear in Jajikonian children's rhetoric makes some readers uneasy. But children's rhetoric of fear actually reflects stable social systems and supportive families tied to hierarchical age relationships (Berman 2018). First, while people in Jajikon speak a lot about corporal punishment, they engage in it much more rarely (Berman 2018). Second, evaluations of corporal punishment, like ideologies of age, are culturally specific. Views of what benefits or harms children vary widely around the world (Korbin 2003). In Jajikon, only limited amounts of physical punishment are acceptable. People criticized adults who hit too hard or often as "harming" (*kaeñtaan*) their children. Many adults said that one should only hit children with one's hand (as opposed to a stick or a knife) so that one can feel how much it hurts and will know when to stop (see also Opie 1991). But while corporal punishment must be limited, some is considered necessary for producing children as

moral persons who work and respect their elders (Berman 2018). Jajikonian views here reflect Korbin's (1990) account of Hawai'ian Americans who view corporal punishment as appropriate but listen with horror to accounts of white mothers who make their children sleep by themselves. The Hawai'ian Americans Korbin spoke with saw such sleeping practices as abusive.

7. In Jajikon talk about force is much more common than physical punishment itself (Berman 2018). Lari never hit anyone during the forty-five-minute video of him in the church. In fact, significantly older children often avoid hitting younger children both because doing so can bring adult retribution and because they view hitting small children as wrong. "Don't hit children," a man scolded a boy who hit his younger sibling. "Don't hit children," Kinta scolded another girl. This greater proportion of signs of force relative to uses of force reflects the important role that signs play in the construction of power and age relationships (Berman 2018). It also shows that these many discussions and threats of force do not mean that Marshallese children are constantly being hit.

5 AGED AGENCY

WHAT CHILDREN CAN DO THAT ADULTS CANNOT (AND VICE VERSA)

The machete sliced into the back of his leg. Blood welled up along its saltwater-rusted edge. Leny cried.

A couple of weeks later, the boy still had a wide, ugly scar running down his leg.

'What is that?' I asked.

He crossed his legs to hide the scar. 'A wound.'

'What is that?' a child insisted. Leny would not answer.

If it had been entirely up to Leny, no one would have found out about his cut. A short child still many years from puberty but who already spent much of his time on family chores, Leny did not talk much about his home life. But Leny's neighbor Ryan had other ideas. 'Jujan cut him,' he said, referring to Leny's adoptive mother with whom Leny lived (see Figure 5.1). If true, this would be a serious charge that adults would unequivocally condemn. Cutting a child is an example of what many Marshallese call *kaeñtaan*, a phrase that literally means "cause to suffer" and can be translated as "abuse" (Berman 2014a).

'Lie!' Jujan cried. 'Leny ran into a machete.'

What actually happened? Was Leny's cut an accident, or did Jujan purposely cut him? If the cut was an accident, Leny would stay with Jujan. But if Jujan intentionally harmed Leny, then Leny's birth mother had not only an excuse but also a duty to take Leny away.

Leny's future hung in the balance. Where he would live depended on who people believed: Ryan or Jujan.

In turn, people's beliefs were profoundly influenced by Ryan's status as a child and Jujan's status as an adult. In the RMI as elsewhere people evaluate children's and adults' speech and actions differently. For example, while adults criticize other adults who walk

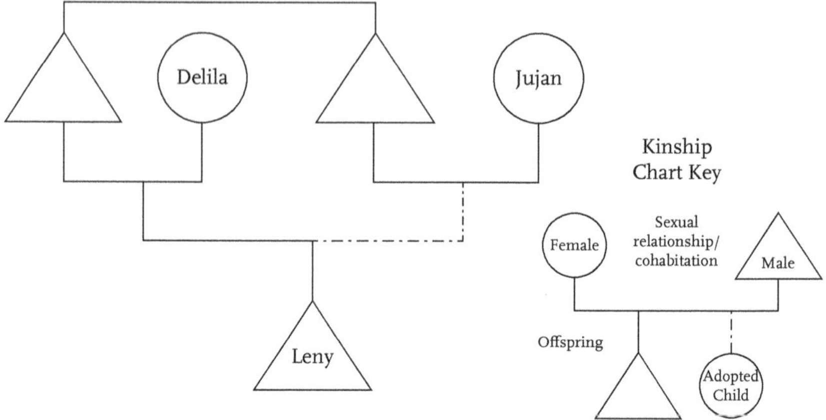

FIGURE 5.1 Leny's mothers.

with ready-to-eat food, they do not criticize children who walk with such food. Instead, adults say that children are too young to feel shame and are not responsible for the food that they carry. Such children have no obligation to share that food with others.

These differing interpretations, statuses, roles, and subjectivities give children and adults the ability to do different things and produce "aged agency." Agency refers to people's abilities to act and speak, abilities mediated by culture (Ahearn 2010, 28). I define "aged agency" as modes of acting particular to children as children or adults as adults.[1] Just as children can do things that adults cannot, adults can do things that children cannot. All agency is aged; all people's actions shaped by views of and their place in the life course.

Jajikonian children have three different types of agency specific to their status as children. First, they have "negative agency," or the ability to disobey and resist those in power (Wardlow 2006, 14). Their negative agency comes from views of children as particularly "naughty" (*bōt*) and naturally inclined to play rather than work. Children regularly disobey their elders, ignore commands and requests, and run away from work. While similar forms of resistance by adults would generate criticism, adults often dismiss children's behavior as mere "naughtiness," giving children more leeway than adults to break such rules.[2] Second, children have "encompassed agency," where the things that they do are encompassed by or attributed to others (Wardlow 2006, 13). Their encompassed agency comes from views of children as lacking both thoughts (*l̹ōmn̹ak*) and shame (*āliklik*). Children physically produce many things, circulate many goods, and speak many words. But since children lack shame and thoughts, adults and children alike largely do not see children as responsible for that which they create or circulate. This view gives children the ability to carry dangerous food and speak difficult words since neither the food nor the words are their own.

Finally, children's negative agency and encompassed agency are both parts of their "nonmoral agency." I define "nonmoral agency" as the ability to act that people have precisely because others do not see them as moral persons responsible for their actions.[3] Views of children as irresponsible, insignificant, and lacking in shame produce children's actions as nonactions, as actions that either are not children's own or do not count. Ironically, such views of children's actions as nonactions give children the ability to act. Jajikonian children are agents not in spite of the fact that they are children but precisely because they are children, because their nonmoral agency lets them do things that adults cannot.

This term, *nonmoral agency*, is "adultcentric." "Adultcentrism" refers to when people view the world from an adult perspective and take adult values and practices as the norm (Goode 1986). Jajikonian children are only "nonmoral agents" relative to adult ideas of morality. When judged on their own terms, Jajikonian children are extremely capable moral actors. They may walk with food, but they also make sure to share with their friends. Nonetheless, I use this adultcentric term because people in Jajikon are often adultcentric themselves and such adultcentric views shape child behavior. In Jajikon, evaluations of children as lacking some attributes of adults—thoughts and shame—lend children some of their aged agency.

The crucial role adultcentrism plays in shaping children's agency challenges typical accounts of agency in childhood studies. One main development in childhood studies has been to argue that children are not just adults in the making but also cultural agents themselves (Alanen 1994; Honwana and De Boeck 2005; James 2007; James and Prout 1997b; Qvortrup 1994, 1997; Stephens 1995). But most such arguments try to present children as the same types of agents as adults. Jajikonian children do indeed have agency, but they are not the same types of actors as adults. Rather, Jajikonian children's contributions to society depend partly on different forms of action than are available to adults, just as adult contributions depend on forms of action unavailable to children. All agency, child or adult, is aged.

Children's aged agency means that people's opinions concerning how Leny got that cut on his leg were affected by Ryan's status as a child and Jujan's status as an adult. Ryan and Jujan, quite simply, had different abilities both to speak and to be believed.

Jujan was a Bad Mother

People's evaluations of Jujan's words and actions began long before Leny was cut. Jujan had a relatively marginal position in the Jajikonian community. While her father was a Jajikonian, her mother was not, so Jujan lacked strong clan ties and close matrilineal relatives. She rarely visited other women, she avoided volleyball games at dusk, and she spent most of her time on her property by herself or talking to her friend, Kati, a self-described stranger (*ruwamãejet*).

Perhaps it is not surprising, therefore, that people said Jujan was a bad mother. One day Raina—an older grandmother—came upon Leny pushing a large wheelbarrow of mature coconuts down the road. Raina frowned. 'What is your mother doing?'

'Watching her children.'

Raina sniffed. 'What is your mother doing?'

Leny raised his voice, annoyed at the implicit criticism: 'Watching her children!'

'She should be helping with the work. You should not be hauling copra.'

According to Raina and many other women in the community, Jujan constantly made Leny collect copra and thus was a bad mother. His excessive copra work, Raina told me, made Leny "tired" and physically "short." Leny was also—according to various different adults—a poor speaker, bad at school, and bad at various games. Like Raina, several adults attributed Leny's problems to his mother's poor care. "Leny . . . will not learn and grow," a woman said, if he gathers copra too much. Ryan's mother was particularly critical. "For example, [Ryan's brother] is almost, wow! Big and tall. But [Leny] is still small."

Constant copra duties are one form of *kaeñtaan*, abusing children by giving them "no time to rest" and difficult, heavy work, like constantly taking care of younger siblings or gathering "coconuts from morning to [night] even if they are really tired." While children can do some of this work, they should not work too much, because "their bodies are weak" and they get "tired." If children work too hard, then their "bodies don't know how to grow" and their minds are "slow." At the extreme, children's health suffers, and they "could die."

But although many people criticized Jujan's parenting, they could have just as easily praised it. In many contexts in Jajikon, telling your children to work or babysit is a *good* thing to do. Elders are supposed to "send" (*jilkin*) children to do things and make them work for their family. "Everyone sends [children]. . . . The Marshallese custom is like I say, 'Hey! Go and . . . can you go and bring that thing?' Even though you are not my child." This work benefits the child as well as the family. Children who are not sent, adults told me, "would not know how to work" or "how to live."

Consequently, all children (male or female) in Jajikon were at the beck and call of their elders. "Pour me some water." "Just come here." "Just bring me the flashlight!" "Rake!" "Clean up!" "Fill this plate." "Get my shoes!" Adults tell children to pick up the trash, clean up the yard, carry things, cook, deliver messages, transport goods, collect coconuts, do the dishes, cut the lawn, and scratch their back (literally). For example, a man told an eight-year-old girl, "Take this to Corey."

The girl carried the pipe to Corey.

Corey said, "Bring a little fire."

The girl went to the cookhouse to get a coconut shell that was partially on fire. She handed it to Corey.

"Go and bring my shoes at the start of the path on the lagoon side."

The girl went to the lagoon and got the shoes.

As she was walking back into the house another woman said, "Please bring the coconut shells here. So that you can throw the things away in the lagoon."

Again, the child obeyed.

Younger people move for older people, an association between lower status and mobility that exists in a number of other places in Oceania as well as in the Philippines and Madagascar (Morton 1996; Rosaldo 1982). The child's purpose or need is always subordinate to the needs of their elders.

Both girls and boys work for their elders, but the particular type of work that they do is often gendered. Girls tend to wash clothes and help cook, while boys tend to mow the lawn and help fish. Adults expect children of both genders to collect copra and fetch and transport things, although they are more likely to send a boy on an errand at night since boys are supposed to be stronger and better able to protect themselves against spirits. Although children of both genders care for their younger siblings, this burden tends to fall to girls. While many who grow up in upper-middle-class households in North America or Europe may be astonished to see young children taking care of babies, sibling caretaking is an extremely common childcare practice worldwide. The arrangement benefits everyone. Adults get help. Older children learn responsibility and build deep bonds with their siblings. In turn, their younger charges spend time in a rich social environment, learn quickly from their elders, and develop close familial ties that last a lifetime (Rogoff 2003; Weisner and Gallimore 1977).

Jujan's crimes were a matter of degree and not kind. Raising children is a balancing act between ordering them enough but not too much. But Leny, many people claimed, was off-balance. "He gathers and makes copra all day," Ryan's mother criticized. Moreover, Jujan's reasons for making Leny work were bad. 'She smokes a lot,' Lacy accused. 'She is always . . . making Leny do a lot of work so that she can go off and smoke.'[4]

Evaluations of Jujan's truthfulness thus began even before Leny's cut, with criticisms of Jujan's caregiving. Such criticisms gained strength after the incident. People used Jujan's supposed prior faults to support their opinions of her speech. As one young woman told me, Jujan was a "bad" mother. She was "always hitting Leny" and pulling his hair. Clearly, Jujan could not be trusted.

Ryan Was a Liar

On the other hand, neither could Ryan. Ryan, his mother Barbra said to me during an interview, "really knows how to lie."

As did all the children. Like their parents they had a love of jokes, a concern for language's social effects, and a relative indifference toward referential accuracy. They lied because it was fun. "Elise!" a six-year-old called. "They have stolen your candy!" They lied to tease. "That boy is not your boyfriend," Leny teased me, referring to my fiancé, who had visited the village. "Do you know whose boyfriend he is? Allison's!" They lied to save face. "I am not going to rehearsal!" a girl insisted as she walked down the road toward the church where the rehearsal was taking place. (She was late.) They lied to get themselves out of trouble. 'I was in school,' claimed a child who had skipped. Sometimes they seemed to lie for no clear reason at all. 'Where did you sleep last night?' I asked a girl. 'My house,' she said, grinning, as she walked out of my host parents' house. (My host mother later confirmed that the girl had spent the night there.)

Roughly the same age as Leny, Ryan was particularly loose with the truth. A short, stocky boy with a wide grin, Ryan seemed to be laughing at a world that frequently fell for his pranks. 'Nomi sometimes lies,' Leny complained: 'Ryan always lies.' Indeed, my field notes and recordings are littered with Ryan's lies. "Elise!" Ryan said: "Abraham says that you smell like poop." (Abraham didn't say it.) "Leny loses!" Ryan declared. (His ball was within the lines.) "Girl, I got drunk!" (He hadn't.) "It is my banana." (He stole them from a cookhouse.)[5] 'He lies to his mother,' Leny said to me, 'and says he is going fishing, but then he goes swimming.'[6]

His mother agreed. "If I say, 'Ryan, have you raked the lawn?' "

"It's done!"

"Then I go [and see], and he hasn't raked; the boy is very bad."

"What about Nita [Ryan's younger sister]?" I asked. (See Figure 5.2.)

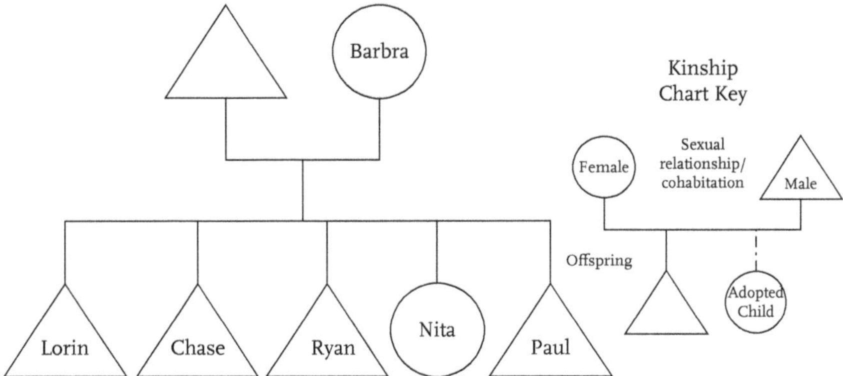

FIGURE 5.2 Ryan's family.

"Nita doesn't because she is scared. Because I hit her and say, It is bad to lie."

"What about Chase [Ryan's older brother]?"

"Chase doesn't."

"Only Ryan?"

"Ryan because Ryan's ways are very bad."

Both Jujan and Ryan, therefore, were untrustworthy sources of information. Jujan was known to harm Leny, and Ryan was a liar.

"Children Do Not Lie": Ideologies of Childhood and Speech

And yet, Ryan's mother's concerns about her son's truthfulness seemed to disappear when Leny's leg was cut.

Barbra and I were sprawled on the floor of her house, enjoying a cool breeze and some privacy. She leaned toward me eagerly, apparently unaware that I had already heard about the incident from numerous other people. 'Ryan saw it,' she whispered. Talking about Leny was not without its dangers. This story had the potential to tear a rift between families and split the village apart.

'Jujan yelled at him to go away,' Barbra continued.

Apparently, Ryan ran home. Barbra was asleep, but Ryan woke her up.

'Mama,' Ryan said, 'Jujan is cutting Leny!'

Barbra and Ryan walked over to Leny's house. Although she and Jujan lived next door to each other, they did not seem to spend much time together. When Barbra got to Jujan's house, she saw Jujan cleaning the blood off of Leny's leg.

The blood could be the result of either a deliberate or accidental cut. But Barbra was convinced. 'Jujan is crazy. She is a bad *caretaker*.'

After all, the story Ryan told her must be the truth. As many people told me, "Children do not lie."

This idea that children cannot lie was a widely held ideology of language and childhood among Marshallese adults. Adults know that children regularly say things that are not true. They expect children to lie (*riab*) about whether or not they went swimming, attended school, did their homework, or said that a person smells like poop. But such statements, like all of children's behavior, are insignificant but not morally bad. As we discovered in chapter 2, it is not telling falsehoods itself that is wrong in Jajikon but, rather, using speech to cause social harm to adults. While children may of their own accord hide information to get out of trouble or tease another child, adults believe that children are too immature to themselves try to harm adults through their speech or actions. Since one definition of *riab* (lie) refers only to such morally bad speech, children cannot lie.[7]

Ideologies of childhood and speech differ drastically across cultural groups (Paugh 2012a; Riley 2012). For example, many Anglo-American middle-class parents believe that children learn language through explicit instruction (Blum 2015; Heath 1983; Ochs and Kremer-Sadlik 2015). Many Kaluli of Papua New Guinea also think that their children learn through explicit (albeit different) routines in which adults elicit complete, socially appropriate sentences (Schieffelin 1990). In contrast, members of a black working-class community in North Carolina believe that children could not be explicitly taught to speak. They think that children teach themselves to speak by imitating adults and "coming up" on their own (Heath 1983). In situations of language shift adults often believe that although children may need help learning a prestigious language variety such as English, they naturally learn the vernacular on their own (Garrett 2012). Such ideologies affect how people treat children. Members of the working-class community do not point things out to their children or ask them to label pictures in books. Their children end up being very successful at storytelling, imitation, analogies, and getting other people's attention. In contrast, middle- and upper-class American parents spend hours scaffolding speech—pointing things out to children and saying, "What is that?" As a result, such children are quite good at labeling but often poor at linguistic play and rapid oral improvisation (Heath 1983). Beliefs that the vernacular is naturally learned may lead parents to emphasize the prestigious language variety instead of vernacular or indigenous languages, often resulting in language shift away from the vernacular (Augsburger 2004; Garrett 2012; Howard 2008).

In Jajikon, growing up entails becoming "able to think" and pay attention to work and Marshallese customs. Children "do not know anything." If they think,

they think only about play. Consequently, children are inclined to play instead of work, making them "naughty" (*bōt*). "All children are naughty," a man told me.

"All?" I asked.

"All children are naughty."

Many people see children's naughtiness as both natural and potentially influenced by their elders and society. Many adults said that children today were worse than children in the past. "Children today, they play and don't help their mama . . . because they are only thinking about play." Since women do not work and cook as much as in the past, another woman explained, their children do not learn. On the other hand, even if children in the past were better, children in general are seen as naturally less likely to think about work than adults. 'Why are some kids naughty?' I asked a woman. "Too much play," she responded. It is not common, another woman explained, for people to grow up and remain naughty as adults.

As children grow they will start to develop thoughts and eventually choose work instead of play on their own. This transformation requires good models but not necessarily explicit instruction. Ryan's mother Barbra had five children (see Figure 5.2). The three youngest "just lie around. . . . The children are very bad." In contrast, Barbra's older child, Chase, helped her around the house.

"Why do they work less than Chase?" I asked.

"I think that it is because they are still too small for me to really sit them down. Chase has grown and knows how to think. I say come and learn this thing, and he learns it. But Ryan, he goes over there; he is still a little child." She continued, "When Chase was small, he was also obstinate."

"Yeah?"

"But then he grew up and knew how to think. I said, 'Come!' He didn't want to. I said, 'Come! So that I can teach you.' And he came."

Since children lack thoughts, they "do not know" enough to be ashamed (*āliklik*). They "do not know shame, because they are small," "because they are children." As with thoughts, children slowly gain shame as they grow. So, Barbra said that her daughter, Nita was sometimes ashamed, revealed by the fact that she sometimes avoided eating in front of a group of people. Barbra also said that Ryan sometimes hid food in his pocket if he saw people coming. But Nita and Ryan still felt less shame than adults. Explained a man, even his son who was almost starting puberty "may [only] feel a little, a little shame. Because shame is for grown-ups, grown-ups only. Only adults." As an eighth-grade teacher explained, his students do not feel shame, "because children do not have any thoughts."

Children's relative lack of thoughts and shame means that they are not concerned with things that matter to adults such as hiding food from others so as to protect their reputation or damaging another adult's reputation through speech.

'Children do not lie,' a man said. Then he corrected himself. 'Okay, well they do a little bit. But they do not lie about goods.' Instead of hiding goods, children talk about them, a woman explained, "because they see it." For example, a man contrasted himself with a child younger than Ryan. Both he and the child saw someone steal a lighter. The man did not say anything, presumably because he did not want to make people mad at him. But the child, the man claimed, said, "That other man over there, he took it." This adult saw the child as free to speak the truth because it did not occur to him to lie. This inability to lie is relative: older children are more responsible than younger ones. But even they tell fewer morally bad falsehoods than adults. "It's like Nomi," one man said, referring to his daughter who was a little older than Ryan. "Maybe 2 percent of the time she lies. . . . But people like me, it could be 50 percent."

If a child were to say something untrue or do something bad, moreover, the act or speech would belong not to them but to an elder. As two women explained, although some children do lie about goods, they only do so because they are scared of their parents. In effect, therefore, their speech is not their own, and they are not the ones who lied. Similarly, said another,

> in Marshallese culture, if you steal, your family stole. If it was you who stole, for example, and now you have a baby, she or he will grow up with what you did. You stole, so the child is going to steal.

Children are not responsible for their behavior and speech and cannot be truly bad. Any goods they take or withhold, any lies they tell, are not real acts of doing wrong or failing to give. Relatedly, although children frequently say to each other, "I hate you" (in contrast to adults, who rarely directly express hatred toward each other), many adults claim that children do not hate. Explained a woman, "Children, okay they are joking, but adults they are not. . . . If adults say they hate them, they will hate them forever, but children just today, and tomorrow all is well." Children's hate, like their lies, is not real.

'Children don't have any sin,' Celia said, shifting back onto her heels. With relatively few chairs, Marshallese women often crouched near the ground, able to stay in that position for hours as they weeded, did laundry, or cooked. Young girls learned the technique early. In contrast, I could only crouch for a couple of minutes. I usually resorted to simply sitting on the ground and getting dirty.

'So,' Celia continued, children 'have an angel.' Many people told me that children either were "angels" or had an "angel" watching over them.

'But,' I protested, 'children are very naughty [*bōt*]!'

Celia scoffed. 'Naughtiness is not a sin!'

Bran, a man sitting next to Celia, broke in. "The main point is that children do not know how to *kōm̧m̧an nana*."[8] A phrase that literally means "make bad," *kōm̧m̧an nana* is a euphemism for sex.

As the euphemism implies, the prototypical sin (*jerǫwiwi*) in Jajikon is sex. Other sins include drinking, smoking, lying, and stealing, practices that adults also classify as moral wrongs (*bōd*). Children, however, do not have sex, drink, or smoke; nor do they lie or steal, since any acts of real lying or stealing are not their own. Children can neither sin nor purposely avoid sin. This lack of sin is why children cannot become "Christian" (*Kūrjin*). Although all Marshallese go to church, the word *Christian* (*Kūrjin*) typically refers to people who become members in good standing of their church through swearing an oath and avoiding sin (Abo et al. 2016). Many adults are not Christian, either because they have not sworn the oath or because, despite the oath, they sin. There are no Christian children for a different reason—the label simply does not apply.

Although children may joke, falsely claim to have run an errand, disobey their elders, or even gossip about other children, they will not themselves choose to hide either goods or words to harm adults or their reputation. Children such as Ryan cannot lie about things that matter, such as Jujan cutting Leny.

Therefore, Ryan must have told the truth. Jujan must be guilty.

Ideologies as Social Acts

Unless Ryan lied.

Shortly after Leny was cut, Jujan's friend Kati accosted some children on their way to school. She started with Cara, a girl slightly older than Leny who lived next door to Leny's birth mother Delila (see Figure 5.3). 'Why did you lie and say that Jujan cut his leg?' Kati scolded.

The girl ducked her head. 'I didn't!'

Kati, the young woman, was not satisfied. 'Why are you making trouble?'

Kati turned to a gaggle of boys also on their way to school. 'Why are you making trouble between women?' Kati demanded. 'Did you say that Jujan cut Leny's leg?'

'I didn't!'

'Delila said that you did. You and Cara and Amy. . . .'

'It wasn't me! It was Chase [Ryan's older brother]! Chase . . . Ryan! Ryan was the one who told me.' In other words, the boy did tell Delila, but he only passed on Ryan's words, so really it was Ryan who told Delila. 'Ryan told me, Ryan told me!' The boy grabbed Kati's arm to make sure that she was listening. 'I am being really truthful!'

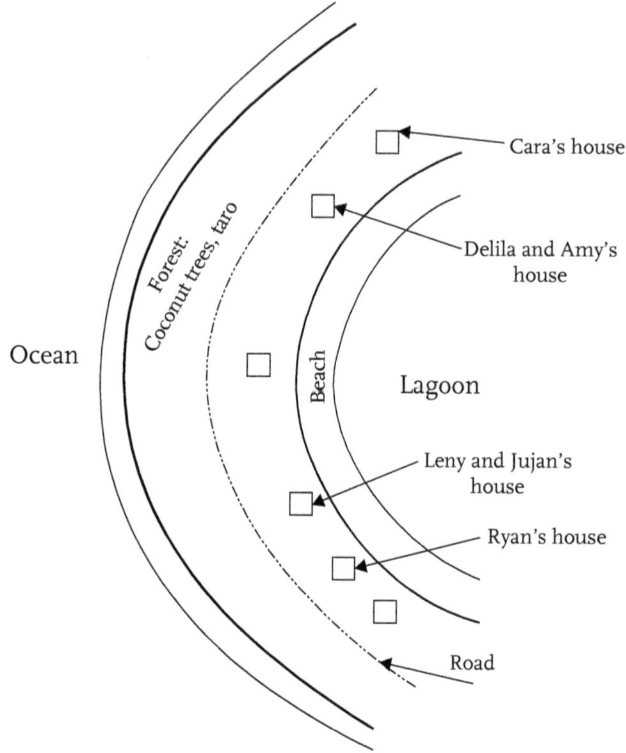

FIGURE 5.3 Organization of people's houses.

'I only said . . . ,' Cara said.

'I didn't say anything!'

'It wasn't me!'

Kati surveyed the children, her hands on her hips. 'Do you know whose house that is?' she said sternly. 'Leny's house. Did any of you see it?'

Eventually Kati and I left the children behind. 'What did Jujan do?' I asked her.

'Nothing,' Kati responded. 'Leny cut himself. [But] the children told Delila that Jujan cut him.'

'Is it true?'

'You heard the children,' Kati responded, implying that their stories did not add up. 'Do you think that they are telling the truth?'

Kati did not agree that children do not lie. She was not the only one. "If a child says something," one of the teachers told me, "the Marshallese, they say that he or she will not lie." He continued: "In Marshallese culture, if [a fourth grader] says,

'Papa that dude threw rocks at me,' according to the older Marshallese, the moms and dads, they say that he is not lying, not even a little."

But, the teacher said, "I do not believe [it]."

"Why do they say that?" I asked.

"I do not know. . . . I [myself] know that children today, they are very smart now, and they know how to lie."

As Kati and this teacher's reactions reveal, people's evaluations of children's speech shift with context. Since all communities contain a certain diversity of opinion, no ideologies are set in stone. For example, this teacher spent his day with children who were constantly declaring that they had lost their homework, that they did not cheat on a test, or that they did not steal a pencil. Such interactions could easily make him more concerned than other adults with what some call mere naughtiness, leading him to think about children as liars.

Beyond the inevitable variation in any given population, however, people often invoke ideologies in some contexts and not others. Consider an interaction among Kati, Ryan, and me several months after Leny's leg was cut. Kati happened to be looking out her window one day. She claimed that she saw Ryan fighting with another boy. But later that day Ryan told Kati and me that he did not fight.

"He is lying!" Kati exclaimed. 'I saw you run from [the other boy].'

'We were playing tag.'

Kati turned to me. 'He knows how to lie.'

'Yes,' I responded.

'Are you surprised?' Kati asked.

'No. Are you?'

'I am surprised!' Kati declared.

'Why?'

'People say children "don't know how to lie." '

Kati's shifting statements about whether children lie reveal that, rather than reflections of people's inner thoughts or beliefs, ideologies are social acts. When the man claimed that "children today" do in fact lie, he challenged elders' status as knowledge keepers and positioned himself as someone with a modern outlook on life who has information that elders lack. When Kati claimed that children do not lie and expressed surprise at Ryan, she realigned herself with many others in the community whom she had indirectly challenged months earlier when she chose to believe that the cut was an accident. In addition, she positioned Ryan as a child. Since *child* (*ajri*) is a relative term that changes with context, whether or not any given individual falls into the category of people who do not lie also changes with context. Finally, when Kati criticized the children for lying to Delila about Jujan, Kati constructed herself as a responsible adult who avoids causing trouble between families and as a loyal friend to Jujan. Prior to this incident I frequently found Kati at Jujan's house chatting, sharing coconut oil, and exchanging food.

But although ideological statements are social acts, they do reflect underlying—albeit constantly shifting and inconsistent—culturally specific attitudes that influence how people interpret interactions. For example, in Great Britain before the 1990s children were not allowed to serve as witnesses in court to their own child abuse. People assumed that, unlike adults, children were not capable of speaking truthfully for themselves. Therefore, people used physical evidence from children's bodies as opposed to verbal evidence from children's speech to determine whether or not abuse had occurred (Lee 1999). Many parenting books from the United States claim that children pass through a lying stage at the age of four (Bronson 2009). These views of children as unable to be truthful contrast directly with the Marshallese ideology that children are naturally transparent and that they are much more likely than adults to talk about what they see.

Ideologies serve as discourses that people can, but are not required to, access to explain a situation. Moreover, the presence or absence of ideologies in a given cultural environment makes some interpretations possible and others impossible. In Britain before the 1990s people would never say "Children do not lie" to support their evaluations of whether a child was abused. In contrast, people in Jajikon who aligned themselves with Delila and against Jujan supported their interpretations of this incident by referencing this ideology. 'I believe it,' Onin said. 'I see Jujan hitting Leny all the time.' Onin continued, 'Children do not lie.'

Onin herself had eight children, one of whom sat next to her. Nomi, slightly older than Leny, calmly fanned the sputtering fire. Corners of a coconut husk burst into flame. Ironically, Nomi spent much of her own time working and caring for her younger sibling, a small boy who had just learned to walk.

'Children don't lie?' I asked.

'They lie!' Nomi declared. Children held a somewhat different ideology of childhood—and adulthood—than adults.

'They lie sometimes . . . ,' Onin reluctantly agreed. She continued, 'I would not have believed it if I had not seen Jujan hitting Leny a lot. Not with a machete, but a lot. Her hands would get swollen.'

Unlike Kati and Jujan, Onin and Jujan were not friends. Perhaps Onin did not like Jujan. Perhaps Onin was close to Delila. Or perhaps Onin did previously see Jujan hitting Leny and believed Ryan's story because it was consistent with her experience. What is clear is that, unlike Kati, she had reasons to access and affirm the ideology that children do not lie. "Children do not lie"—except when they do.

Childhood, Power, and Aged Agency

Although ideologies are instrumental and context-dependent, they nonetheless transform people's social environment. This particular ideology reflects children's supposed lack of moral personhood and gives children a great deal of child-specific agency.

'Did you tell Delila?' I asked Onin about all the times that she saw Jujan hitting Leny.

'No.'

'Why not?'

Onin hesitated, looking at the flames. 'I did not want to make trouble.' 'And,' she continued, 'I did not think that she would believe me.'

'But all the children told Delila about Jujan cutting his leg,' I said.

'Yes.'

'And Delila believed them. . . .'

'They [Delila's family] said that children do not lie.'

There is no ideology—contested or not—that adults do not lie. Quite the opposite: adults implicitly distrusted each other's words (see chapter 3). Consequently, Onin could not speak. First, she did not want others to accuse her of spreading gossip. Second, she assumed that other adults would interpret anything she said as a lie. In contrast, according to Onin, the children could speak. Indeed, by invoking children's observations Onin was able to validate her own intrinsically untrustworthy opinion.

Ryan's power, and Onin's lack of power, to speak and be believed reflects the unique, child-specific forms of agency available to Ryan by virtue of being a nonmoral person. This nonmoral agency gives children the ability to do all sorts of things that adults cannot: gather and spread information, say things that adults (although not children) interpret as true, transport material goods in public without having to give them away, and ask for goods.

First, as we have seen with Ryan and Onin, children can both gather information that adults fear to collect and talk when adults fear to speak. It was Ryan, not an adult, who spied on Leny. When a ghost possessed a woman one night, it was children who peered into the woman's window the next day to see what she was doing. Such invasions of privacy are inappropriate for adults. But children are nonmoral persons who can do things that their elders may not.

Second, once children gather information they can also more easily spread it. The children who peered in through the window had information that they could then distribute. Adults regularly plied their children with questions. 'Where is grandfather?' 'What was he doing?' 'Who came on the boat?' 'What did they bring?' 'What are they eating?'

Like adults, many children also wanted to avoid taking responsibility for talking about Leny. For example, some older children would not let me record them when they discussed what happened to Leny, aware that they could get into trouble for talking about adults. But while children often fear to speak about adults because they fear their elders, adults often fear to speak about adults because they are concerned with their own reputations. Thus, in contrast to adults some children—and particularly younger children—were willing to brave the consequences of speaking. 'Did you say that Jujan cut his leg?' I asked Ryan.

His grin reflected innocence, mischief, or both. 'Yes.'

'Did you see it?'

'Yes.'

Children's greater ability to speak comes partly from the fact that adults have the option of interpreting children's words as true even when children contradict themselves. Several people supported their belief in Jujan's guilt by referring to the fact that not only Ryan but also 'Leny said it, and Ryan saw it.' In fact, however, as the story goes, Leny actually said multiple, contradictory things. Supposedly Delila questioned Leny about the incident. According to several sources, at first Leny did not speak. Then, after some more questions, Leny defended Jujan and claimed that the cut on his leg was an accident. Delila asked Leny again what happened. Finally, a friend told me, Leny "told the truth." He implicated Jujan in the cutting of his leg, marking Jujan as a bad mother who abused her child. By calling Leny's final statement "true" and also insisting that children "do not lie," my friend erased children's inconsistencies and gave Leny and Ryan more power to speak than Jujan.

Third, children are also able to carry things that adults cannot. Every adult I asked said that adults give things to children to carry when they are too ashamed to carry those things themselves. As one woman said, when she feels ashamed to carry food she tells her children, "Take it." It is better for the children to carry the food, she continued, because "they are small . . . and they do not have any thoughts." For example, a woman once gave her son (who was roughly the same age as Ryan) a plate of cooked bread to carry to her relatives across the street. The boy walked right past numerous men sitting in the yard. He did not offer them any food. Rather than the exception, this boy's behavior was the norm. One grandfather sent his granddaughter to buy Spam. Two other children transported a big container of donuts, rice, and other goodies across the village. Two girls carted a big basket of chicken back to their house. These children never offered the food they carried to anyone. Explained another man,

> Sometimes I give [the food] to children. The reason that I am ashamed is because if my brother or sister is there, I am ashamed . . . because I don't give them their food. In truth, I should have given them their food. But now I am ashamed because if there is only a small amount of the food left and I take it over there . . . they [will] say, "You are bad." Now I am ashamed. So I give it to the children so that they will take it. And maybe [my friends] will say [that I am bad], but the children do not pay any attention.

Adults believe that when they carry food children can refuse to give in ways that adults may not. As one woman said, "If you ask for something from a child, he or she will not give it to you. Because he or she is not ashamed. But if you ask for something from an adult, they are ashamed, and they say, 'Here.'"

Finally, children can ask for things adults can not. Just as with carrying goods, every adult I asked (ten) said that adults send children to ask for things when they are too ashamed to do so. "The main thing that we see among people," a woman told me, "is that they send their child to say, 'Grandpa says give me that thing.' The real reason is because they are ashamed."

For example, a man told his wife to go and ask for cooking oil from a relative. "Go and say," he said, "that I said they should give it to us." He was uncomfortable with the errand and wanted to pass it on to his wife.

But, of course, his wife also did not want to ask for the oil. She stalled, "But why is the oil in that house?"

"It is for us to fry that thing."

The woman hesitated, tossing some grass she had unearthed over her shoulder into a growing pile of weeds. "Ugh," she complained, "I am scared. Why don't you send [our son]?" Just as the man tried to pass the errand off to his wife, she wanted to pass it off to her son.

Coming from a nonmoral agent, her son's words would not be his own. Slightly older than Ryan, the boy did not need to be ashamed to ask. Indeed, he was too young to feel shame, since he was too young to be responsible for his words. Because his words and goods belonged to others, he could mediate economic and political life for his parents. He could ask for things, transport food, gather information, and speak the truth.

Delila's Decision

It is not clear exactly who told Delila, Leny's birth mother, about the cut on Leny's leg. Some people said that it was Cara, a girl who lived next door to Delila.

Others said that it was Dean, who lived on the other side. Some fingered Josie. All agreed that it was a child. And all agreed that the child got his or her information from another child—from Ryan.

It only took five minutes for Delila to storm over to Jujan's house.

'She yelled at Jujan.' The younger woman's face was flushed with excitement as she related the story. 'She told her, "I gave you my child when he was little! And now that he is grown, you are destroying him." '

Kati told me, 'She said, "I am taking Leny because you murdered him!" '

'What did Jujan say?' I asked the younger woman.

'She cried and said, "Lie." '

But Delila's family said, a third woman explained to me, 'Children do not lie.'

'So,' the younger woman continued, 'Delila slapped Jujan in the face and punched her in the chest.'

And Delila took Leny away.

Child-Specific Agency and the Transformation of Signs

Jujan and Ryan were both flawed characters in the realm of trust. Jujan had a history of harming Leny; Ryan had a history of mischief and lies. Nonetheless, Jujan was an adult, while Ryan was a child. As a result, Ryan was implicitly more trustworthy than Jujan and had more agency than Jujan, in this specific instance, to shape Leny's fate.

As did all the children involved in this story. Only Ryan—or another child—could gather the evidence of Leny's supposed abuse. And only a child could be believed. Ryan told his mother as well as other children about what he saw. But either only the children spoke to Delila (the public story), or Delila claimed that only the children spoke to her. Delila had to rest her evaluation of Leny's cut on children's words if she was to support her decision to take Leny away.

At the same time, there were many things that adults could do that children could not. Ryan could not physically remove Leny from his household. Children could not order an adult to run an errand for them, to pass on a message, or to cook rice. Leny, when Jujan told him to make copra, largely had to obey. Jujan could punish Leny, sometimes physically. While children could talk about Jujan and Leny, they nonetheless feared their elders, who could punish them for talking about adults. Leny could not run his own household. He had to live with a relative—be it Jujan or Delila.

Ryan, Leny, and the other children did not have more agency than adults but, rather, a different type of agency: their agency was aged. All agency—child or adult—is aged. Despite the push in childhood studies to discuss children as active agents, for the most part such studies talk about child and adult agency as the same (James 2009; James and Prout 1997b; Porter 1996; Tisdall and Punch 2012). As I show here, however, children in Jajikon have agency not in spite of the fact that they are children but precisely because of it. As children they are different from adults and can do different things.

Local views of children as not responsible produce children in Jajikon as nonmoral agents—they can do things that are inappropriate for adults. Adults can also fail to work, ignore their own elders, or neglect their duty to care for their children. But when adults such as Jujan do such things, other adults criticize them as moral failures. Jujan's reputation as a poor mother and woman contributed to the loss of her child. In contrast, when Ryan broke implicit privacy boundaries and spied on Jujan and Leny, people essentially rewarded him by believing his story. Such actions are not without risks—children may be scolded or disciplined for disobedience. Nonetheless, the consequences of such forms of action on the part of children are distinctly different than those for adults. All of Ryan's failures—his lies, his acts of stealing, his disobedience—were merely examples of *bōt*, naughtiness, a child-typical characteristic that means that children will inevitably do things that mature people should not.

Aged agency comes from the way people's bodies transform the meanings of the signs—both words and goods—that they circulate. Adult bodies mark certain items as up for grabs, while child bodies mark those same items as out of circulation and unattainable. Adult mouths mark speech as probably false, while child mouths mark such speech as probably true. Children's and adults' bodies serve as indices that change the status of the things that they hold or the words that they speak.

Through their speech and actions children transform relationships, possessions, and statuses. Seen as not responsible for their words or actions, children do all sorts of things that adults should not. They say no, they walk with food, they spy, and they make requests. They do some of these things on their own. On other occasions, however, adults explicitly command children to do things that they would never do themselves. Children play a major role in transporting food around the village, since, given the option, all adults would rather send a child than carry something themselves. Many requests take place through children as mediators, just as much gossip and information travels via children's mouths. A family without children in Jajikon cannot function, not only because they need labor but also because they need people who follow different social and moral rules. Families need nonmoral agents.

Leny's Future

Leny stayed with Delila. He did not have to. Other adoptive children whose birth parents reclaimed them returned of their own accord to their adoptive family. In contrast, some adoptive children chose to run away back to their birth parents. All people in the RMI—adults and children—exercise this ability to vote with their feet and move away from difficult social situations. People's abilities to move, however, are constrained by their relationships with their other relatives. Leny may have stayed with Delila because he was afraid that Jujan would not take him back. Alternatively, he may have stayed with Delila because he actually preferred to live there.

Leny also avoided Jujan. For a couple of weeks Leny stayed far away from his former house and anything that was near it. He skipped church, Sunday school, and choir rehearsals. When I interviewed him a couple of months after the incident he rejected his adoptive family as his relatives, refusing to include them in a drawing of his family.

Leny slowly came out of his shell. Eventually he returned to church, Sunday school, and the choir. He started talking about his experience, repeating the line that everyone eventually came to accept as the truth.

'Is Delila better than Jujan?' I asked.

'Yes.'

'Why?'

'Because Jujan cut my leg.'

From my perspective—colored by all my friends who thought that Jujan had cut Leny's leg—Leny seemed to play and laugh more than he did before. 'I think he is happier now,' I remarked to Kati.

Interestingly, Kati—Jujan's main supporter early in the controversy—agreed. 'Yes,' Kati said. 'I am surprised. He is playing with other children.'

'Now do you think that it is good that Delila took him back? Because before you did not.'

'Now,' Kati said, 'I think it is good.'

A month after our conversation I found Leny playing with some other children outside of his new house. He yelled commands to his teammates as he stood at home base, ready to bat. The bat connected and he bounded off but, to the hysterical amusement of everyone around, he deliberately went in the wrong direction. After completing the circuit he collapsed on the ground, rolling in laughter.

Three years after I left Jajikon, I returned. Leny still lived with Delila who, like Jujan, depended on copra for her livelihood. Like before, Leny spent much of his time gathering and processing copra, hauling wheelbarrows of coconuts back to the house.

Notes

1. I draw this definition of aged agency from Wardlow's definition of gendered agency as "particular modes of exerting power or producing effects that are particular to women as women or men as men" (2006, 9).
2. Similarly, Botswanan adults call youth community organizing "just playing," allowing them to dismiss such actions as insignificant (Durham 2005).
3. Although nonmoral agency may seem like a contradiction in terms, across cultures many people are able to do things precisely because others do not see them as socially relevant. Servants often fall into this category, as do, of course, children (Berman 2011; Carsten 1991; Gaskins and Lucy 1987; Haviland 1977, 189; Hotchkiss 1967; Kulick 1992, 230–34; Lancy 1996, 158; Mead 1930, 40; Rasmussen 1994; Reynolds 2008; Schildkrout 1978). K'iche' Maya children run errands, carry messages, and buffer feelings of resentment between adults (Berman 2011); children in Kano run errands for women who are in purdah and cannot leave their homes (Schildkrout 1978).
4. Lacy's accusation reflects a gender inequality. While men could smoke, women were not supposed to. Hence, Jujan had to hide her smoking (if indeed she was smoking) and send Leny to work. A man could have made copra and smoked at the same time.
5. The stealing occurs earlier in the video.
6. Marshallese adults believed that swimming made children sick. Therefore, they often told children not to swim.
7. Throughout this chapter I refer to adult ideologies of whether or not children lie or tell the truth. I do not make any claims about what children actually say or their actual abilities to lie or speak the truth.
8. The underlined words were in English, Bran spoke all the rest of the sentence in Marshallese.

6 SOCIALIZING AGE DIFFERENCES

Jackie hid in the dark.

The height of a grown woman, she slumped behind the door, leaving only her head and one arm visible to the men in the room. She raised her hand palm forward and then flicked fingers downward. People use this gesture when they want to surreptitiously get someone's attention. *Come.*

No one responded. Frustrated, Jackie retreated. She took refuge in the safe invisibility of the night.

To people lacking knowledge of Marshallese gender norms Jackie's mission would have seemed simple. Jackie's relative, Kirinrose, was preparing dinner for her household—a rambunctious, crowded, constantly changing throng of between ten and twenty family members.[1] Kirinrose did not have any meat. So, following the principle that younger people move for their elders, Kirinrose sent Jackie to find her partner, Michael, and tell him to buy a can of tuna (see Figure 6.1).

Unfortunately for Jackie, Michael was out with a bunch of other young men enjoying an evening coffee at a small household store nearby. Although no explicit rules bar most interactions between people of different genders, in practice both women and men are extremely shy (*jook* or *abje*) of groups of people of the opposite gender.[2]

Children break these gender boundaries all the time and regularly play in mixed-gender groups. But Jackie, apparently, was no longer completely a child. She made one more half-hearted attempt. "Michael. . . ."

It was no use. So Jackie did what adults do when they have trouble asking for something themselves: she gave the errand to a child who could do what she could not. "Nomi," Jackie pleaded with her younger relative, "go and say it."

Unfortunately for Jackie, Nomi ignored her.

But luckily Nomi's younger sibling Sisina did not. "OK, I will say it." The short, petite girl strode up to the doorway, letting the light fall directly on her body. "Hey Michael!" Sisina said in a loud, clear voice.

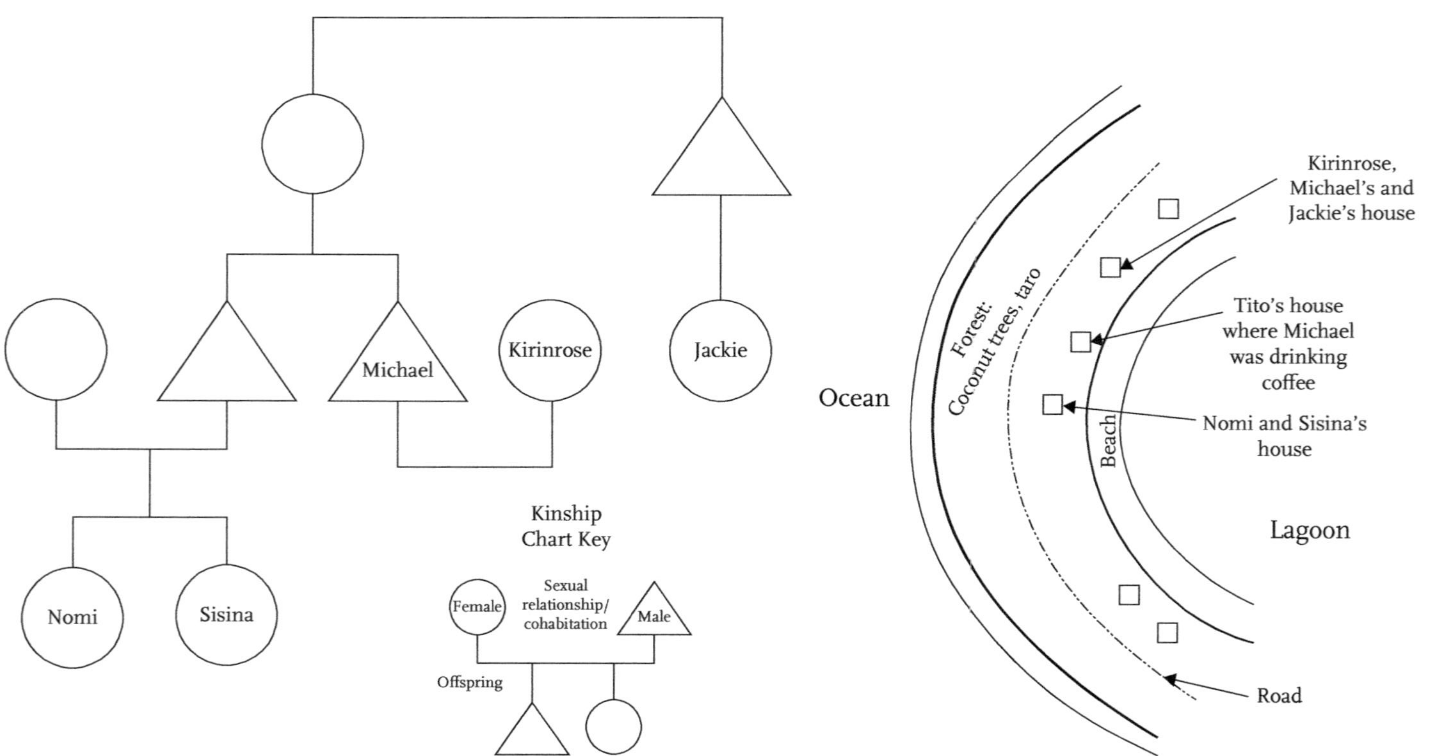

FIGURE 6.1 Jackie's household and relationships.

How did Sisina and Jackie become different from one another?

One answer is biology. But although biological changes over time may have created their bodily differences, they probably did not create the social or subjective differences between the two girls. It was no more natural for Sisina to stand in the light than for Jackie to hide in the dark and no more natural for Sisina to speak than for Jackie to remain silent. Around the world many children are silent and hide, while many youth are unafraid to speak.

This chapter analyzes two interrelated questions: (1) How and why did Jackie learn to feel shyness and shame? (2) How and why did Sisina learn *not* to be shy or ashamed? Jackie's and Sisina's different subjective responses to the prospect of approaching men in the night were socialized through interaction. It was not only Jackie who learned to be mature and to conform to adult gender and interactional norms; Sisina also learned to be immature and to be different from her elder Jackie.

My first question—how Jackie learned to feel shame and to conform to the taboos that govern Marshallese adult life—is a typical question for a language socialization study. Often conceptualized as the analysis of how "particular culturally meaningful practices become acquired (or not) by children and other novices" (Ochs and Schieffelin 2012, 1), many such studies (although not all) focus on practices seen as mature in a given context such as politeness, shame, or indirectness (Berman 2014b; Burdelski 2012; Burdelski and Mitsuhashi 2010; Fung 1999; Lo and Fung 2012). In Marshallese adult ideologies of childhood, as we saw in chapter 5, babies and very young children naturally feel no shame and do not hide. Both of these things require thoughts, which babies supposedly lack. While Marshallese adults disagree as to how often different children lie, hide, and feel shame, they all agree that the general trajectory is from no thoughts to thoughts, no shame to shame, revealing to hiding. In this ideology, the second of each of these pairs must be socialized, but the first is natural.

My second question is less common but equally relevant: How did Sisina learn to lack shame and to do things that Jackie would not? In Jajikon, as in many other places, people view children as not yet fully social.[3] According to many Jajikonians children are immature; they lack some capacity of their elders. But we now know that infant and child behavior is, at least partly, cultural (Rogoff 2003): Inuit and Zinacantán babies do not cry (Crago 1988; Rogoff 2003), Digo infants in East Africa are toilet trained by the time they are five or six months old (deVries and deVries 1977), and Beng babies do not have separation anxiety (Gottlieb 2004). Children's inabilities—their inabilities to control their temper, inabilities to be responsible caregivers, inabilities to be by themselves—are at least partly cultural. Not only the presence but also often the absence of behavior is socialized.

The social production of difference takes place through language and interaction. In Sisina's and Jackie's case, these interactions include times when people recruit younger individuals to run errands that they wish to avoid, such as this errand to pass a message on to Michael. Interactions such as these exhibit "dual indexicality"—they simultaneously index two opposing subject positions (Kulick 2003; Kulick and Schieffelin 2004). As an example of dual indexicality, consider when adults explicitly try to socialize politeness through instructing children to say "please." Such instructions do teach politeness, but they also teach children how to be rude—that is, by not saying please (Billig 1999, 94–95). Thus, instructions to say please "manifest both their surface propositional content and the simultaneous inverse of that concept" (Kulick and Schieffelin 2004, 358). Similarly, elders' commands to youth in Jajikon to "go and say" things that the elders themselves avoid point to people who avoid speaking while also teaching children such as Sisina to speak; simultaneously indexing both shame and the lack of it. These interactions recruit people into different subject positions. People who speak, like Sisina, lack shame (*āliklik*). People who avoid speaking, like Jackie, are ashamed (*āliklik*). Through this dual indexicality differences come to be.

Dual indexicality is involved in both social change and cultural reproduction. Kulick and Schieffelin (2004) focus on culturally unpredictable outcomes, such as Hasidic children who become immodest, liberal children who become evangelical Christians, or white children in the antebellum South who fight for civil rights.[4] But if culture itself—people's beliefs, practices, and subjectivities—constantly changes not only across historical periods but also across the life course, then changing cultural practices are necessary features of not only change but also continuity.[5] Cultural continuity includes within it life course variation; cultural reproduction requires people who, before they learn to be like their elders, learn to be different from them.

Socialization, therefore, is not the acquisition of cultural practices by children and other novices but, rather, the constant and continuous production of differences. Neither Sisina nor Jackie was a novice (although they were children). Instead, Sisina's and Jackie's movements through life took them through different subject positions. Socialization takes place as people such as Sisina and Jackie continuously take on, modify, and discard age-specific modes of being and speaking, as they construct themselves as different from both those who they used to be and those who they are yet to (and may never) become.

This chapter explores Jackie's attempt to run her errand and the various interactions that produce people such as Sisina and Jackie as different from one another. I start first with the similarities between Sisina and Jackie and then turn to their differences. Finally, I examine times in which people encourage children to display, demand, refuse, and criticize: to be children who lack shame and are different from their elders.

Similarities

"Oh baby I love you. . . ."

Children's voices floated in the night air above the sounds of the five-dollar convenience store ukulele. It was around ten minutes before Jackie found herself cowering outside the door.

"I don't want to go with you, because you are married. . . ."

One of the children recognized Jackie's silhouette in the distance. "Jackie!"

"Fuck Jackie," the youngest boy swore, grinning. Only a couple of years into his elementary schooling, Tito was a rascal. Who knows why he cursed Jackie. Perhaps they had a disagreement earlier in the day. Or perhaps Tito simply felt like cursing.

"Sisina!" Jackie called. Roughly the same age as Tito, Sisina was technically Jackie's daughter (see Figure 6.1). Jackie's father and Sisina's grandmother were siblings, and their two households were a stone's throw away from each other, close enough for their families to regularly share food, work, childcare, and sleeping spaces. In other words, Sisina was a younger relative whom Jackie could command. "Is Michael," Jackie continued, "is Michael in that house?"

"He is gone," Tito lied.

Jackie ignored him. She commanded Sisina, "Go and say, 'Michael! Come here please. Michael, Kirinrose said to bring. . . .' "

Sisina hesitated. Around thirty seconds later she said, "Oh Jackie! I am scared! Jackie! I am scared!"

Understanding how Sisina and Jackie became different from each other requires first recognizing that in some respects they were more similar than different. Neither Sisina nor Jackie wanted to pass the message on to Michael. Nor did Kirinrose. Although all three were in different stages of life, they shared a desire to stay silent. Adults send children on errands because they say, as we saw in chapter 5, that children can do things that adults may not. But although children are often perfectly willing to ask, refuse, talk about, and display their goods to other children, they frequently do not want to interact in such a way with adults or with adult goods. Adults are older than children and are people whom they should fear.

First, though children are willing to walk around with snack food and candy, they often fear to carry many other types of food. Ten children, most of them close to Sisina's age or younger, said that although it was fine to walk around with snack food such as lollipops or Marshallese apples, it was inappropriate to walk around with meal food such as a plate of rice and fish.

"Is it okay to walk and eat?" I asked a girl slightly older than Sisina.

"It is bad."

"With pandanus [a snack food]?"

"No problem."

Such comments reflect some adults' statements that it is only bad to walk with "real" food.

Second, most children said that they were scared to refuse to give to adults. As one child said, if an adult asks, "I give." On the other hand, if a child should ask, "sometimes I give and sometimes I do not." As another girl explained to me, children are often willing to say no to another child. But they prefer to "give [to adults] because they are scared of adults."

Third, children say that they are willing to talk about children but are scared to talk about adults. One girl, younger than Sisina, said that if she saw two children fighting, she would say to others, "Two children are fighting." She continued, "It is not [bad], because they are children." In contrast, she said that if she overheard two adults gossiping, she would not say anything, because "they would get mad at me." Tito insisted that a hypothetical story I told about him overhearing two adults gossiping was impossible. He never hears adults speaking, he claimed implausibly, because the lawnmower is too loud. Tito later contradicted himself and told me a story he overheard when listening to adults, suggesting that he did in fact listen to adults but did not want to admit it. As Tito explained, it is "bad" to talk about what adults say because "we are children." In practice, of course, children did frequently talk about adults, but they tried to keep their gossip under the radar of the adult in question. For example, several children refused to let me record them when they were talking about the fight between Jujan and Delila about Leny (see chapter 5).

Fourth, children are often willing to demand things from other children but fear to approach adults. For example, two girls—older than Sisina but younger than Jackie—hovered on the edge of a gathering. They wanted cake. "I went closer and closer," one of the girls said, telling the story to some friends. "Then I was scared. I immediately told Coline [her friend] that she should come away from there." On another day, I sat with another girl roughly the same age as those two children. We watched some women approach from a neighboring town. 'Elise,' the girl said, 'ask them where they are going.'

'Why don't you ask?' I asked her.

"Children are scared to ask adults."

These declarations and performances of fear mark children as good children who know their place in society and appropriately respect their elders (Berman 2018, see also Meek 2011). Consequently, both adults and older children often view declarations of fear such as Sisina's as legitimate reasons why they should not force children to run errands. "I am scared!" Tito said to his grandmother when she told him to ask the preacher's wife for a cooking pan. Rather than criticizing or threatening Tito, his grandmother accepted his excuse. (She sent me instead.) Children often emphasize the legitimacy of their fear by using the first-person inclusive plural *je*. "*Jemijak*!" Sisina said, which literally means "We are scared." "We are scared of him [*jemijake*]," a boy said when his mother told him to pass a message along to his father. This inclusive first-person plural pronoun is a common rhetorical strategy for resisting authority. The pronoun shifts the responsibility for resisting away from the individual and onto society as a whole. I occasionally translate such statements as "I am scared" because my research assistants typically translated them as such. But other appropriate translations of such statements would be "It is a scary situation" or "He/she is a scary person." Through their grammar children emphasize the problems with asking others for things and encourage their elders to release them from their errand.

Jackie was frustrated. "Argh Sisina!" she exclaimed. Nonetheless, she accepted Sisina's excuse and tried someone else. "Oh Nomi," Jackie said, turning to Sisina's older sister. "You just say, 'Hey Michael. . . .'"

By trying to outsource her errand first to Sisina and then to Nomi, Jackie was using a tried and tested model among both adults and children to accomplish unpleasant tasks. Children frequently used this same method when they had no choice but to run an errand that they feared.[6] One child asked a friend of his to purchase goods for him at a household store. "Just go and buy it here. One corned beef and three cans of tuna." Children often tried to pass an errand on to someone who was closer to the adult in question and less scared of that adult. As one girl explained, when her parents sent her to get firewood from Mariana (an adult), she would try to give the errand to Mariana's children, either "Ruto or if not him, Chris. Or if not him, Cake." Neither Jackie's hesitation nor her methods of negotiating her fear differentiated her from Sisina.

Jackie and Sisina were also similar in another way: they were to a certain extent peers. Jackie was obviously older than Sisina. But while Jackie was tall, about to start high school, occasionally hung out with women, and like women avoided swimming, she was also still a child. She went to school and sang in Sunday school. Although she occasionally stood in the adult line for food at parties, she also sometimes stood in the children's line.

Consequently, the children were not scared of Jackie.

"Ugh girl," Nomi complained. She was not going to run the errand.

"You should go by yourself," another boy said.

Jackie tried a third person. "Tito," she pleaded, "go and say, 'Hey Michael!'"

"I am/we are scared [*jemijak*]," Tito responded.

Of course, Tito was not scared. At least, not according to my research assistant who reviewed this video with me. Tito had no reason to be scared: not only was he male, but he also lived in the house where Michael was drinking coffee. But children had many reasons other than fear to refuse an errand. Sometimes they were lazy. 'My legs are tired,' a girl complained when her grandfather told her to pass a message to her grandmother. Sometimes they wanted to play. "Go and bring that thing and wash so that I can rest," a mother commanded her daughter. Her small daughter ignored her, concentrating on throwing rocks with a friend. Sometimes, like Tito, they were too busy "talking" (the reason suggested by my research assistant). But since none of those reasons are legitimate, children may claim "fear" even when they are not afraid.

Jackie seemed to suspect that Tito was not actually scared. "Just go and say it," she commanded.

"Ooooh," Tito teased.

When they cannot find someone to run their errand for them, children, youth, and adults alike often try to find a way to minimize the dangerous aspects of the errand. For example, many children claimed that they would try to hide food away from the eyes of others. A boy slightly younger than Tito said that when adults told him to transport food he "put [the food] in a backpack and brought it." If he did not put the food in a backpack, he explained, "they would say, 'Give me our food,' and the food will be gone." A girl slightly older than Tito expressed a fear that others would ask her about what she was carrying. Therefore, "I always bike. If there is no bike, [I will go] on the road, but I will [cover the food] in plastic. . . . They should not see it, because then they will say, 'Hey, what is that?'" A third girl said that when carrying food she goes on the "beach! . . . So that they will not ask. Because everybody is greedy."

Finally, despite their mixed playgroups children sometimes prefer to talk to people of their own gender. Children frequently enforce gender segregation. "Girls don't play basketball," a boy said to a girl who wanted to join some boys in a game. "The reason he is more effeminate/weak [than another boy]," Kinta teased, "is because he is always staying with the girls." 'Don't spy on girls!' a girl criticized a younger boy. By shaming children of the opposite gender, children start creating the largely gender-segregated peer groups of adulthood. Hence, just as girls such as Sisina may fear to approach a group of men in the night, boys such as Tito may fear to approach a group of women.

Sisina, Jackie, and Kirinrose were not as different from each other as one might think. They all feared to refuse to give to adults, to talk about adults, and to approach Michael among a group of men and ask him for food. They all negotiated their hesitation by declaring fear, outsourcing their errand to others, or hiding things from view. Just as studies of women and men's speech have shown that the similarities between the genders often dwarf the differences (Hyde 2005), in many ways these three people were the same.

Differences

Yet in other ways, Jackie's hesitation to run the errand was very different from Sisina's.

"Nomi, Sisina," Jackie pleaded one last time.

They ignored her.

Jackie was stuck. She had to approach Michael herself. She procrastinated for a few more minutes. Then she slowly headed over to the house.

At this point, as we saw, she cowered in the doorway, hid in the dark, and retreated when her surreptitious attempts to get Michael's attention failed. She gave up. It was, in the end, Sisina who had to speak. "Hey Michael!" she said in a loud, clear voice, letting the light fall directly on herself.

Jackie obviously felt a substantial amount of pressure to run this errand, but she could not do it. Sisina could.

I suspect that, unlike Tito, Sisina was actually somewhat afraid when Jackie first asked her to run the errand. This errand required approaching someone else's house (Tito's) and talking to a crowd of adult men—all things that could feasibly scare a girl. But Sisina's fear was of neither the same quantity nor the same quality as Jackie's. Whereas Sisina demonstrated and claimed fear (*mijak*), Jackie's behavior marked not only fear but also embarrassment (*abje*/*jook*) and/or shame (*āliklik*). *Fear* (*mijak*) is a broad term that encompasses the more specific emotions shy/embarrassed (*jook*/*abje*) and shame (*āliklik*). People use *fear* (*mijak*) to refer to fear for one's physical safety, of the dark, of approaching people of the opposite gender or people whom one does not know well, of challenging or disagreeing with people, or of breaking cultural rules by doing things such as walking while eating (Berman 2012, 110). Almost every time people say that they are either shy (*abje*/*jook*) or ashamed (*āliklik*), they are also afraid (*mijak*). For example, Mariana said that she was not "scared [*mijak*]" to ask people where they were going. 'What about the reverend?' I asked. 'I am ashamed [*āliklik*],' she responded, substituting *shame* (*āliklik*) for *fear* (*mijak*).

In contrast, neither shame (*āliklik*) nor shyness (*abje/jook*) necessarily encompasses fear (*mijak*). People who were afraid (*mijak*) of ghosts were not embarrassed (*abje/jook*) or ashamed (*āliklik*) of ghosts. Shame (*āliklik*), as we have seen, refers specifically to the feeling that stops people from doing something that is transgressive or inappropriate. For example, a woman said that she was ashamed (*āliklik*) during a festival to go bathe in the bathhouse because she was surrounded by many male relatives. *Abje* as well as its synonym *jook* connote shyness and embarrassment. People typically, although not exclusively, associated these words with cross-gender interactions. "It is like she is embarrassed [*abje*] to go over there," a woman commented about another woman who hesitated to bring food to the men outside, a situation very similar to Jackie's. When watching this video my research assistant said that Jackie "was embarrassed" (*abje*) when Jackie did not want to ask Michael for the food.

Both shame (*āliklik*) and embarrassment (*abje/jook*) stem from the mere fact of speaking or acting, and there is no way to avoid the emotions except to avoid the encounter entirely. Regardless of to whom the food belongs, adults who carry food in public by definition are not ashamed (*āliklik*). In other words, to recall terminology from chapter 3, such adults are not mere animators but are necessarily also authors and principals—people who must take responsibility for their words and actions. Similarly, if Jackie were to approach Michael, she would be the one approaching a group of men even though she was doing it on behalf of someone else. Jackie could not separate herself from her words.

In fact, she had already gotten too close to the men to avoid responsibility for her actions and speech.

"Michael," Sisina said, "Kirinrose says to bring her a bottle of soy sauce. A . . . a bottle of soy sauce and a can of tuna."

"Jackie or Kirinrose?" Michael asked.

Sisina did not hesitate. "Kirinrose."

"Where is she?"

Sisina giggled. "Over there . . . ," she collapsed with laughter, unable to finish.

"She is lying!" Nomi said. "Jackie."

Michael knew that Sisina was speaking for Jackie and Jackie for Kirinrose. He viewed Sisina as a child, a mere animator who had no responsibility for her speech. In contrast, even though Jackie was carrying a message for someone else, Michael forced Jackie to own her own words, to be mature and take responsibility for her speech. Jackie was right to be embarrassed (*abje*).

But while adults (and Jackie) cannot separate themselves from their actions or words, children can. Sisina—who like every child with whom I spoke during my first visit did not know the word *shame* (*āliklik*)—was neither embarrassed nor ashamed. As one woman explained to me, fear (*mijak*) is not the same as shame (*āliklik*), because children are simply "afraid [*mijak*] of elders."[7] Moreover, since children are afraid as opposed to ashamed or embarrassed, through marking themselves as not responsible for what they carry or say they can alleviate that fear and complete their tasks. One child explained how she would get out of a request to give by saying, "I will say it is Siera and her husband's food." Another girl said that when people ask for the food she is carrying she simply says, "It is not my food." When children carried food in public often others did not ask for the food at all, since they automatically assumed that what children were carrying did not belong to them. As an older boy said, "They don't [ask], because the food belongs to others."

Unlike adults, children can run errands and reduce their fear by marking themselves as animators who are not responsible. Children often manage this through what anthropologists and linguists call reported speech. Reported speech is a way of attributing one's own words to someone else by saying things such as "he said . . ." (Basso 1986, 1987; Besnier 1992; Goffman 1974, 1981; Hill and Irvine 1993a, 1993b; Hill and Zepeda 1993; Lucy 1993; Tannen 1995; Urban 1986). As we saw, Sisina marked her request as belonging to Kirinrose when she said, "Kirinrose says to bring her a bottle of soy sauce." Jajikonian adults know that children can mitigate their fear of an errand by using reported speech. For example, when a boy protested passing a message on to his father because "I am scared of him," his mother agreed that his father was scary but then suggested a way to minimize his fear: "Go and say that I said it." When children ran errands and attributed their errands to another they reproduced themselves as children who were not responsible and need not hide—need not be embarrassed or ashamed.

That is, running errands requires not only using reported speech but also internalizing one's status as a child and taking on child-specific subjectivities (fear as opposed to shame) as well as a child-specific sense of self.[8] Among girls, at least, these child senses of self are explicit: girls know that they are children, so they can do and feel things that adults do not. As a girl only slightly younger than Jackie said about running an errand, "Adults will send me because they are scared. But me, I am a child, so I am not scared." Another girl roughly the same age explained that her mother was scared because she is an "adult, but me, I am a child," so she was not scared. A slightly younger girl agreed. Adults are shy, but 'children aren't shy [*jook*] . . . because they are children.' A girl even younger than Sisina had a similar perspective, explaining that adults do not ask for things as much as children, because they "are scared."

Jackie's problem was that she, unlike Sisina, no longer had a child's subjective responses. She no longer felt herself to be a child, to be someone who was able to detach herself from her actions. She was different from Sisina, and Sisina was different from Jackie.

Socializing Shame: Becoming Different from Sisina

Where did these differences come from? I rarely heard adults tell people like Jackie that they were too old to run an errand. The change was more organic. Sometimes adults started sending younger children on errands. Often, however, adults like Kirinrose continued sending people like Jackie on errands as long as they agreed to go. Eventually, youth refuse to comply. Or, like Jackie, they recruit still younger people to do what they themselves will not. What transformed Jackie from someone who, when she was younger, would speak but now would not?

Paradoxically, it is partly by doing things that are inappropriate for adults that children such as Jackie eventually take on mature subjectivities that lead them to pass errands on to younger individuals. When Kirinrose sent Jackie on this errand, she commanded Jackie to act like a child while simultaneously modeling the opposite. Her command manifested "dual indexicality," as did Jackie's commands to Nomi, Sisina, and Tito. The command to "go and say" is an explicit command to do something immature, speaking. At the same time, such commands also mark elders such as Kirinrose or Jackie as people who will not "go and say" themselves. When people such as Kirinrose and Jackie command younger people to run errands, they provide models of the future, models of people who cannot "go and say," who cannot act like children. These representations of the life course play a central role in shaping choices and making "certain paths, certain social trajectories, easier to imagine than others" (Cole 2010, 16). Kirinrose helped Jackie, and Jackie helped Nomi and Sisina, imagine a future in which they too would be unable to approach Michael in the night, making that future more likely.

Such errands provide not only models of the future but also opportunities for people such as Jackie and Sisina to either run the errands or avoid them, reproducing themselves as children or adults. Jackie already interacted with youth and women as well as children and was clearly on her way to seeing herself as more similar to people like Kirinrose rather than people like Sisina. She had also already been teased about and/or propositioned by boys: I saw the former and heard about the latter. Such interactions could easily lead Jackie to feel less like a child and more like a woman who was uncomfortable breaking gender norms. Kirinrose put Jackie in an uncomfortable situation and encouraged her to further develop her feelings of shame and embarrassment. Moreover, when Jackie found herself unable to enter the doorway or step into the light, she pulled herself closer to Kirinrose and further away from Sisina. When Sisina spoke (while Jackie would not) she reinforced Jackie's already developed sense that she was no longer the same as Sisina, no longer entirely a child. Finally, when Michael insisted that Jackie take responsibility for her speech, he embarrassed Jackie, reinforced her hesitation, and further encouraged her to take on mature subjectivities. Michael did not let Jackie displace responsibility; he forced her to own her speech like an adult.

Socializing a Lack of Shame: Becoming Different from Jackie

Of course, Jackie not only provided Sisina with a model of the future but also explicitly encouraged Sisina to be immature. She commanded Sisina to "go and say," to do something inappropriate for adults. Just as Jackie commanded Sisina, adults constantly command children to run errands inappropriate for their elders. Whenever they do so, they both provide a model of the future and teach children to do things that adults should not, to be children who are immature and different from adults.

There are many other ways in which people, directly or indirectly, encourage children to become immature. First, older children constantly model adult-inappropriate behavior. Consider the lesson two small children received from their older kin. The two little children—one had not yet started speaking, and the other spoke but had not started school—watched a slightly older girl (she was about to start kindergarten) eat some breadfruit nuts. The older girl paraded around with the nuts, showing them off to friends. Then she refused to share. "It is Sarah's food," the girl said. "Okay," one of her friends responded, "we hate you!" These children modeled conspicuous consumption, refusing, and direct insults, all indices, as we saw in chapter 4, of immaturity.

Second, elders indirectly encourage children to demand food by interpreting children's first words as demands. Two people told me that, in addition to "mama" and "papa," children's first words are the baby talk versions of demands for food and drink, *jōjō* and *mōmō*.[9] *Jō* and *mō* are the last syllables of "my food" (*kijō*) and "my drink" (*limō*), the part that means "my." Sometimes children just said *jō* or *mō*, and sometimes they reduplicated it, saying *jōjō* or *mōmō*. Kuba and Ron, two "little children" who could walk but had only recently started to speak, frequently wandered around their house saying, "*Jōjō* [My food]!" Interpretations of early speech as demands for food probably help to socialize children into demanding food. Similarly, Ochs (1993) argues that interpretations of Samoan children's first words as "shit" are part of a range of practices that socialize such children into the cursers that Samoan adults expect them to be.

Moreover, whenever Kuba and Ron demanded food or drink, they got it. For example, after feeding Kuba and Ron dinner their grandmother said that the boys were done.

"My food my food my food [*jō jō jō*]," Kuba demanded.

His grandmother relented and gave him more food. 'All done,' she said again, trying to give food to the rest of her family.

"My food my food my food [*jō jō jō*]," the children again demanded. They ate all of the food, likely learning that such demands get results. Their act of speaking in ways that their elders would not was reinforced, reproducing it.

Finally, older children and adults also actively encourage little children to display goods in public. One day Kuba and Ron's grandfather returned from Majuro with a box full of treats. Most of the family ate those treats inside their house. But the grandfather gave Kuba and Ron each their own bag of chips and permitted them to go outside. Holding their open bags as they happily stuffed chips into their mouths, Kuba and Ron wandered around the crowded yard as they displayed their wares to everyone around (see Figure 6.2). Similarly, a teenager once picked up a little boy who was eating a lollipop and carried that boy down the

FIGURE 6.2 Kuba and Ron eating chips in public.

road, helping that boy show his lollipop to others. In all of these situations, adults could have acted differently. Just as adults regularly bar little children from swimming because they are scared that they might drown, they could have closed the door to the house or waited until the boy finished the lollipop before carrying him down the road. Instead, these elders actively helped the children display their food to others—they helped them engage in conspicuous consumption.

Adults encourage conspicuous consumption probably not only because they think that displaying things is simply part of small children's unchangeable nature but also because people are supposed to give little children food and anything else they want.[10] Women sleep with their infants and breastfeed on demand.[11] As babies grow into "little children" (*ajri jidikdik*), everybody else continues to give them everything they want. For example, several adults became very angry with an older boy whom they thought had taken a little girl's food. This girl, roughly the same age as Kuba and Ron, wandered around a dock with a bag of Cheetos. Her older sibling—still in elementary school—took a tiny Cheeto from her bag and slowly ate it, staring at the girl. The little girl shrieked. Adults heard and thought that the boy had taken all of her food. They scolded the boy, gave him money, and told him to go buy the girl another bag of chips. She should have treats because she was a small child.

As this boy's behavior with the girl reveals, these lessons in immaturity always also point toward maturity and convey multiple conflicting messages at once (see also Mageo 1991). While the adults saw the girl as someone who should have everything she wanted, her older sibling complicated that message by taking her food. Even though he took only one piece, he implied that her food was not entirely her own but, rather, that she too had a responsibility to share, albeit only with other children (as opposed to with adults). Like Jackie's command to Sisina, these interactions encourage both immaturity and its opposite.

Consider how an older child reacted to Kuba and Ron when they were wandering around in the yard with their chips. Kevin, a relative close to Jackie's age, said to one of them, "Give me my food."

The child did not give.

"Okay I hate you," Kevin said.

"Show-off," Kevin criticized another child wandering around in the yard. In this interaction, he embarrassed a very small child for displaying food, taught that child that displaying food has the consequence that other children will ask for it, and modeled child-specific modes of demanding and criticizing. He modeled immaturity while also making that immaturity potentially dangerous.

After encouraging children to display goods, people often (as did Kevin) label such behavior as showing off. For instance, one day Kuba walked toward his family, precariously carrying a tub of food.

"Ulalala!" another family member, an older boy, yelled toward him, encouraging Kuba to imitate the nonsense speech.

"Ulalala!" Kuba said.

Everybody laughed.

"Ulalala!" Kuba said again. "Ulalala!"

"Come here," his older relative, a girl around Jackie's age, commanded. Then she pulled down his pants. "Showing your penis!" she crowed.

"Aaah!" the boy screamed as he ran away.

Everyone laughed.

"Kuba is such a show-off," another woman commented.

From the Marshallese perspective, Kuba was indeed showing off. He was calling attention to himself. But, of course, everybody encouraged Kuba to do so by yelling nonsense at him and getting him to repeat it, by laughing when he spoke, and by pulling his pants down and making him into a spectacle.

Displays of power are embedded in such encouragement and criticism of showing off. In all of these interactions children and adults reinforced the general Marshallese age hierarchy system and its basis in the fear of elders. For example, on another occasion people told Kuba and Ron to dance to the music. Kuba refused. "We hate you," Kevin told him. 'Dance.'

Kuba did not move.

'Show-off,' someone criticized.

'Come and eat,' an adult commanded.

Kuba did not move.

'We hate you,' she criticized. Whereas before Kuba was a show-off because he drew attention to himself, now he was a show-off because he disobeyed the command to draw attention to himself. The only consistent messages he got was that he must obey and, regardless of what he did, he was a show-off.

Success: Socializing Age

Jackie and Nomi joined Sisina at the door of the house. Perhaps the company of other children created an association between Jackie and childhood, giving her some sanctuary. Bold and unafraid, Nomi talked to some of the men, her child-sized body framed by the light. But despite Nomi and Sisina's company Jackie remained in the dark. She peeked only her head around the door. "Michael," she complained.

"Go and say . . . ," Michael mumbled the rest of his command.

"They say that you should. Kirinrose said you should . . . Kirinrose said that you should go."

"Okay, I will go with you. I will bring it to you."

"She said now."

"Okay, you should go to tell her."

"Ugh!"

Painstakingly slowly, Michael eventually went to find some food. He brought it back to the door, allowing Jackie to remain outside. "Here."

"Not a can of mackerel!" Kirinrose had said tuna. Mackerel was cheaper, but tuna was tastier.

"Take it!" Michael brushed Jackie off, blaming her for Kirinrose's commands. He forced her again to own her words. "You are such a. . . ."

The girls took their prize and left.

Finally, after twelve minutes of begging three different children to help her out, Jackie had what she came for. She could return to Kirinrose as an obedient younger relative. And it was all due to Sisina, a child who was not embarrassed or ashamed.

In Jajikon, numerous influences combine to encourage children to become different from their elders and elders to become different from children. People encourage children to carry their food in public, to show off, to demand, to declare hatred, and to refuse. By indicating that children should often display, demand, and refuse, elders imply that children need not be ashamed of such behavior. They encourage children to take on child-specific subjectivities: a lack of shame and a willingness to reveal themselves and their possessions to others. When children present themselves as different from their elders, moreover, they highlight the differences between immaturity and maturity, encouraging people like Jackie to no longer feel like children.

This production of difference comes partly from the fact that all interactions teach (at least) two things at once: display and its dangers. These conflicting messages teach not only immaturity but also its opposite; they provide children with a model of the future and pull them through cultural practices as they change across the life course. In early childhood, these conflicting messages create practices that adults assume to be natural consequences of immaturity—revealing food rather than hiding it, demanding rather than quietly waiting. As children grow they move through different subject positions with different demands. Older children have to wait their turn to eat, share with those younger than them, and do the bidding of everyone older than them.[12] But although children such as Sisina frequently declare "Give me my food" to their peers, they fear adults and often do not want to ask things of them or refuse them. Consequently, children like Sisina continue to feel themselves to be children who are able to separate themselves from their words and actions in ways that their elders cannot. As a result, they continue to speak and act differently than their elders and can do things that elders cannot, such as ask Michael for food. As people move through the life course those who are younger or older than them change, creating changes in behavior as well.

Before children learn to be adults they learn to be different from adults. They take on child-specific subjectivities, practices, forms of speech, and senses of self. The nature and characteristics of such practices change with context and as children grow. But they are all culturally produced. Immaturity is not natural; it is socialized. Socialization is the process of taking on, modifying, and discarding constantly changing age-specific modes of being.

Being Different

"Shit!" Jackie yelled. Perhaps she had stumbled and dropped the food.

"It is on the video!" Nomi taunted. "On the video! Ha ha, look at you."

"Ugh," Jackie grumbled.

"I am going to show [the video] to Michael," Nomi laughed.

"I am not scared of Michael," Jackie boasted.

"Hey," Nomi countered, "I am going to say to him. . . ."

"He didn't even hit you," Sisina teased, "but you were scared."

Nomi laughed. "Her eyes were really wide. . . ."

Nomi and Sisina reinforced Jackie's difference from them. Jackie had been scared, while they were not.

Nomi and Sisina knew that Jackie had been scared. She had modeled the future for them, giving them an image of who they would eventually become.

Notes

1. See Burton, Nero, and Hess 2002 for a description of variability in Marshallese household arrangements.
2. Explicit gender taboos exist for the most part only between siblings. They relate to sexual intercourse and marriage, talk about sex, and seeing each other walk to the bathroom or with wet hair. Outside of siblings, individual women and men are technically allowed to interact with each other. In the familiar environment of her own home my host mother frequently chatted with men who visited for a variety of reasons. Groups, however, are different. Despite the lack of explicit rules, women tended to sit on one side of the church, and men, on the other. As another example, when I gave English lessons only women showed up. The men told me that they were too shy to join since they saw only women. But while avoiding groups of the opposite gender often applied to both men and women, some limitations were not

equally shared. For example, women were less likely to walk and gather at night than men. It was typically men who gathered for coffee at this house, not women, and thus typically women and/or girls who feared to approach.

3. This view is by no means universal; consider places where people think that children are reborn ancestors (Gottlieb 2004; Gupta 2002).
4. Althusser called such people who fail to conform "bad subjects" (1971, 169).
5. Toren (1990, 1993) argues that children necessarily invert adult cultural models because of the way the mind interprets the social environment. Her perspective also discusses inversions and opposites, but does so through analyzing cognitive features of the mind as opposed to the meaning of signs.
6. Although adults and elders typically did not hit or criticize children for declaring fear, they could still put pressure on them to complete an errand. "Go and say that I said it," a mother urged her son, who resisted an errand because he was afraid. Thus, children often did end up running errands that they feared.
7. It is not entirely true that children only hid goods or avoided errands out of fear of adults. Several children also said that they were worried about being embarrassed by other children. For example, children both Tito's age and only a little younger than Jackie said that they might transport food on the beach because they were worried that other children would embarrass (*kajook*) them by saying, "Look at the boy who is carrying food" or "Look at that girl!" Nonetheless, children's experiences differ in three ways from adults' shame (*aliklik*). First, although children do talk about others shaming them, they use a verb, *embarrass* (*kajook*), that does not have exactly the same meaning as *shame* (*āliklik*). *Embarrass* (*kajook*) refers to the use of speech to criticize and embarrass others and differs from *shame* (*āliklik*), which refers to a feeling that prevents people from getting into such embarrassing situations in the first place. Second, although children talked about other children embarrassing (*kajook*) them, when they talked about what they themselves feel that causes them to hide they cited fear (*mijak*). Third, the children were largely worried about being embarrassed by other children as opposed to adults. They were merely afraid of adults, which meant that they could get around that fear by separating themselves from their words and actions.
8. Just as Jajikonian children present themselves as children through running errands and using reported speech, Kwara'ae children have a child-mode presentation of self in which they mark themselves as not adult (Watson-Gegeo 2001).
9. One person also said that children's first words are *kaka* and *meme*, baby talk words for "drink" and "chew." I never heard any children actually say these two words. Other people told me that these are words that adults say to small children but not words that the children themselves speak.
10. Such indulgence of young children is common throughout the Pacific and in many other parts of the world (Briggs 1998; Chapin 2014; Gallimore, Boggs, and Jordan 1974; Howard 1970; Jordan et al. 1969; Morton 1996; Ritchie and Ritchie 1979).

11. People thought that separating babies from their mothers at night would harm the baby for several reasons: the baby should eat whenever he or she wants, the baby would be lonely, and ghosts would attack and kill the baby. Babies were particularly vulnerable to the ghosts who come out in the night. But although babies may be the most vulnerable, ghosts can take anyone who is alone, so communal sleeping continues throughout the life span. Everybody was surprised that I was not scared to sleep alone. It seems likely that these beliefs teach children to want others near them. Many people also thought that if I was reading alone, I must be sad or angry.
12. This expectation that older children indulge younger children is also common in the Pacific (Morton 1996; Ritchie and Ritchie 1979; Schieffelin 1990).

CONCLUSION

TOWARD AN ANTHROPOLOGY OF AGE

Shortly after her struggle to pass a message on to Michael, Jackie left Jajikon for Majuro. Many girls and boys her age do the same. School in Jajikon only goes up to grade 8, so anyone who wants to go to high school has to leave.

Jackie's journey did not stop in Majuro. After attending Marshall Islands High School she left the RMI and traveled to Enid, Oklahoma, where she joined a large Marshallese community. Several thousand Marshallese live in Enid, exponentially more than on Rōrin atoll. Several hours away from Enid in Springdale, Arkansas there is an even larger Marshallese community. More Marshallese live in Springdale than on any Marshallese atoll other than Majuro and, potentially, Kwajalein.[1] In 2010 an estimated 22,400 Marshallese lived in the United States as a whole, roughly one third of the population of the RMI itself (EPPSO 2012; Jimeno S. 2013; Schwartz 2015).

Marshallese come to the United States for many reasons. They come because of the unique Compact of Free Association between the RMI and the United States, an agreement that gives any Marshallese citizen the right to enter the United States as an "alien authorized to work" (U.S. Citizenship and Immigration Services 2016). They come in search of an education: Marshallese migration in the 1970s began with youth enrolling in American schools (Hess, Nero, and Burton 2001, 95–97). They come in search of jobs (Duke 2014; Schwartz 2015). They come because their family is already in the United States, and family is important. Perhaps, one day soon, they will come because rising sea levels due to climate change are devouring their low-lying islands (Andrews 2016; Davenport 2015).

Jackie may or may not stay in Oklahoma. Many of the people I met in Jajikon had themselves returned from the United States or from other atolls. I heard about others who had recently left Jajikon, an example of the circular migrations that are common throughout the Pacific (Alkire 1989; Hess, Nero, and Burton 2001; Hezel 1983, 203; Nero 1997; Small and Dixon 2004). But wherever Jackie goes, her children's lives are bound to differ from her own. Culture always changes.

This book has been an account of one form of cultural change: people's movement through the life course. Attention to age differences, I have argued, is essential to our understanding of socialization and cultural reproduction. But change over the life course necessarily interacts with another type of cultural change: change over historical time. Since culture and cultural practices are always aged, attention to age has implications for our understanding of both cultural continuity and historical change. The ways in which people produce themselves as different in age from one another provide new ways to think about cultural reproduction, cultural change, and culture itself.

Age and Cohort Variation

In any study of age, the question inevitably arises: Do the observed patterns represent age differences or cohort differences? Are the differences between Jackie and Sisina caused by their movement through the life course or by a historical shift in Jajikonian society that has reduced the importance of shame?

If the differences that I observed reflect the latter, then one would expect either (1) that past Marshallese children felt more shame (*āliklik*) or (2) that the children with whom I worked will continue to lack shame (*āliklik*) as they get older. Unfortunately, there are no data relating to the first of these possibilities. This book is the first in-depth study of Marshallese children. It is also the first study based on a large corpus of nonelicited Marshallese speech. As for the second, the available data point in multiple directions. On the one hand, I frequently saw people in Majuro carrying food or eating in a taxicab without offering the food to others, exemplifying my friends' claims that people in Majuro "do not know custom." Relatedly, Carucci (2015) says that members of the community on Majuro with whom he worked now do not offer food to visitors, although in the past they did. One could hypothesize that Jajikonian children's lack of shame and their display of food in public could reflect the transfer of these Majuro patterns to Jajikon.

On the other hand, this hypothesis has numerous problems. First, rural villages such as Jajikon do not necessarily reflect Majuro's past, and present practices in Majuro do not necessarily represent Jajikon's future. Claims that rural villages are windows into the past erase the historical changes such villages always experience. Second, Carucci (2015) argues that the changes he observed are tied to increasing poverty—a basic lack of goods to give. But even if this were true, and people in

Jajikon are poorer than they were in the past (claims for which I have no evidence either way), a lack of goods does not explain the age differences between children and adults in Jajikon. Jajikonian children carried goods in public because they lacked shame—not because their families were too poor to have goods at all.

Finally, the one clear change that I observed between the end of my first visit in 2009–10 and my return trip in 2013 points to successive cohorts of children becoming more knowledgeable about shame (*āliklik*) rather than less. In 2010, *shame* (*āliklik*) was an adult vocabulary word: although every adult could talk about it at length, every child I spoke with was unfamiliar with its meaning. For example, I said to one girl who was a little younger than Jackie, "Are you ashamed [*āliklik*] sometimes?" She did not appear to understand me and did not answer, even when an older sibling broke in and said that the girl was not ashamed (*āliklik*), because she was "small." In contrast, in 2013 many of the children I spoke with knew the word. One child, who was roughly the age of Sisina during her errand at Michael's house, said that adults "send their children because they [the adults] are ashamed [*āliklik*]." This change in the children's vocabulary could have been my doing (my obsessive interest in the word could have increased children's knowledge), or it could reflect an unrelated cohort shift. Regardless, successive cohorts' vocabulary knowledge of *shame* (*āliklik*) was increasing rather than decreasing, the opposite of what one would expect if the differences recounted in this book reflected cohort rather than age variation.

Thus I do not know what role historical change plays in this story. But whether or not the observed patterns represent historical change, they *do* reflect culturally specific age differences. First, the differences I have discussed are not natural but social. Children do not naturally parade around in public with food or have the boldness to carry messages to elders; adults do not naturally avoid carrying food or speaking. Second, these differences create differing interpretations of people's actions and utterances, giving people of different ages the socially produced ability to do different things. Jackie and Sisina were not equally able to complete Kirinrose's errand; Ryan and Jujan were not equally likely to be believed. Third, these differing interpretations help give people of different ages different subjective reactions to similar situations. Jackie was ashamed (*āliklik*); Sisina was merely afraid (*mijak*).

Finally, the differences that I observed reflect age differences because that is how people on Jajikon see them, interpret them, and use them in their daily life. Marshallese adults do say that children today are different from the children of yesterday. "Children today," a woman told me, "are very bad. . . . The children of the past knew how to work. Children today, they don't know how to work. They just play." Explained another woman, "Children today are very naughty. . . . They wake up, from morning till night they play. . . . Children in the past worked." But the differences that they discuss do not include children's feelings or their lack of shame, children's activities running errands that their elders avoid, or children's inability to engage in meaningful or important deceptions. Rather, people imagine these differences as natural products of the process of development and aging—and help produce them as such.

The relevant question is not whether differences between children and adults represent age or cohort variation but whether they represent cohort variation *as well as* age variation. The differences that I discuss here, regardless of their role in historical change, are interpreted as and function as age differences.

Age and Anthropology

Age is a basic social variable, and age differences are ever-present forms of socially produced variation. Yet age is often erased, not only in anthropological and linguistic studies of culture but also in political analyses of difference and inequality. With respect to the latter, while gender and racial gaps in educational achievement generate rallying cries for social change, most formal education systems segregate children according to chronological age and expect aged forms of difference and inequality. I do not necessarily argue against age-segregated classrooms (although such a shift would be a dramatic educational reform). Rather, this example merely reveals the discontinuity between people's views of gender and race and their views of age. Segregation based on gender and race is discrimination, but people often view segregation based on age as natural, inevitable, and right.[2]

Consider also the interdisciplinary field of childhood studies and its basic tenet that children are relevant to the study of culture and society. This orienting framework comes partly from James and Prout's influential edited volume *Constructing and Reconstructing Childhood* (1997a), which argues that childhood is a social construction, children are important social agents, and social science research needs to include children's lives, voices, and experiences. My data here both build on and reaffirm these arguments, as well as their claim that children have been marginalized in the social sciences partly because of children's powerlessness. But my data also challenge James and Prout's emphasis on childhood and children in particular as opposed to age in general. They write, "Childhood is a variable of social analysis. It can never be entirely divorced from other variables such as class, gender, or ethnicity" (1997b, 9). But "childhood," a stage of life, is not analytically similar to class, gender, or ethnicity. Rather, the analogy to overarching categories such as class, gender, or ethnicity would be another overarching category: age. The problem is not just that children have been ignored but also that culture and social life have been constructed as ageless.

Here childhood studies, like anthropology as a whole, often erases age in favor of other variables of analysis.

This erasure of age limits our ability to understand culture and social life. Take two central anthropological concerns that I have discussed in this book, gift exchange and agency. Studies of gift exchange tend to exclude children: of twelve profoundly influential studies of gift-giving in Oceania over the past century, none mention children as playing any significant role (Firth 1929, 1940; Gregory 1982; Lederman 1986; Malinowski 1961; Merlan and Rumsey 1991; Munn 1986; Strathern 1988; Sykes 2005; Thomas 1991; Weiner 1976, 1992).[3] But gift exchange in Jajikon cannot take place without children: a woman cannot give fish to her mother if she has to give it to everyone she passes along the way. Moreover, children are invaluable economic agents precisely because they are people who are different from adults *in age* and thus can do different things. But most studies of child agency assume universal definitions of agency as either resistance or independent action and present children as the same types of agents as adults.[4] Children are not the same types of agents as adults. Sisina was able to animate Jackie's errand because she was *different*—she was different in age and different in agency. Agency, like culture, is aged.

Just as understanding gift exchange and agency requires considering age differences, understanding cultural reproduction and change requires considering how those differences are produced. Like all aspects of culture, age differences come into being through interaction (Duranti, Ochs, and Schieffelin 2012). Through interaction, people learn to be not only similar to some but also different from others, including those ahead of them and behind them in the course of life. This production of age differences is embedded in cultural continuity, since cultural reproduction requires the reproduction of variation. Paradoxically, it is partly through commands to do things that their elders should not that Marshallese children eventually take on mature modes of speaking, acting, and being. But at the same time, if children are learning first to be different from their elders, this production of difference can lead people not only to reproduce the future but also to take an alternative path (Cole 2010). Linguistic anthropologists have shown that language shift results partly from ideologies of childhood and speech that frame certain languages or codes as more appropriate for children (Garrett 2005, 2012; Meek 2007, 2011; Paugh 2012b). As they grow, such children sometimes continue speaking the languages of childhood rather than discarding them in favor of adult modes of speaking. This type of process could also potentially produce other forms of change, making the socialization of age differences a key mechanism of both cultural reproduction and historical change.

Socialization is not the acquisition of cultural practices but, rather, the continuous production of different cultural practices. It should be the study of not how novices acquire practices but how people take on and discard age- or life-course-specific modes of being—how people produce themselves as different from others. This view of socialization highlights the fact that almost everything changes over the life course—not only exchange practices and agency but also familial relationships, modes of speech, gender and racial identities, subjectivities, forms of violence, and political interactions. For example, Indian women become more masculine as they grow older, and youth in the United States age into and out of crime (Lamb 2000; Wakefield and Apel 2016). On the one hand, it seems obvious that all such things change over the life course. After all, constant change is a central feature of the field of life course studies (Elder, Shanahan, and Jennings 2015). On the other hand, life course change has never been fully integrated into the study of culture, language, or even social change (Cole 2010; Toren 1993). As a result, for most life course scholars (outside of anthropology), age is inevitably chronological, whereas within anthropology neither gift exchange nor agency (not to mention many other practices) has been studied from a life course perspective. Thus, a linguistic anthropological analysis of how age comes to be has much to offer life course studies, anthropology, and linguistics. If everything changes over the life course, then our understandings of social structures, cultural reproduction, and language socialization must be revised, as must our analysis of culture itself. Culture is aged.

Some people in this book are still in Jajikon. Karlin and Ronji both live there, although Karlin has told me that she wants to move to the United States. But while some remain in Jajikon, many others do not. Some, like Jackie, went to the United States. Pinla and Deina live in Hawai'i. There, Pinla has given birth to four more children. Giving away her child to Terij, she told me, made her sad, so she held onto these younger infants despite numerous familial requests. Leny lives in Seattle along with Delila; Sisina's older brother is in Majuro looking for a seat on a plane, trying to get to Texas. Many others live in Majuro: Kinta, Kyle, Sisina, Nomi, and Lari are all there attending high school or college. After these children finish school, they may return to Jajikon, stay in Majuro, or move to a different atoll. I suspect that many of them will leave the RMI.

I do not know what is ahead for these children (now youths). I do know that the forms of immaturity that I observed in 2009–10 and 2013 are culturally produced and culturally specific. As these youths move around the world, they will continue to produce themselves as different from others and take on age-specific modes of being, feeling, and acting. They will continue to produce age.

Notes

1. The only atolls in the RMI with a population of more than two thousand people are Kwajalein, population 11,408, and Majuro, population 27,797 (EPPSO 2012). According to the 2010 Census there were 4,726 Marshallese in Springdale, Arkansas (U.S. Census Bureau 2012). Virtually everyone with whom I have spoken believes that this number underestimated the size of the population. Approximately 59 percent of Native Hawai'ian and Pacific Islanders in the region did not report an ethnicity on the 2010 Census survey (Empowering Pacific Islander Communities and Asian Americans Advancing Justice 2014, 56). In addition, migration has continued and increased since 2010 (Empowering Pacific Islander Communities and Asian Americans Advancing Justice 2014; Jimeno S. 2013). The Marshallese Educational Initiative (2017) claims that roughly twelve thousand Marshallese live in the greater region and eight thousand live in Springdale.
2. The main exception is the prohibition of age discrimination. In the United States, however, the Age Discrimination in Employment Act of 1967 (29 U.S.C. 621–34) prohibits discrimination only against older people (over forty) and is not concerned about age differences or inequalities at the beginning of the life course (e.g., Posthuma, Wagstaff, and Campion 2012).
3. For example, Strathern (1988) discusses children only in the context of childbirth or as people produced by adults. Most studies that do discuss children in detail focus either on peer exchanges between children, the socialization of exchange practices, education and the family, or children as objects of exchange (adoption), as opposed to children as agents of gift-giving and relationship negotiation within the overall kin network (Brady 1976; Carroll 1970; Dickerson-Putnam and Schachter 2008; Howard 1970; Morton 1996; Schieffelin 1990). This absence also exists in studies of exchange outside of Oceania and in general theoretical discussions of the gift (Godelier 1996; Graeber 2001; Sahlins 1972). One exception is Carsten (1991), who, within a broader discussion of kinship, mentions children as people who mediate household economic interactions.
4. For example, Tanzanian children "strategize and negotiate the terms and content of their work" and have "agency . . . in selecting the details of their own work strategies" (Porter 1996, 10, 12). Swedish preschool children often use "a strategy of silence and avoidance" when "they want to resist an adult's or another child's remarks" (Markström and Halldén 2009, 116). This view of agency is similar to earlier accounts of women's agency that assumed universal ideas of agency as exhibited by independence or resistance (Mahmood 2005; McNay 2000).

APPENDIX

TRANSCRIPTS

Below are the transcripts that are the basis for the main stories in the introduction, chapter 4, and chapter 6. Transcription conventions:

Italics: Marshallese words
Empty parentheses (): Incomprehensible speech
Parentheses with words (walking): Nonverbal action or additional explanation
Brackets []: Overlapping speech (if necessary for clarity, a space is placed below the overlapping speech to separate it from non-overlapping speech).
@: Burst of laughter

Transcript 1. Introduction: Kori Walking Half Naked and Carrying Food

Scene: Five children—Bini, Lisa, James, Mark, and Simpson—are playing outside in the yard of a household compound. All are young; Jason, the oldest, just started school. Bini, who has not yet started school, is wearing the head camera. The children play with a plastic container, claiming that it is the food of a pig and that it smells like pigs. As the children play, they overhear Kori calling to his mother. Below I have transcribed only the conversation that the children overhear, not the conversation between the children who are playing.

1	Kori	*Lim̧am̧a!* Mama!
2		*Ejjeļo̧k aō jedoujij ak elōñ ad jiiñlij wōt!* I don't have any pants I only have a shirt!
3	Kori's mother	*Etal im kōkōņak am jedoujij m̧weo!* Go and wear the pants that are in the house!
4	Kori	*Eh?*

		Huh?
5	Kori's mother	*Etal im kōkōņak m̧weo ippān libubu bwe elōñ jedoujij ie!* Go and wear them (the pants) in the house with grandma because there are pants there!
6		*Bōkļo̧k men kaņe kijen libubu mār* ()! And take grandma and grandpa their food ()!
7	Kori	*Utkōkļo̧k?* Go naked?
8	Kori's mother	*Eañ utkōkļo̧k im kōm̧m̧an am jedoujij* Yes go naked and put on your pants
9		*Etal ļo̧k!* Go on!
10		(Three minutes and twenty-five seconds pass. Bini plays with the other children for a while, while Kori probably puts his shirt on and goes to get the food to take to his grandparents. The children play with the piece of plastic for a while, pretending that it is a mouse. The older children seem to annoy Bini and Simpson, Kori's younger brother. Bini and Simpson leave.)
11	Simpson	*Eaaah!* Aaah!
12	Bini	(Walks away from the children.)
13	Kori's mother	*LaKori ah* Kori
14		*LaKori!* Kori!
15		*Ewi laKori?* Where is Kori?
16	Bini	*Eñiō ah* Here he is
17		(Looks back toward the house, sees Simpson walking away from the house and toward Kori, who is standing in the road. Simpson is also half naked with only a shirt and no pants.)
18	Simpson	*Kori ah!* Hey Kori!
19		*Kori!*
20	Lisa	*Simpson itok* Simpson come
21	Simpson	*Kori eh* Hey Kori (Continues walking toward Kori on the road.)

22 Kori *Eh?*
Huh?
23 Simpson *Kori!*
24 Kori *Eh?*
Huh?
25 Bini (Follows Simpson. Bini can now see Kori, who is standing and waiting for Simpson in the road. Kori is wearing a yellow shirt and no pants. He carries a pink bowl on his head, presumably with the food for his grandparents. Kori waits in the road as Simpson runs to catch up. Bini follows Simpson.)
26 (Twenty-four seconds pass. Bini runs to the road. Then he stops, looks down the road in the other direction, and then looks back at Kori and Simpson, who are walking next to each other. Bini starts to follow them.)
27 Kori (Stops and talks to Simpson. They are almost in front of another cookhouse.)
28 Simpson (Turns around and looks back at Kori.)
29 Kori and Simpson (Walking)
30 Kori (Stops, turns around, and looks at Bini.)
31 *Kwe tal ke?*
Are you going?
32 Simpson (Lifts his hands under his shirt, shows his belly and genitals.)
33 Bini (Doesn't answer. Looks toward the cookhouse.)
34 (Walks toward the cookhouse. Several women sit in the cookhouse: Bini's grandmother, Stacey, and Lorin.)
35 *Ruo katan aō kōņake*
I have worn this (the video camera) twice
36 Bini's grandmother *Ro̧o̧lkake*
Go away with that thing
37 *Etal etal im pija ilo iaļ kaņe*
Go, go and film the road with that thing.
38 Stacey *Ah itok im pijaik an jibwūm babu!*
Hey, come back and film your grandmother lying down!
39 Bini's grandmother *Ej roñ wōt*
He is only listening (A criticism—Bini is listening but not obeying.)
40 Lorin *Etal im pijaik an John kwanjin*
Go and film John scraping and preparing breadfruit

41	Bini	(Looks back toward the road. Simpson and Kori had been shielded from view from the cookhouse by some banana trees. But at this moment, Simpson walks forward, coming into view.)
42	Bini's grandmother	() *bōk ñan Mōn Morin* () take it to House Morin.
43		*Bwe l̦ōm̦araņ ren kwanjin mā* Because the men are preparing breadfruit. (This is funny because it is typically a woman's job.)
44	Stacey	*Etal l̦o̦k!* Go on!
45	Stacey/Bini's grandmother	*Etal im pijaiki aer kwanjin!* Go and film them preparing breadfruit!
46	Bini	(Doesn't move. Looks at Kori and Simpson in the street, who are looking back at Bini and waiting for him.)
47		*Itok kōjeañ tin* Come we will. (to Kori and Simpson)
48		*Etal im kōkāāl im* Go and change, and
49	A woman	()
50	Bini	*Jol̦o̦k mōñā ņe im* Give them that food and
51		*Kōkōņak am jedoujij im* Put on your pants and
52		*Tok kōjeañ* Come we will all
53		*Etal im pijaiki* Go and film them
54	A woman	() (Sees Kori and Simpson.)
55		*Rejjab jedoujij@@* They aren't wearing pants!
56	Simpson	*Eh?* Huh?
57	Women	@@@
58	Bini's grandmother	*Erro ej kotak juon bowl ñan ion bōraerro*! They are carrying a bowl on their heads!
59	Women	()
90		(Kori and Simpson continue down the road. Bini follows them.)

Transcript 2. Chapter 4: Children in Church Trying to Get Rōka's Lollipop

Scene: Many children have gathered in church, waiting for their rehearsal to begin. Members of the Sunday school, they will be rehearsing their Christmas songs. One child in the church, Trint, is wearing the head camera. I had placed the camera on Trint earlier when he was at his house. Then Trint remembered the rehearsal and walked to the church.

Around a minute passes after Trint enters the church and talks to other children. Lari is sitting on the right side of the church; Kinta, Kyle, and Rōka are on the left. Kinta is sitting on the front bench; Kyle is sitting in the fourth row over by the window; Rōka is sitting in the third row in the middle. Wearing a yellow shirt and sucking on a lollipop, Rōka does not speak. The stick of the lollipop hangs out of his mouth.

Kinta stands up, turns around, and looks at Rōka.

1	Kinta	*ĻaRōka ah letok kijed*! Hey, Rōka, give me my food!
2		(Walks to the right, to kneel on the front bench facing Rōka.)
3	Kyle	*ĻaRōka ah lelok kijen liKinta* Hey, Rōka, give Kinta her food
4	Lari	*Rōka ah tok kijō* () Hey Rōka give me my food. (Either now or at some point before line 12 Lari gets up and walks over to Rōka, standing on the bench behind him.)
5	Kinta	*Koban lale eni* You won't watch us playing tag
6		(Leans forward over the back of the bench seat toward Rōka. She has a rolled-up piece of paper in her hand. She taps Rōka's hand with it.)
7	Rōka	(Turns away from Kinta to face behind him, potentially toward Lari to give him some food.)
8	Kyle	*Jab leļo̧k kijen ĻaLari!* Don't give Lari his food!
9	Lari	*Ah ah* Aah
10	Kinta?	*Tok kijō* Give me my food
11	Kinta	(Taps Rōka's hand with the roll of paper again.)
12	Lari	(Walks on the seat behind Rōka, bending over something. His back is to the camera.)

13	Rōka	(Leans back on the bench toward Lari.)
14	Kinta	*ĻaRōka ah* Hey Rōka
15		(6.4 seconds pass as Trint and Lila continue to talk.)
16	Kinta	*ĻaRōka ah!* Hey Rōka!
17	Rōka	*Eñe ippa* Here it is with me! (brandishing the lollipop in the air)
18	Kinta	*Ah ñe kobōke jim̧m̧am enaj m̧ane eok* Ah if you take it your grandfather will hit you
19	Lari or Kyle	() *jedike eok* We hate you.
20	Kinta	(Stretches out her hand toward Rōka.)
21	Rōka	*Ah iban!* Ah I won't!
22	Kinta	()
23	Rōka	*Iban!* I won't!
24	Kinta	(Pulls her hand back.)
25	Lari	()
26	Rōka	(Looking up behind him, presumably at Lari. Kinta's and Lari's next words suggest that Rōka shared the lollipop with Lari.)
27	Kinta	*Kijō!* My food! (as she stretches her hand back toward Rōka again)
28	Children	(unrelated conversation)
29	Lari	*Etan bar kain kaņe?* What is the name of that kind of thing again? (still standing behind Rōka on the bench)
30		*Ah ña kij jidik wōt* Ah I am only biting off a little.
31	Kyle	(singing)
32		*Letok kijō ļo ĻaRōka ļo* Rōka, dude, give me my food, dude
33	Lari	*Ah! jijet* Hey, sit down!
34		(Strides off the bench holding his stick.)
35		*Ña ij m̧an kom̧eañ* I am going to hit y'all.
36		(Using the stick menacingly as a walking stick, he advances toward five children playing in some chairs at the front of the church.)

37		(Four of the children at the front of the church run away from Lari back toward the benches.)
38		*Jijet ejjab bar kukure loan m̧wiin* Sit, don't play again in the building
40	Krino	() (to Lari)
41	Lari	(Pretends to swing his stick at Krino.)
42	Krino	(Flinches and backs away toward the benches.)
43	Lari	(Holding the stick in two hands like a baseball bat, walks back to the side of the church where Rōka, Kinta, and Kyle are.)
44	Kinta?	*Ekōk letok kijō* Ugh, give me my food
45	Lari	(Climbs back onto the bench. Walks to the window where Kinta is and, presumably, Rōka—later on the video shows Rōka here.)
46		() (potentially asks for food, but Rōka doesn't give any)
47	Lari	*Kwōn baj miin wōt ļe* Man, you are really stingy
48	Kinta	(Walks away from Rōka and looks at something in her hand. She climbs over the bench and then puts her hand to her mouth, presumably eating something.)
49	?	()
50	?	()
51	?	()
52	?	()
53	Lari	()
54		(Turns away from the window with his stick and walks away.)

Transcript 3. Chapter 6: Jackie Trying to Pass on a Message to Michael

Scene: It is nighttime. A group of children sit singing songs and talking near a house that also functions as a small store. The children present (all are younger than Jackie):

- Nomi and Sisina live in the house next door. They are both technically Jackie's daughters. Nomi is wearing the head camera and records everything that follows.
- Kyle and Tito live in the house nearby. They are brothers. Tito is the only child present who is younger than Sisina.
- Sylvia and Kinta are Kyle and Tito's relatives. They both live elsewhere in Jajikon but often spend the night at Kyle and Tito's house.

1	Children	(Singing. They sing through many different songs.)
2		*Oh baby ña ij iọkwe eok*
		Oh baby I love you (singing)
3		(They continue to sing and then switch songs.)
4	Sylvia	*Ijjab kōnaan iwōj ippām̧ bwe kwe ri-m̧are*
		I don't want to go with you, because you are married (singing)
5		*Ah kwōn mōk lale emat ke raij ṇe*
		Ah you should see if the rice is ready! (not singing)
6		*Ah ejjab al eṇ men kōjro kijoñ al kake*
		Hey, not that song, we should all really sing like this.
7	Sisina	[*LiJackie ah*]
		Jackie! (Sees Jackie coming in the distance.)
8	Sarah	[*Me ej ba*]
		The song that goes
9		[*Kurin*]
		(the name of a boat)
10	Tito	[*Kolem liJackie won*]
		Fuck Jackie
11	Sarah	*Ah*
		Hey
12	Sylvia	*Ah kwōn jab kanijnij ijeṇe*
		Hey you shouldn't swear!
13	Sarah	[*Ah*] (Continues singing.)
		Hey.
14	Tito	[*Ilukkuun kile liJackie*]
		I really recognize Jackie.
15		(ukulele music)
16	Sylvia	*Al "Ñan Kōjro"*
		Sing "For the Two of Us"
17	Kyle	*Iñak*
		I don't know it
18	Sylvia	*Kom̧i jab al ippam̧ro Kinta*
		Don't sing just me and Kinta
19		(20.03 seconds pass. The children sing and talk about songs.)
20	Sylvia	*Ah key eo am̧ ṇe ke?*
		Hey, are we going to sing in your key?
21	Sarah	*Eo kwōn key eo am*
		Okay, you should pick your key
22	Jackie	*LiSisina!*
		Sisina!
23	Nomi	*Eh?*
		Huh?
24	Kyle	*Ej riab*

		She is lying.
25	Sylvia	*Lio ta ṇe bōjrak?*
		Girl, why have you stopped (singing)?
26	Kyle	*Ball*
		Ball (talking about a marble)
27	Sisina	()
28	?	()
29	Jackie	*Michael epād lo . . .*
		Is Michael . . .
30		*Michael epād ilo m̧weieṇ?*
		Is Michael in the house?
31	Tito	[*Ejako*]
		He is gone
32	Jackie	[*Etal im ba*]
		Go and say
33		*"Michael ah"*
		"Hey Michael"
34		[*"itok m̧ōk"*]
		"come here please"
35	Sarah	[()]
36		[*LiSylvia iñak key ṇeṇe*]
		Sylvia I don't know that key
37	Jackie	[() *"Michael ah. Kirinrose ej ba bōk juon" etan le, "bōk juon . . ."*]
38		"Hey Michael. Kirinrose says to bring a" what was it again? "bring a . . ."
39		(27.3 seconds pass. The children sing songs and then start playing marbles.)
40	Sisina	[*Ah liJackie jemijak*]
		Ah, Jackie, I am (we are) scared
41	Jackie	[*Eñṇeṇe*]
		There it goes (talking about the marbles game)
42	Sylvia/Kyle	[*Ōkkōk*]
		Darn
43		(sound of marbles shaking)
44	?	[*Im̧ōk lale*]
		Can I see?
45	Sisina	[*LiJackie jemijak*]
		Jackie I am (we are) scared
46	Jackie	*Ōrra LiSisina*
		Arg Sisina!
47	Sarah	*Kwe im ña*
		You and me (marbles clang together)

48	Jackie	*LiNomi ah* Hey Nomi
49	Sarah	[*Sylvia im ña uklele*] Sylvia and I will play the ukulele and sing
50	Jackie	[*Kwe m̧ōk ba "Michael ah"*] You just say, "Hey Michael"
51	Nomi	*Ah liō ōkkōk* Darn girl
52	Kyle	*Kwōn make etal* You should go yourself
53		(Two minutes and twelve seconds pass. The children talk about marbles and their grandparents' relationship. They sing and discuss the nature of Easter.)
54	Jackie	[*Tito etal*] *im ba "Michael ah"* Tito go and say, "Hey Michael"
55	Sarah	[*Ilu ilu*] Tom . . . , tom . . .
56		*Ilju* [*ejerkakpeje*] Tomorrow he rises from the dead
57		[*Jenaaj l̦ak jar Jabot*] We will pray on Sunday
58	Tito	[()]
59	Nomi	*Ejjab ejjab ilju eo rar kaeñtaan im l̦ak* [()] It's not, it's not, tomorrow is when they made him suffer and then
60	Tito	[*Jemijak*] I am (we are) scared.
61	Jackie	[*Kwōj tal wōt im ba*] You just go and say
62	Tito	[*Ooooh*]
63		(One minute and twenty-three seconds pass. The children dispute Easter. They discuss Jackie's comb and then also talk about marbles.)
64	Sylvia	*Lale m̧ōk ña ñan ij kab bu inne* Like me, I just began to play marbles again yesterday
65	Sisina	*Bar ña* Me too
66	Jackie	*LiSisina* Sisina
67	Nomi	*Bar ña* Me too (She also played marbles yesterday.)

68		(One minute and thirty-two seconds pass. The children continue to play and talk about marbles as well as their current chore of doing the dishes. Dishes clang as the children talk. Then they shift their discussion to their shoes and who has a particular preferred brand—Scotts.)
69		(Playing the ukulele.)
70		(The discussion peters out, and the children sit listening to the ukulele. At some point now, Jackie leaves the children and walks toward the house.)
71	Kyle	()
72	Nomi	*Ej* It . . .
73	Kyle	*Ekūñ* It smells like poop.
74	Nomi	(Looks at the house and then begins to walk toward it.)
75	Sisina	*LiNomi ah!* Hey Nomi!
76		*Kwōj etal ñan ia ke ij rol?* Where are you going because I need to go back?
77	Nomi	(Does not answer, drawing near the house. Nomi sees Jackie cowering behind a wall, poking her head into the doorframe and talking to someone in the house.)
78	Sisina	*Ekwe eṃṃan ña ij rọọl!* (yelling from across the yard) Okay fine I am going to go back!
79		(Nomi does not answer. Jackie is still hiding behind the wall.)
80	Sisina	*Ñe kwōjjab itok!* If you don't come!
81		(Nomi moves forward to stand in the center of the doorway, looking at all the men inside.)
82	Sisina	*Bwe liṃaṃa mār retōn bar katak im* Because mama and them are going to go to rehearsal and then
83		*LiNomi itok!* Nomi come!
84	Nomi	(Looks in the door of the house where the men are talking. Jackie is in front of her but to the side, hidden behind the wall.)
85		(One minute and twenty seconds pass. Sisina and Nomi continue to call out to each other, but Nomi does not leave. Nomi starts to talk to Jackie about Nomi's parents and where they are. Then, Jackie asks Nomi questions about the camera she is wearing and if anything will appear on it since it is dark. Throughout the conversation, Nomi is in the doorway, while Jackie is behind the wall. Then Sisina shows up and joins in the conversation. Finally, Jackie tries to continue with her errand.)

86	Jackie	*LaMichael e* Hey Michael
87		(Rubs her hands over her face.)
88		*LiNomi etal im ba* Nomi go and say it
89	Sisina	[*Ekwe ña itōn ba*] Okay I will say it
90	Nomi	[*Pijaik* ()] I am filming . . .
91	Sisina	*Michael ah* Michael
92		*Kirinrose ej ba* [*bōk juon joiu*] Kirinrose says to bring one bottle of soy sauce
93	Nomi	[*liJackie karuan kij ñan mwenmōnmō*] Jackie accompany us to my house.
94	Jackie	*Im ña naj et tok?* And what will I do to get back?
95	Nomi	*Kōmro enaj karuan eok tok* We will accompany you back.
96	Sisina	*Juon im juon joiu im juon tuna* One and one bottle of soy sauce and a can of tuna
97	Nomi	(Looks toward Sisina, showing her standing in the middle of the doorway.)
98	Michael	*LiJackie ke Kirinrose?* Jackie or Kirinrose?
99	Sisina	*Kirinrose*
100	Nomi	(Turns her head to look back at Jackie, who is still behind the wall.)
101	Jackie	(smiles)
102	Michael	*Ewi?* Where?
103	Sisina	@@@@@
104		*@@eñiō@@* Here (through laughter)
105	Nomi	*Ej riab* She is lying
106		*LiJackie!* Jackie!
107	A man	[*LiNomi ah bōktok m̧ōk teeñki ne am*] Nomi, bring me that flashlight of yours
108	Sisina	[*LiJackie letok juon ad pāāñkōl bwe em̧ōj am . . .*] Jackie give me a bracelet because I am finished your . . .

109	Nomi	*Ewi?*
		Where?
110		*Ejjab teeñki men e!*
		This isn't a flashlight!
111	A man	*Akō?*
		But what?
112	Nomi	*Kein jerbal* @@
		A work tool! (what they called the camera)
113	Jackie	(Pokes her head around the doorway, her body still out of sight.)
114		*ĻaMichael ah*
		Hey Michael
115	Michael	*Etal im ba* ()
		Go and say . . .
116	Jackie	*Rej ba kwōn*
		They said that you should
117		*Kirinrose ear ba kwōn* ()
		Kirinrose said that you should ()
118	Michael	()!
119	A man	*An limana ke?*
		It's the gossiper's huh? (This was their nickname for me.)
120	Jackie	*Akō Michael*
		But Michael
121		*Kirin*
122		*Kirinrose ej ba kwōn etal*
		Kirinrose says that you should go
123	Michael	()
124	Nomi	*Pijaiki Michael*
		Filming Michael.
125		(Jackie is still poking her head around the door. Nomi is in the middle of the door, and Sisina is in the middle of the door in front of Nomi.)
126	Michael	*Ekwe ña naaj awōj*
		Okay I will go to you.
127		*Inaaj būkiwōj*
		I will bring it to you (over at Kirinrose's house).
128	An older woman	*LaTito jeuwaroñ*
		Tito we are annoyed by your noise.
129	Jackie	*Ej ba kiō* ()
		She said now

130	Michael	*Ah ekwe kwōn tōn ba* Hey you should go and say
131	Jackie	*Ōrrōr* Ugh
132		(One minute and fifty-four seconds pass. A man, known as someone a little slow, passes the girls into the house and talks to them. They laugh as he leaves and then make fun of his speech. Then they talk about the prize Nomi will pick after she is done wearing the camera. I pass by, and they talk to me for a minute.)
133	Michael	(Approaches the door from inside the house.)
134		*Eo* Here (Gives Jackie a can and a bottle of soy sauce.)
135	Jackie	*Ejjab juon mackeral!* She didn't say mackeral!
136	Michael	*Bōke* Take it
137		*Kwelukkuun* You are so
138		(Lightly pushes Jackie off.)
139	Sisina	*@@ ekor ah* She is scared (while laughing)
140		(Two minutes and four seconds pass. The three girls walk away toward Jackie's house. They talk about where they are going. They pass Sarah and Sylvia from earlier and chat briefly about ukuleles and marbles. They make fun of the man and his speech again. Apparently Jackie farts, because Sisina and Nomi start to make fun of her. They enjoy some toilet humor and then discuss a pregnant dangerous spirit who often appears in the night. Then Jackie either falls or trips.)
141	Jackie	*Eo* Oh
142	Nomi	*Epija!* It is filmed!
143		*Epija!* It is filmed.
144		*Ekaka!* Ha ha look at you!
145	Jackie	*Ōrrōr* Ugh
146	Nomi	*Inaaj kowaļọk ñan Michael @@* I am going to show it to Michael

147	Jackie	*Ijjab mijak laMichael*
		I am not scared of Michael
148	Nomi	*Ah*
		Ah
149		*N̄a inaaj ba ñan e*
		I am going to say to him
150	Sisina	*Emōj rar*
		They
151		*Rejjab tō deñōte eok ak kokor @@*
		He wasn't going to beat you, but you were scared (laughing)
152	Nomi	@@
153		[*Lukkuun ļap mejen an*]
		Her eyes were very big and
154	Jackie	[*Kōnke ijjab leļo̧k peū ñan e ñe im̧ane elukkuun jañ*]
		I don't lay my hand on him, but if I hit him, he would really cry
155	Nomi	@@
156		*Bwe kwōlāj?*
		Because you are strong?
157	Jackie	*Aet*
		Yes
158	Sisina	*N̄e relukkuun*
		If he really went
159		[*One two kwe kōlukkuun jañ*]
		One two (smack), you would really cry
160	Nomi	[*Bwe ña ij ba ñan Kirinrose*]
		I am going to tell Kirinrose.
161	Jackie	*Ba*
		Say
162	Nomi	[*Ekwe @Kirinrose uweo*] *Kirinrose uweo@*
		Okay Kirinrose is over there, Kirinrose over there
163	Jackie	[*N̄a tōn kar baran Kirinrose*]
		I am going to throw rocks at Kirinrose's head
164	Sisina	*Ah liō ñe relukkuun one two tañ eok kwejañ @@*
		Hey girl, if they really went one two smack, you would cry
165	Jackie	*Bwe in one two tañe komeañ*
		Because I am going to one two smack you guys!
166		(They keep walking and eventually reach Jackie's house.)

REFERENCES

The Age Discrimination in Employment Act of 1967 (ADEA). 1967. 29 U.S.C. 621–634.

Abo, Takaji, Byron Bender, Alfred Capelle, and Tony DeBrum. 2018. *Marshallese-English Online Dictionary*. http://www.trussel2com/mod/index.htm.

Addo, Ping-Ann, and Niko Besnier. 2008. "When Gifts Become Commodities: Pawnshops, Valuables, and Shame in Tonga and the Tongan Diaspora." *Journal of the Royal Anthropological Institute* 14: 39–59.

Ahearn, Laura. 2010. "Agency and Language." In *Handbook of Pragmatics*, edited by Jan-Ola Östman Verschueren and Jürgen Japsers, 28–48. Amsterdam: John Benjamins Publishing.

Alanen, Leena. 1994. "Gender and Generation: Feminism and the 'Child Question.'" In *Childhood Matters: Social Theory, Practice, and Politics*, edited by Jens Qvortrup, Marjatta Bardy, Giovanni Sgritta, and Helmut Wintersberger, 27–41. Brookfield, Vt.: Avebury.

Alkire, William. 1989. *Lamotrek Atoll and Inter-island Socieconomic Ties*. Urbana: University of Illinois Press.

Allen, Linda. 2002. "Maintaining Marshallese Fundamentals with Christian Fundamentalism." *Pacific Studies* 25 (1/2): 95–116.

Allen, S. E. M., and Martha B. Crago. 1996. "Early Passive Acquisition in Inuktitut." *Journal of Child Language* 23: 129–55.

Althusser, Louis. 1971. "Ideology and Ideological State Apparatuses (Notes towards an Investigation)." In *Lenin and Philosophy and Other Essays*, 127–86. New York: Monthly Review Press.

Altman, Jon, and Nicholas Peterson. 1988. "Rights to Game and Rights to Cash among Contemporary Australian Hunter-Gatherers." In *Hunters and Gatherers: Property, Power, and Ideology*, edited by Tim Ingold, David Riches, and James Woodburn, 50–67. Oxford: Berg.

Andrews, Sally. 2016. "Drought in the Marshall Islands." *Diplomat*, February 16.

Augsburger, D. 2004. "Language Socialization and Language Shift in an Isthmus Zapotec Community of Mexico." Ph.D. dissertation, University of Pennsylvania.

Australian Government. 2011. *Current and Future Climate of the Marshall Islands*. Aspendale, Victoria: Marshall Islands National Weather Service Office, Pacific Climate Change Science Program.

Bargiela-Chiappini, Francesca. 2003 "Face and Politeness: New (Insights) For Old (Concepts)." *Journal of Pragmatics* 35(10-11): 1453–1469.

Barker, Holly. 2013. *Bravo for the Marshallese: Regaining Control in a Post-nuclear, Post-colonial World*. Belmont, Calif.: Cengage Learning.

Barnett, Jon, and W. Neil Adger. 2003. "Climate Dangers and Atoll Countries." *Climatic Change* 61 (3): 321–37.

Basso, Ellen. 1986. "Quoted Dialogues in Kalapo Narrative Discourse." In *Native South American Discourse*, edited by Joel Sherzer and Greg Urban, 118–69. New York: Mouton De Gruyter.

Basso, Ellen. 1987. *In Favor of Deceit: A Study of Tricksters in an Amazonian Society*. Tucson: University of Arizona Press.

Basso, Keith. 1970. "'To Give Up on Words': Silence in Western Apache Culture." *Southwestern Journal of Anthropology* 26 (3): 213–30.

Baxter, P. T. W., and Uri Almagor. 1978. *Age, Generation, and Time: Some Features of East African Age Organizations*. New York: St. Martin's Press.

Beall, Cynthia. 1984. "Theoretical Dimensions of a Focus on Age in Physical Anthropology." In *Age and Anthropological Theory*, edited by David Kertzer and Jennie Keith, 82–98. Ithaca: Cornell University Press.

Bender, Bryon. 1963. "Marshallese Phonemics: Labialization or Palatalization?" *Word* 19 (3): 335–41.

Berman, Elise. 2011. "The Irony of Immaturity: K'iche' Children as Mediators and Buffers in Adult Social Interactions." *Childhood* 274–88.

Berman, Elise. 2012. "Children Have Nothing to Hide: Deception, Age, and Avoiding Giving in the Marshall Islands." Ph.D. dissertation, University of Chicago.

Berman, Elise. 2013. "Passive First-Person Recordings: A New Way to Study Children." *Anthropology of Childhood and Youth Interest Group Newsletter* 5 (1): 3–4.

Berman, Elise. 2014a. "Holding On: Adoption, Kinship Tensions, and Pregnancy in the Marshall Islands." *American Anthropologist* 116 (3): 1–13.

Berman, Elise. 2014b. "Negotiating Age: Direct Speech and the Sociolinguistic Production of Childhood in the Marshall Islands." *Journal of Linguistic Anthropology* 24 (2): 109–32.

Berman, Elise. 2018. "Force Signs: Ideologies of Corporal Discipline in Academia and the Marshall Islands." *Journal of Linguistic Anthropology* 28 (1): 22–42.

Berman, Elise. Forthcoming. "Avoiding Sharing: How People Help Each Other Get Out of Giving." *Current Anthropology*.

Besnier, Niko. 1990. "Language and Affect." *Annual Review of Anthropology* 19: 419–51.

Besnier, Niko. 1992. "Reported Speech and Affect on a Nukulaelae Atoll." In *Responsibility and Evidence in Oral Discourse*, edited by Jane Hill and Judith Irvine, 161–81. Cambridge: Cambridge University Press.

Billig, Michael. 1999. *Freudian Repression: Conversation Creating the Unconscious*. Cambridge: Cambridge University Press.

Bjorklund, David. 1997. "The Role of Immaturity in Human Development." *Psychological Bulletin* 122 (2): 153–69.

Bledsoe, Caroline. 2002. *Contingent Lives: Fertility, Time, and Aging in West Africa*. Chicago: University of Chicago Press.

Blitvich, Pilar Garcés-Conejos. 2010. "A Genre Approach to the Study of Im-politeness." *International Review of Pragmatics* 2: 46–94.

Blitvich, Pilar Garcés-Conejos. 2013. "Introduction: Face, Identity, and Im/politeness. Looking Backward, Moving Forward: From Goffman to Practice Theory." *Journal of Politeness Research* 9 (1): 1–33.

Bluebond-Langner, Myra, and Jill Korbin. 2007. "In Focus: Children, Childhoods, and Childhood Studies." *American Anthropologist* 109 (2): 241–306.

Blum, Deborah. 1997. *Sex on the Brain: The Biological Differences between Men and Women*. New York: Penguin.

Blum, Susan. 2015. "'Wordism': Is There a Teacher in the House?" *Journal of Linguistic Anthropology* 25 (1): 74–75.

Blum-Kulka, S., and C. E. Snow. 2004. "Introduction: The Potential of Peer Talk." *Discourse Studies* 6 (3): 291–306.

Boggs, Stephen. 1985. *Speaking, Relation, and Learning: A Study of Hawaiian Children at Home and at School*. Norwood: Apex Publishing Corporation.

Bourdieu, Pierre. 1984. *Distinction: A Social Critique of the Judgment of Taste*. Cambridge: Harvard University Press.

Brady, Ivan. 1976. *Transactions in Kinship: Adoption and Fosterage in Oceania*. Honolulu: University of Hawai'i Press.

Briggs, Charles. 1986. *Learning How to Ask*. Cambridge: Cambridge University Press.

Briggs, Jean. 1971. *Never in Anger: Portrait of an Eskimo Family*. Cambridge: Harvard University Press.

Briggs, Jean. 1998. *Inuit Morality Play: The Emotional Education of a Three-Year-Old*. New Haven: Yale University Press.

Brodkin, Karen. 2000. "Global Capitalism: What's Race Got to Do with It?" *American Ethnologist* 27 (2): 237–56.

Bronfenbrenner, Urie. 1979. *The Ecology of Human Development*. Cambridge: Harvard University Press.

Bronson, Po. 2009. *NurtureShock: New Thinking about Children*. New York: Hachette Book Group.

Brown, Penelope, and Suzanne Gaskins. 2014. "Language Acquisition and Language Socialization." In *Cambridge Handbook of Linguistic Anthropology*, edited by N.

J. Enfield, Paul Kockelman, and Jack Sidnell, 187–226. Cambridge: Cambridge University Press.

Brown, Penelope, and Stephen Levinson. 1978. "Universals in Language Usage: Politeness Phenomena." In *Questions and Politeness: Strategies in Social Interaction*, edited by Esther Goody, 56–289. Cambridge: Cambridge University Press.

Bucholtz, Mary. 2002. "Youth and Cultural Practice." *Annual Review of Anthropology* 31: 525–52.

Bucholtz, Mary. 2011. *White Kids: Language, Race, and Styles of Youth Identity*. Cambridge: Cambridge University Press.

Burdelski, Matthew. 2012. "Language Socialization and Politeness Routines." In *The Handbook of Language Socialization*, edited by Alessandro Duranti, Elinor Ochs, and Bambi Schieffelin, 275–95. West Sussex: Wiley-Blackwell.

Burdelski, Matthew, and Koji Mitsuhashi. 2010. "'She Thinks You're *Kawaii*': Socializing Affect, Gender, and Relationships in a Japanese Preschool." *Language and Society* 39: 65–93.

Burton, Michael, Karen Nero, and Jim Hess. 2002. "Who Can Belong to a Micronesian Household: Representations of Household Compositions across Social Contexts." *Field Methods* 14: 65–87.

Butler, Judith. 1999. *Gender Trouble: Feminism and the Subversion of Identity*. London: Routledge.

Cameron, Deborah. 2007. *The Myth of Mars and Venus*. Oxford: Oxford University Press.

Cameron, Deborah, Fiona McAlinden, and Kathy O'Leary. 1988. "Lakoff in Context: The Form and Function of Tag Questions." In *Women in Their Speech Communities*, edited by Jennifer Coates and Deborah Cameron, 74–93. London: Longman.

Campbell, Colin. 1995. "Conspicuous Confusion? A Critique of Veblen's Theory of Conspicuous Consumption." *Sociological Theory* 13 (1): 37–47.

Capps, Lisa, and Elinor Ochs. 1995. *Constructing Panic: The Discourse of Agoraphobia*. Cambridge: Harvard University Press.

Carr, E. Summerson. 2010. *Scripting Addiction: The Politics of Therapeutic Talk and American Sobriety*. Princeton: Princeton University Press.

Carroll, Vern, ed. 1970. *Adoption in Eastern Oceania*. Honolulu: University of Hawai'i Press.

Carsten, Janet. 1991. "Children In Between: Fostering and the Process of Kinship on Pulau Langkawi, Malaysia." *Man*, New Series, 26 (3): 425–43.

Carsten, Janet. 1995. "The Substance of Kinship and the Heat of the Hearth: Feeding, Personhood, and Relatedness among the Malays in Pulau Langkawi." *American Ethnologist* 22 (2): 223–41.

Carucci, Laurence. 1985. "Concepts of Maturing and Dying in the 'Middle of Heaven.'" In *Aging and Its Transformations: Moving Toward Death in Pacific Societies*, edited by Dorothy Ayers Counts and David R. Counts, 107–129. Lanham, MD: University Press of America.

Carucci, Laurence. 1988. "Small Fish in a Big Sea: Geographical Dispersion and Sociopolitical Centralization in the Marshall Islands." In *State and Society: The Emergence and Development of Social Hierarchy and Political Centralization*, edited by J. Gledhill, B. Bender, and M. T. Larsen, 31–40. New York: Routledge.

Carucci, Laurence. 1997a. "Irooj Ro Ad: Measure of Chiefly Ideology and Practice in the Marshall Islands." In *Chiefs Today: Traditional Pacific Leadership and the Postcolonial State*, edited by Geoffrey White and Lamont Lindstrom, 197–210. Stanford: Stanford University Press.

Carucci, Laurence. 1997b. *Nuclear Nativity: Rituals of Renewal and Empowerment in the Marshall Islands*. De Kalb: Northern Illinois University Press.

Carucci, Laurence. 2008. "The Making and Nurturing of Relationships: An Ujelang/Enewetak Model in the Context of Change." *Pacific Studies* 31 (3/4): 32–57.

Carucci, Laurence. 2015. Stinging While Giving: An Historical Consideration of Stinging in Relation to the Giving of Gifts. Unpublished manuscript.

Chapin, Bambi. 2014. *Childhood in a Sri Lankan Village: Shaping Hierarchy and Desire*. New Brunswick, N.J.: Rutgers University Press.

Chayanov, Alexander V. 1966. *The Theory of Peasant Economy*. Homewood, Ill.: Richard Irwin.

Cherry, Louise, and Michael Lewis. 1976. "Mothers and Two-Year-Olds: A Study of Sex-Differentiated Aspects of Verbal Interactions." *Developmental Psychology* 12 (4): 278–82.

Chin, E. 2001. *Purchasing Power: Black Kids and American Consumer Culture*. Minneapolis: University of Minnesota Press.

Chisolm, James. 1996. "Learning 'Respect for Everything': Navajo Images of Development." In *Images of Childhood*, edited by C. P. Hwang, M. E. Lamb, and I. E. Sigel, 167–84. Hillsdale, N.J.: Erlbaum.

Chudacoff, Howard. 1986. *How Old Are You? Age Consciousness in American Culture*. Princeton: Princeton University Press.

Clancy, Patricia. 1986. "The Acquisition of Communicative Style in Japanese." In *Language Socialization across Cultures*, edited by Bambi Schieffelin and Elinor Ochs, 213–50. Cambridge: Cambridge University Press.

Clark, Cindy Dell. 1995. *Flights of Fancy, Leaps of Faith: Children's Myths in Contemporary America*. Chicago: University of Chicago Press.

Cleveland, David. 1989. "Developmental Stage Age Groups and African Population Structure: The Kusasi of the West African Savanna." *American Anthropologist* 91: 401–13.

Cole, Jennifer. 2010. *Sex and Salvation: Imagining the Future in Madagascar*. Chicago: University of Chicago Press.

Cole, Jennifer, and Deborah Durham. 2007. "Introduction: Age, Regeneration, and the Intimate Politics of Globalization." In *Generations and Globalization: Youth, Age, and Family in the New World Economy*, edited by Jennifer Cole and Deborah Durham, 1–28. Bloomington: Indiana University Press.

Coleman, Linda, and Paul Kay. 1981. "Prototype Semantics: The English Word *Lie*." *Language* 57 (1): 26–44.

Cook-Gumperz, Jenny, and William Corsaro. 1986. "Introduction." In *Children's Worlds and Children's Language*, edited by Jenny Cook-Gumperz, William Corsaro, and Jürgen Streeck, 1–11. Berlin: Mouton de Gruyter.

Coupland, Nikolas. 2004. "Age in Social and Sociolinguistic Theory." In *Handbook of Communication and Aging Research*, edited by Justine Nussbaum, 69–90. Mahwah, N.J.: Lawrence Erlbaum.

Crago, Martha B. 1988. "Cultural Context in the Communicative Interaction of Young Inuit Children." Ph.D. dissertation, McGill University.

Cukor-Avila, Patricia, and Guy Bailey. 2013. "Real Time and Apparent Time." In *The Handbook of Language Variation and Change*, 2nd ed., edited by J. K. Chambers and Natalie Schilling, 237–62. Chichester: John Wiley and Sons, Inc.

Danely, Jason, and Caitrin Lynch. 2013. "Introduction: Transitions and Transformations: Paradigms, Perspectives, and Possibilities." In *Transitions and Transformations: Cultural Perspectives on Aging and the Life Course*, edited by Caitrin Lynch and Jason Danely, 3–20. Berghahn.

Davenport, Coral. 2015. "The Marshall Islands Are Disappearing." *New York Times*, December 1.

Davey-Smith, George, Carole Hart, David Blane, and Victor Hawthorne. 1997. "Lifetime Socioeconomic Position and Mortality: Prospective Observational Study." *British Medical Journal* 314: 547–52.

De Leon, Lourdes. 2007. "Parallelism, Metalinguistic Play, and the Interactive Emergence of Zinacantec Mayan Siblings' Culture." *Research on Language and Social Interaction* 40 (4): 405–36.

Department of Marshallese Studies. 2017. *Kilen Karōk Keyboard in M̧ajeļ Ņe (Guide to Setting Up Your Marshallese Keyboard)*. https://sites.google.com/site/marshallesestudiesdepartment/home/marshallese-keyboard-files-spellchecker. Last accessed 7/30/2018.

deVries, Marten W., and M. Rachel deVries. 1977. "Cultural Relativity of Toilet Training Readiness: A Perspective from East Africa." *Pediatrics* 60 (2): 170–77.

Dickerson-Putnam, Jeanette, and Judith Schachter, eds. 2008. "Relative Power: Changing Interpretations of Fosterage and Adoption in Pacific Island Societies." Theme issue, *Pacific Studies* 31 (3/4).

Du Bois, John. 1993. "Meaning without Intention: Lessons from Divination." In *Responsibility and Evidence in Oral Discourse*, edited by Jane Hill and Judith Irvine, 48–71. Cambridge: Cambridge University Press.

Duke, Michael. 2014. "Marshall Islanders: Migration Patterns and Health-Care Challenges." Washington, D.C.: Migration Policy Institute. https://www.migrationpolicy.org/article/marshall-islanders-migration-patterns-and-health-care-challenges.

Duranti, Alessandro. 1992. "Language and Bodies in Social Space: Samoan Ceremonial Greetings." *American Anthropologist* 94 (3): 657–91.

Duranti, Alessandro. 1997. *Linguistic Anthropology*. Cambridge: Cambridge University Press.

Duranti, Alessandro, Elinor Ochs, and Bambi Schieffelin, eds. 2012. *The Handbook of Language Socialization*. West Sussex: Wiley-Blackwell.

Durham, Deborah. 2005. "'They're Only Playing': Song, Choirs and Youth in Botswana." In *Makers and Breakers: Children and Youth in Postcolonial Africa*, edited by Alcinda Honwana and Filip De Boeck, 150–71. Oxford: James Curry.

Eberhart, Nancy. 2006. *Imagining the Course of Life: Self-Transformation in a Shan Buddhist Community*. Honolulu: University of Hawai'i Press.

Eckert, Penelope. 1987. *Jocks and Burnouts: Social Categories and Identity in the High School*. New York: Teachers College Press.

Eckert, Penelope. 1998. "Age as a Sociolinguistic Variable." In *The Handbook of Sociolinguistics*, edited by Florian Coulmas, 151–67. Malden, Mass.: Blackwell.

Eckert, Penelope. 2014. "Language and Gender in Adolescence." In *Handbook of Language, Gender, and Sexuality*, edited by Susan Ehrlich, Miriam Meyerhoff, and Janet Holmes, 529–45. Malden, Mass.: John Wiley and Sons, Inc.

Elder, Glen. 1974. *Children of the Great Depression: Social Change in Life Experience*. Boulder: Westview Press.

Elder, Glen. 1998. "The Life Course as Developmental Theory." *Child Development* 69 (1): 1–12.

Elder, Glen, and Linda George. 2016. "Age, Cohorts, and the Life Course." In *Handbook of the Life Course*, edited by Michael Shanahan, Jeylan Mortimer, and Monica Kirkpatrick Johnson, 59–85. Cham, Switzerland: Springer.

Elder, Glen, and Richard Rockwell. 1979. "The Life Course and Human Development: An Ecological Perspective." *International Journal of Behavioral Development* 2 (1): 1–21.

Elder, Glen, Michael Shanahan, and Julia Jennings. 2015. "Human Development in Time and Place." In *Handbook of Child Psychology and Developmental Science*, vol. 4, edited by Marc Bornstein and Tama Leventhal, 6–54. John Wiley & Sons, Inc.

Ellis, Sarah, and Robert S. Seigler. 1997. "Planning as a Strategy Choice, or Why Don't Children Plan When They Should?" In *The Developmental Psychology of Planning: Why, How, and When Do We Plan?* edited by Sarah L. Freidman and Ellin Kofsky Scholnick, 183–208. Mahwah, N.J.: Lawrence Erlbaum Associates.

Empowering Pacific Islander Communities and Asian Americans Advancing Justice. 2014. *A Community of Contrasts: Native Hawaiians and Pacific Islanders in the United States, 2014*. Los Angeles: Empowering Pacific Islander Communities and Asian Americans Advancing Justice.

EPPSO, 2012. *Republic of the Marshall Islands 2011 Census Report*. Majuro, MH: Economic Policy, Planning and Statistics Office. http://prism.spc.int/images/census_reports/Marshall_Islands_Census_2011-Full.pdf.

Evaldsson, Ann-Carita. 2005. "Staging Insults and Mobilizing Categories in a Multiethnic Peer Group." *Discourse and Society* 16 (6): 763–86.

Evaldsson, Ann-Carita. 2007. "Accounting for Friendship: Moral Ordering and Category Membership in Preadolescent Girls' Relational Talk." *Research on Language and Social Interaction* 40 (4): 377–404.

Fader, Ayala. 2009. *Mitzvah Girls: Bringing Up the Next Generation of Hasidic Jews in Brooklyn*. Princeton: Princeton University Press.

Fagot, Beverly. 1978. "The Influence of Sex of Child on Parental Reactions to Toddler Children." *Child Development* 49 (2): 459–65.

Fajans, Jane. 1983. "Shame, Social Action, and the Person among the Baining." *Ethos* 11 (3): 166–80.

Ferguson, Ann. 2001. *Bad Boys: Public Schools in the Making of Black Masculinity*. Ann Arbor: University of Michigan Press.

Finch, Janet. 1986. "Age." In *Key Variables in Social Investigation*, edited by Robert G. Burgess, 12–30. London: Routledge.

Firth, Raymond. 1929. *Economics of the New Zealand Maori*. Christchurch: Whitcombe and Tombs Limited.

Firth, Raymond. 1936. *We, the Tikopia: A Sociological Study of Kinship in Primitive Polynesia*. London: Allen and Unwin.

Firth, Raymond. 1940. "The Analysis of Mana: An Empirical Approach." *Journal of the Polynesian Society* 48: 483–510.

Fortes, Meyer. 1984. "Age, Generation, and Social Structure." In *Age and Anthropological Theory*, edited by David Kertzer and Jennie Keith, 99–122. Ithaca: Cornell University Press.

Fung, Heidi. 1999. "Becoming a Moral Child: The Socialization of Shame among Young Chinese Children." *Ethnos* 27 (2): 180–209.

Gallimore, Ronald, Joan Boggs, and Cathie Jordan. 1974. *Culture, Behavior, and Education: A Study of Hawaiian-Americans*. Beverly Hills: SAGE Publications.

Gammino, Victoria, Joel Gittelsohn, and Justina Langidrik. 2007. "Dietary Intake in Infants and Children in the Marshall Islands." *Health Promotion in the Pacific* 14 (2): 13–21.

Gardiner, Judith Kegan. 2002. "Theorizing Age with Gender: Bly's Boys, Feminism, and Maturity Masculinity." In *Masculinity Studies and Feminist Theory: New Directions*, edited by Judith Kegan Gardiner, 90–118. New York: Columbia University Press.

Garrett, Paul. 2005. "What Language Is Good For: Language Socialization, Language Shift, and the Persistence of Code-Specific Genres in St. Lucia." *Language in Society* 34 (3): 327–61.

Garrett, Paul. 2007. "Language Socialization and the (Re)production of Bilingual Subjectivities." In *Bilingualism: A Social Approach*, edited by Monica Heller, 233–56. Hampshire: Palgrave Macmillan.

Garrett, Paul. 2012. "Language Socialization and Language Shift." In *The Handbook of Language Socialization*, edited by Alessandro Duranti, Elinor Ochs, and Bambi Schieffelin, 515–35. West Sussex: Blackwell.

Garrett, Paul, and Patricia Baquedano-Lopez. 2002. "Language Socialization: Reproduction and Continuity, Transformation and Change." *Annual Review of Anthropology* 31: 339–61.

Gaskins, Suzanne, and John Lucy. 1987. "The Role of Children in the Production of Adult Culture: A Yucatec Case." Paper presented at the 109th Annual Meeting of the American Ethnological Society, held jointly with the Society for Psychological Anthropology, San Antonio, May 1.

Gay y Blasco, Paloma and Huon Wardle. 2007. *How to Read Ethnography*. New York: Routledge.

Gittelsohn, Joel, Heather Haberle, Amy Vastine, Wiliam Dyckman, and Neal Palafox. 2003. "Macro- and Microlevel Processes Affect Food Choice and Nutritional Status in the Republic of the Marshall Islands." *Journal of Nutrition* 133 (1): 3105–35.

Gittelsohn, Joel, Leslie Mass, Victoria Gammino, and Neal Palafox. 1998. *Overnutrition and Undernutrition in the Republic of the Marshall Islands: Report of a Pilot Study and Future Directions*. Baltimore: Johns Hopkins University School of Hygiene and Public Health.

Giudice, Marco Del, Romina Angeleri, and Valeria Manera. 2009. "The Juvenile Transition: A Developmental Switch Point in Human Life History." *Developmental Review* 29: 1–31.

Godelier, Maurice. 1996. *The Enigma of the Gift*. Chicago: University of Chicago Press.

Goffman, Erving. 1959. *The Presentation of Self in Everyday Life*. New York: Doubleday.

Goffman, Erving. 1967. *Interaction Ritual*. New York: Anchor Books.

Goffman, Erving. 1974. *An Essay on the Organization of Experience*. Boston: Northeastern University Press.

Goffman, Erving. 1981. *Forms of Talk*. Philadelphia: University of Pennsylvania Press.

Goode, David. 1986. "Kids, Culture, and Innocents." *Human Studies* 9: 83–106.

Goodman, Alan H., and George J. Armelagos. 1985. "Disease and Death at Dr. Dickson's Mounds." *Natural History* 94 (9): 12–18.

Goodwin, Charles. 2000. "Action and Embodiment within Situated Human Interaction." *Journal of Pragmatics* 32 (10): 1489–1522.

Goodwin, Charles, and Marjorie Goodwin. 2004. "Participation." In *A Companion to Linguistic Anthropology*, edited by Alessandro Duranti, 222–44. Oxford: Blackwell.

Goodwin, Marjorie. 1980. "He-Said-She-Said: Formal Cultural Procedures for the Construction of a Gossip Dispute Activity." *American Ethnologist* 7 (4): 674–95.

Goodwin, Marjorie. 1990. *He-Said-She-Said: Talk as Social Organization among Black Children*. Bloomington: Indiana University Press.

Goodwin, Marjorie. 2006. *The Hidden Life of Girls: Games of Stance, Status, and Exclusion*. Malden, Mass.: Blackwell Publishing.

Goodwin, Marjorie, and H. Samy Alim. 2010. "'Whatever (Neck Roll, Eye Roll, Teeth Suck)': The Situated Coproduction of Social Categories and Identities through Stancetaking and Transmodal Stylization." *Journal of Linguistic Anthropology* 20 (1): 179–94.

Goodwin, Marjorie, and Amy Kyratzis. 2007. "Children Socializing Children: Practices for Negotiating the Social Order among Peers." *Research on Language and Social Interaction* 40 (4): 1–11.

Goodwin, Marjorie, and Amy Kyratzis. 2012. "Peer Language Socialization." In *The Handbook of Language Socialization*, edited by Alessandro Duranti, Elinor Ochs, and Bambi Schieffelin, 365–90. West Sussex: Wiley-Blackwell.

Gorenflo, L. J., and Michael Levin. 1989. "The Demographic Evolution of Ebeye." *Pacific Studies* 12: 91–128.

Gottlieb, Alma. 1998. "Do Infants Have Religion? The Spiritual Lives of Beng Babies." *American Anthropologist* 100 (1): 122–35.

Gottlieb, Alma. 2004. *The Afterlife Is Where We Come From: The Culture of Infancy in West Africa*. Chicago: University of Chicago Press.

Graeber, David. 2001. *Toward an Anthropological Theory of Value: The False Coin of Our Own Dreams*. New York: Palgrave.

Gregory, Christopher. 1982. *Gifts and Commodities*. New York: Academic Press.

Grice, H. P. 1989. *Studies in the Way of Words*. Cambridge: Harvard University Press.

Gupta, Akhil. 2002. "Reliving Childhood? The Temporality of Childhood and Narratives of Reincarnation." *Ethnos* 67 (1): 33–55.

Hanks, William. 1990. *Referential Practice: Language and Lived Space among the Maya*. Chicago: University of Chicago Press.

Hansen, K. C., and L. E. Hansen. 1974. *Pitcheri*. Papunya, Australia: SIL Bilingual Programme.

Harkness, Sara, and Charles Super. 1992. "Parental Ethnotheories in Action." In *Parental Belief Systems: The Psychological Consequences for Children*, edited by Irving E. Sigel, Ann V. McGillicuddy-DeLisi, and Jacqueline J. Goodnow, 373–91. Hillsdale, N.J.: Erlbaum.

Haviland, John. 1977. "Gossip as Competition in Zinacantan." *Journal of Communication* 27 (1): 186–91.

Heath, Shirley Brice. 1983. *Ways with Words: Language, Life and Work in Communities and Classrooms*. Cambridge: Cambridge University Press.

Hess, Jim, Karen Nero, and Michael Burton. 2001. "Creating Options: Forming a Marshallese Community in Orange County, CA." *The Contemporary Pacific* 13 (1): 89–121.

Hewlett, Barry. 1992. "The Parent-Infant Relationship and Social-Emotional Development among Aka Pygmies." In *Parent-Child Socialization in Diverse Cultures*, edited by Jaipaul Roopnarine and Bruce Carter, 223–43. Norwood, N.J.: Ablex.

Heywood, Colin. 2001. *A History of Childhood: Children and Childhood in the West from Medieval to Modern Times*. Cambridge: Polity Press.

Hezel, Francis. 1983. *The First Taint of Civilization: A History of the Caroline and Marshall Islands in Pre-colonial Days, 1521–1885*. Honolulu: University of Hawai'i Press.

Hezel, Francis. 1987. "Truk Suicide Epidemic and Social Change." *Human Organization* 46 (4): 283–91.

Hezel, Francis. 1995. *Strangers in Their Own Land: A Century of Colonial Rule in the Caroline and Marshall Islands*. Honolulu: University of Hawai'i Press.

Hill, Jane, and Judith Irvine. 1993a. "Introduction." In *Responsibility and Evidence in Oral Discourse*, edited by Jane Hill and Judith Irvine, 1–23. Cambridge: Cambridge University Press.

Hill, Jane, and Judith Irvine, eds. 1993b. *Responsibility and Evidence in Oral Discourse*. Cambridge: Cambridge University Press.

Hill, Jane, and Ofelia Zepeda. 1993. "Mrs. Patricio's Trouble: The Distribution of Responsibility in an Account of Personal Experience." In *Responsibility and Evidence in Oral Discourse*, edited by Jane Hill and Judith Irvine, 197–225. New York: University of Cambridge Press.

Hogan, Dennis. 1978. "The Variable Order of Events in the Life Course." *American Sociological Review* 43 (4): 573–86.

Hogbin, H. Ian. 1943. "A New Guinea Infancy: From Conception to Weaning in Wogeo." *Oceania* 13: 285–309.

Honwana, Alcinda, and Filip De Boeck, eds. 2005. *Makers and Breakers: Children and Youth in Postcolonial Africa*. Oxford: James Curry.

Hotchkiss, John. 1967. "Children and Conduct in a Ladino Community of Chiapas, Mexico." *American Anthropologist*, New Series, 69 (6): 711–18.

Howard, Alan. 1970. *Learning to Be Rotuman: Enculturation in the South Pacific*. New York: Teachers College Press.

Howard, Kathryn. 2007. "Kinterm Usage and Hierarchy in Thai Children's Peer Groups." *Journal of Linguistic Anthropology* 17 (2): 204–30.

Howard, Kathryn. 2008. "Language Socialization and Language Shift among School-Aged Children." In *Encyclopedia of Language and Education*, edited by P. A. Duff and Nancy Hornberger, 187–99. New York: Springer.

Howard, Kathryn. 2009. "Breaking In and Spinning Out: Repetition and Decalibration in Thai Children's Play Genres." *Language in Society* 38 (3): 339–63.

Howard, Kathryn. 2012. "Language Socialization and Hierarchy." In *The Handbook of Language Socialization*, edited by Alessandro Duranti, Elinor Ochs, and Bambi Schieffelin, 341–64. Malden, Mass.: Wiley-Blackwell.

Huijsmans, Roy, Shanti George, Roy Gigengack, and Sandra Evers. 2014. "Introduction: Theorising Age and Generation in Development: A Relational Approach." *European Journal of Development Research* 26: 163–74.

Hyde, Janet Shibley. 2005. "The Gender Similarities Hypothesis." *American Psychologist* 60 (6): 581–92.

Irvine, Judith. 1990. "Registering Affect: Heteroglossia in the Linguistic Expression of Emotion." In *Language and the Politics of Emotion*, edited by Catherine Lutz and Lila Abu-Lughod, 126–61. Cambridge: Cambridge University Press.

Irvine, Judith, and Susan Gal. 2000. "Language Ideology and Linguistic Differentiation." In *Regimes of Language: Ideologies, Polities, and Identities*, edited by Paul Kroskrity, 35–83. Santa Fe, N.M.: School of American Research Press.

Jacobs-Huey, Lanita. 2006. *From the Kitchen to the Parlor: Language and Becoming in African American Women's Hair Care*. Oxford: Oxford University Press.

Jacobs-Huey, Lanita. 2007. "Learning through the Breach: Language Socialization among African American Cosmetologists." *Ethnography* 8 (2): 171–203.

James, Allison. 2007. "Giving Voice to Children's Voices: Practice and Problems, Pitfalls and Potentials." *American Anthropologist* 109 (2): 261–72.

James, Allison. 2009. "Agency." In *The Palgrave Handbook of Childhood Studies*, edited by Jens Qvortrup, William A. Corsaro, and Michael-Sebastian Honig, 34–45. Basingstoke, U.K.: Palgrave Macmillan.

James, Allison, and Alan Prout, eds. 1997a. *Constructing and Reconstructing Childhood.* London: Routledge Falmer.

James, Allison, and Alan Prout. 1997b. "A New Paradigm for the Sociology of Childhood? Provenance, Promise and Problems." In *Constructing and Reconstructing Childhood*, edited by Allison James and Alan Prout, 7–33. London: Routledge Falmer.

James, Allison, and Alan Prout. 1997c. "Re-presenting Childhood: Time and Transition in the Study of Childhood." In *Constructing and Reconstructing Childhood: Contemporary Issues in the Sociological Study of Childhood*, edited by Allison James and Alan Prout, 230–50. London: Routledge Falmer.

James, G. D., and P. T. Baker. 1995. "Human Population Biology and Blood Pressure: Evolutionary and Ecological Considerations and Interpretations of Population Studies." In *Hypertension, Pathophysiology, Diagnosis, and Management*, edited by John H. Laragh and Barry M. Brenner, 115–26. New York: Raven Press.

Jenkins, Michael, and Cleveland McSwain. 2005. "The Republic of the Marshall Islands." In *Social Change and Psychosocial Adaptation in the Pacific Islands: Cultures in Transition*, edited by Anthony J. Marsella, Ayda Aukahi Austin, and Bruce Grant, 187–210. New York: Springer.

Jimeno S., Rafael A. 2013. *A Profile of the Marshallese Community in Arkansas, vol. 3.* Little Rock: Winthrop Rockefeller Foundation; and Fayetteville: University of Arkansas.

Joash, Bernice. 2004. "Mantin Ajri, Children's Customs." In *Life in the Republic of the Marshall Islands*, edited by Anono Lieam Loeak, Veronica Kiluwe, and Linda Crowl, 51–56. Suva: University of the South Pacific Centre and Institute of Pacific Studies.

Johnson-Hanks, Jennifer. 2002. "On the Limits of Life Stages in Ethnography: Toward a Theory of Vital Conjuncture." *American Anthropologist* 104 (3): 865–80.

Jordan, Cathie, Ronald Gallimore, B. Sloggett, and E. Kubany. 1969. "The Family and the School." In *Studies in a Hawaiian Community:* Na Makamaka o Nanakuli, edited by Ronald Gallimore and Alan Howard, 55–63. Honolulu: Bernice P. Bishop Museum.

Kaplan, Sarah. 2015. "Exiled by Nuclear Tests, Now Threatened by Climate Change, Bikini Islanders Seek Refuge in the U.S." *Washington Post*, Morning Mix, October 28.

Katriel, Tamar. 1987. "'*Bexibùdim!*': Ritual Sharing among Israeli Children." *Language and Society* 16 (3): 305–20.

Keane, Webb. 2007. *Christian Moderns: Freedom and Fetish in the Mission Encounter*. Berkeley: University of California Press.

Keenan, Elinor Ochs. 1974. "Norm-Makers, Norm-Breakers: Uses of Speech by Men and Women in a Malagasy Community." In *Explorations in the Ethnography of Speaking*, edited by Richard Bauman and Joel Sherzer, 125–43. Cambridge: Cambridge University Press.

Kehily, Mary Jane. 2007. "A Cultural Perspective." In *Youth: Perspectives, Identities, and Practices*, edited by Mary Jane Kehily, 11–44. London: SAGE.

Kertzer, David, and Jennie Keith, eds. 1984. *Age and Anthropological Theory*. Ithaca: Cornell University Press.

Kiste, Robert. 1974. *The Bikinians: A Study in Forced Migration*. Menlo Park: Cummings Publishing Company.

Kiste, Robert, and Michael Rynkiewich. 1976. "Incest and Exogamy: A Comparative Study of Two Marshall Island Populations." *Journal of the Polynesian Society* 85 (2): 209–26.

Korbin, Jill. 1990. "*Hana 'Ino*: Child Maltreatment in a Hawaiian-American Community." *Pacific Studies* 13 (3): 7–22.

Korbin, Jill. 2003. "Children, Childhoods, and Violence." *Annual Review of Anthropology* 32: 431–46.

Krekula, Clary. 2007. "The Intersection of Age and Gender: Reworking Gender Theory and Social Gerontology." *Current Sociology* 55 (2): 155–71.

Kuhl, Patricia K. 2009. "Early Language Acquisition: Phonetic and World Learning, Neural Substrates, and a Theoretical Model." In *The Perception of Speech: From Sound to Meaning*, edited by Brian Moore, Lorraine Tyler, and William Marslen-Wilson, 103–31. Oxford: Oxford University Press.

Kulick, Don. 1992. *Language Shift and Cultural Reproduction: Socialization, Self, and Syncretism in a Papua New Guinean Village*. Cambridge: Cambridge University Press.

Kulick, Don. 1993. "Speaking as a Woman: Structure and Gender in Domestic Arguments in a New Guinea Village." *Cultural Anthropology* 8 (4): 510–41.

Kulick, Don. 2003. "No." *Language and Communication* 23 (2): 139–51.

Kulick, Don, and Bambi Schieffelin. 2004. "Language Socialization." In *A Companion to Linguistic Anthropology*, edited by Alessandro Duranti, 349–68. Malden, Mass.: Blackwell.

Kyratzis, Amy. 2004. "Talk and Interaction among Children and the Co-construction of Peer Groups and Peer Culture." *Annual Review of Anthropology* 33: 625–49.

Kyratzis, Amy. 2007. "Using the Social Organizational Affordances of Pretend Play in American Preschool Girls' Interactions." *Research on Language and Social Interaction* 40 (4): 321–52.

Lamb, Sarah. 2000. *White Saris and Sweet Mangoes: Aging, Gender, and Body in North India*. Berkeley: University of California Press.

Lamb, Sarah. 2015. "Generation in Anthropology." In *International Encyclopedia of the Social and Behavioral Sciences*, 2nd ed. Vol 9, edited by James D. Wright, 853–56. Oxford: Elsevier.

Lamb, Sarah. 2017. *Successful Aging as a Contemporary Obsession: Global Perspectives*. New Brunswick, N.J.: Rutgers University Press.

Lancy, David. 1996. *Playing on the Mother-Ground: Cultural Routines for Children's Development*. New York: Guilford Press.

Lancy, David. 2015. *The Anthropology of Childhood: Cherubs, Chattels, and Changelings*, 2nd ed. Cambridge: Cambridge University Press.

LaRossa, Ralph, and Donald Reitzes. 2001. "Two? Two and One-Half? Thirty Months? Chronometrical Childhood in Early Twentieth Century America." *Sociological Forum* 16 (3): 385–407.

Laz, Cheryl. 1998. "Act Your Age." *Sociological Forum* 13 (1): 85–113.

Laz, Cheryl. 2003. "Age Embodied." *Journal of Aging Studies* 17: 503–19.

Lederman, Rena. 1986. *What Gifts Engender: Social Relations and Politics in Mendi, Highland Papua New Guinea*. Cambridge: Press Syndicate of the University of Cambridge.

Lee, Nick. 1999. "The Challenge of Childhood: Distributions of Childhood's Ambiguity in Adult Institutions." *Childhood* 6 (4): 455–74.

Lesko, Nancy. 2012. *Act Your Age! A Cultural Construction of Adolescence*. New York: Routledge.

LeVine, Robert A., Suzanne Dixon, Sarah LeVine, Amy Richman, P. Herbert Leiderman, Constance H. Keefer, and T. Berry Brazelton. 1994. *Childcare and Culture: Lessons from Africa*. New York: Cambridge University Press.

LeVine, Robert. 2007. "Ethnographic Studies of Childhood: A Historical Overview." *American Anthropologist* 109 (2): 247–60.

LeVine, Robert, and Karin Norman. 2001. "The Infant's Acquisition of Culture: Early Attachment Reexamined in Anthropological Perspective." In *The Psychology of Cultural Experience*, edited by Holly Mathews and Carmella Moore, 83–104. New York: Cambridge University Press.

Lewis, Michael, and Marsha Weinraub. 1979. "Origins of Early Sex-Role Development." *Sex Roles* 5 (2): 133–53.

Lightfoot, Cynthia, Michael Cole, and Sheila Cole. 2013. *The Development of Children*, 7th ed. New York: Worth Publishers.

Llamas, Carmen. 2007. "Age." In *The Routledge Companion to Sociolinguistics*, edited by Carmen Llamas, Louise Mullany, and Peter Stockwell, 68–76. New York: Routledge.

Lo, Adrienne, and Heidi Fung. 2012. "Language Socialization and Shaming." In *Handbook of Language Socialization*, edited by Alessandro Duranti, Elinor Ochs, and Bambi Schieffelin, 169–89. Malden, Mass.: Wiley-Blackwell.

Lock, Margaret. 1998. "Deconstructing the Change: Female Maturation in Japan and North America." In *Welcome to the Middle Age! (And Other Cultural Fictions)*, edited by Richard Shweder, 45–74. Chicago: University of Chicago Press.

Lowe, Edward D. 2003. "Identity, Activity, and the Well-Being of Adolescents and Youths: Lessons from Young People in a Micronesian Society." *Culture, Medicine, and Psychiatry* 27 (2): 187–219.

Lowe, Edward D. 2016. *Anthropological Engagements of Youths' Mental Health in Contexts of Modernizing Social Change: A Critical Assessment*. Pacific Basic Research Center Working Paper. http://www.pbrc.soka.edu/files/documents/working-papers/lowe.pdf

Lucy, John. 1993. *Reflexive Language: Reported Speech and Metapragmatics*. New York: Cambridge University Press.

Lutz, Catherine. 1982. "The Domain of Emotion Words on Ifaluk." *American Anthropologist* 9 (1): 113–28.

Lutz, Catherine. 1988. *Unnatural Emotions: Everyday Sentiments on a Micronesian Atoll and Their Challenge to Western Theory*. Chicago: University of Chicago Press.

Macaulay, Ronald. 1975. "Negative Prestige, Linguistic Insecurity, and Linguistic Self-Hatred." *Lingua* 36 (2–3): 147–61.

Maddox, Camee. 2015. "'Yes We Can! Down with Colonization!' Race, Gender, and the 2009 General Strike in Martinique." *Transforming Anthropology* 23 (2): 90–103.

Mageo, Jeannette. 1991. "Samoan Moral Discourse and the *Loto*." *American Anthropologist* 93 (2): 405–20.

Mahmood, Saba. 2005. *Politics of Piety: The Islamic Revival and the Feminist Subject*. Princeton: Princeton University Press.

Mahoney, Francis. 1974. *Social and Cultural Factors Relating to the Cause and Control of Alcohol Abuse among Micronesian Youth*. Washington, D.C.: Trust Territory of the Pacific Islands.

Malinowski, Bronislaw. 1961. *Argonauts of the Western Pacific*. New York: E. P. Dutton and Co. (Original edition, 1922.)

Mao, LuMing Robert. 1994. "Beyond Politeness Theory: 'Face' Revisited and Renewed." *Journal of Pragmatics* 21 (5): 451–86

Markström, Ann-Marie, and Gunilla Halldén. 2009. "Children's Strategies for Agency in Preschool." *Children and Society* 23: 112–22.

Marlowe, Frank. 2004. "Dictators and Ultimatums in an Egalitarian Society of Hunter-Gatherers, the Hadza of Tanzania." In *Foundations of Human Sociality: Economic Experiments and Ethnographic Evidence from Fifteen Small-Scale Societies*, edited by Joseph Henrich, Robert Boyd, Samuel Bowles, Colin Camerer, Ernst Fehr, and Herbert Gintis, 167–92. Oxford: Oxford University Press.

Marshall, Mac. 1979. *Weekend Warriors: Alcohol in a Micronesian Culture*. Palo Alto: Mayfield Press.

Marshallese Educational Initiative. 2017. "Marshallese in Arkansas." https://www.mei.ngo/marshallese-in-arkansas.

Mason, Leonard. 1947. *The Economic Organization of the Marshall Islanders*. Honolulu: U.S. Commercial Company, Economic Survey.

Mauss, Marcel. 1990. *The Gift: The Forms and Reason for Exchange in Archaic Societies*. New York: Norton.

Mayer, Enrique, and Manuel Glave. 1999. "*Alguito Para Ganar* (A Little Something to Earn): Profits and Losses in Peasant Economies." *American Ethnologist* 26 (2): 344–69.

Mayer, Karl Ulrich. 2009. "New Directions in Life Course Research." *Annual Review of Sociology* 35: 413–33.

McArthur, Phillip. 1996. "The Social Life of Narrative: Marshall Islands." Ph.D. dissertation, Indiana University.

McClennen, Caleb. 2007. "Environmentally Induced Costs of Urbanization in Small Island States: The Case of the Republic of the Marshall Islands." Ph.D. dissertation, Fletcher School of Law and Diplomacy, Tufts University.

McElhinny, Bonnie. 1994. "An Economy of Affect: Objectivity, Masculinity, and the Gendering of Police Work." In *Dislocating Masculinity*, edited by Andrea Cornwall and Nancy Lindisfarne, 158–70. London: Routledge.

McElhinny, Bonnie. 1995. "Challenging Hegemonic Masculinities: Female and Male Police Officers Handling Domestic Violence." In *Gender Articulated: Language and the Socially Constructed Self*, edited by Kira Hall and Mary Bucholtz, 217–43. New York: Routledge.

McNay, Lois. 2000. *Gender and Agency: Reconfiguring the Subject in Feminist and Social Theory*. Cambridge: Polity.

Mead, Margaret. 1930. *Growing Up in New Guinea*. New York: Perennial Classics.

Meek, Barbra. 2007. "Respecting the Language of Elders: Ideological Shift and Linguistic Discontinuity in a Northern Athapascan Community." *Journal of Linguistic Anthropology* 17 (1): 23–43.

Meek, Barbra. 2011. *We Are Our Language: An Ethnography of Language Revitalization in a Northern Athabaskan Community*. Tucson: University of Arizona Press.

Mehl, Matthias R., Simine Vazire, Nairan Ramirez-Esparza, Richard B. Slatcher, and James W. Pennebaker. 2007. "Are Women Really More Talkative than Men?" *Science* 317 (5834): 82.

Meiu, George Paul. 2015. "'Beach-Boy Elders' and 'Young Big-Men': Subverting the Temporalities of Ageing in Kenya's Ethno-erotic Economies." *Ethnos* 80 (4): 472–96.

Mendoza-Denton, Norma. 2008. *Homegirls: Symbolic Practices in the Making of Latina Youth Styles*. Oxford: Blackwell.

Meredith, Stephanie. 2015. "Comparative Perspectives on Human Gender Development and Evolution." *Yearbook of Physical Anthropology* 156 (S59): 72–97.

Merlan, Francesca, and Alan Rumsey. 1991. Ku Waru: *Language and Segmentary Politics in the Western Nebilyer Valley, Papua New Guinea*. Cambridge: Cambridge University Press.

Miller, Peggy, Michele Koven, and Shumin Lin. 2012. "Language Socialization and Narrative." In *Handbook of Language Socialization*, edited by Alessandro Duranti, Elinor Ochs, and Bambi Schieffelin, 190–208. West Sussex: Wiley-Blackwell.

Minkley, Gary, and Martin Legassick. 2000. "'Not Telling': Secrecy, Lies, and History." *History and Theory* 39 (4): 1–10.

Modell, Judith. 1999. "Freely Given: Open Adoption and the Rhetoric of the Gift." In *Transformative Motherhood: On Giving and Getting in a Consumer Culture*, edited by Linda Layne, 29–64. New York: New York University Press.

Moir, Anne, and David Jessel. 1991. *Brain Sex: The Real Difference between Men and Women*. New York: Delta Books.

Moir, Anne, and Bill Moir. 1999. *Why Men Don't Iron: The Fascinating and Unalterable Differences between Men and Women*. New York: Citadel.

Montgomery, Heather. 2009. *An Introduction to Childhood: Anthropological Perspectives on Children's Lives*. Malden, Mass.: Wiley-Blackwell.

Morton, Helen. 1996. *Becoming Tongan: An Ethnography of Childhood*. Honolulu: University of Hawai'i Press.

Munn, Nancy. 1986. *The Fame of Gawa: A Symbolic Study of Value Transformation in a Massim (Papua New Guinea) Society*. Cambridge: Cambridge University Press.

Nero, Karen. 1997. "The End of Insularity: Islander Paradigms for the Pacific Century." In *The Cambridge History of the Pacific Islanders*, edited by Donald Denoon, Stewart Firth, Jocelyn Linnekin, Malama Meleisea, and Karen Nero, 439–67. Cambridge: Cambridge University Press.

Neugarten, Bernice. 1996a. *The Meanings of Age: Selected Papers of Bernice L. Neugarten*. Edited by Dail Neugarten. Chicago: University of Chicago Press.

Neugarten, Bernice. 1996b. "Time, Age and the Life Cycle." In *The Meanings of Age: Selected Papers of Bernice L. Neugarten*, edited by Dail Neugarten, 114–27. Chicago: University of Chicago Press.

Nguyen, Hanh Thi, and Guy Kellogg. 2010. "'I Had a Stereotype that American Were Fat': Becoming a Speaker of Culture in a Second Language." *Modern Language Journal* 94 (1): 56–73.

Niedenthal, Jack. 2001. *For the Good of Mankind: A History of the People of Bikini and Their Islands*. Majuro: Bravo Publishers.

Nukaga, Misako. 2008. "The Underlife of Kids' School Lunchtime: Negotiating Ethnic Boundaries and Identity in Food Exchange." *Journal of Contemporary Ethnography* 37 (3): 248–380.

Ochs, Elinor. 1986. "Introduction." In *Language Socialization across Cultures*, edited by Bambi Schieffelin and Elinor Ochs, 1–13. Cambridge: Cambridge University Press.

Ochs, Elinor. 1988. *Culture and Language Development: Language Acquisition and Language Socialization in a Samoan Village*. Cambridge: Cambridge University Press.

Ochs, Elinor. 1992. "Indexing Gender." In *Rethinking Context: Language as an Interactive Phenomenon*, edited by Alessandro Duranti and Charles Goodwin, 335–58. Cambridge: Cambridge University Press.

Ochs, Elinor. 1993. "Constructing Social Identity: A Language Socialization Perspective." *Language and Social Interaction* 26 (3): 287–306.

Ochs, Elinor, and Tamar Kremer-Sadlik. 2015. "How Language Became Knowledge." *Journal of Linguistic Anthropology* 25 (1): 72–73.

Ochs, Elinor, and Bambi Schieffelin. 2012. "The Theory of Language Socialization." In *The Handbook of Language Socialization*, edited by Alessandro Duranti, Elinor Ochs, and Bambi Schieffelin, 1–21. West Sussex: Wiley-Blackwell.

Opie, Ellen. 1991. "Parenting Difficulties in the Republic of the Marshall Islands: Toward the Prevention of Child Maltreatment." Master's thesis, Behavioral Sciences, University of California, Berkeley.

Paugh, Amy. 2012a. "Local Theories of Child Rearing." In *Handbook of Language Socialization*, edited by Alessandro Duranti, Elinor Ochs, and Bambi Schieffelin, 150–68. West Sussex: Blackwell.

Paugh, Amy. 2012b. *Playing with Languages: Children and Change in a Caribbean Village*. New York: Berghahn.

Peterson, Glenn. 2009. *Traditional Micronesian Societies: Adaptation, Integration, and Political Organization in the Central Pacific*. Honolulu: University of Hawai'i Press.

Peterson, Nicolas. 1993. "Demand Sharing: Reciprocity and the Pressure for Generosity among Foragers." *American Anthropologist*, New Series, 95 (4): 860–74.

Platt, Martha. 1986. "Social Norms and Lexical Acquisition: A Study of Deictic Verbs in Samoan Child Language." In *Language Socialization across Cultures*, edited by Bambi Schieffelin and Elinor Ochs, 127–52. Cambridge: Cambridge University Press.

Pollock, Nancy. 2003. "Rethinking Marriage and Gender Relations Using Evidence from the Pacific." *Gender and Development* 11 (1): 85–90.

Porter, Karen. 1996. "The Agency of Children, Work, and Social Change in the South Pare Mountains, Tanzania." *Anthropology of Work Review* 17 (1–2): 8–19.

Posthuma, Richard A., Maria Fernanda Wagstaff, and Michael A. Campion. 2012. "Age Stereotypes and Workplace Age Discrimination." In *The Oxford Handbook of Work and Aging*, edited by Jerry Hedge and Walter Borman, 298–312. Oxford: Oxford University Press.

Poyer, Lin, Suzanne Falgout, and Laurence Carucci. 2001. *The Typhoon of War: Micronesian Experiences of the Pacific War*. Honolulu: University of Hawai'i Press.

Qvortrup, Jens. 1994. "Childhood Matters: An Introduction." In *Childhood Matters: Social Theory, Practice, and Politics*, edited by Jens Qvortrup, Marjatta Bardy, Giovanni Sgritta, and Helmut Wintersberger, 1–23. Brookfield, Vt.: Avebury.

Qvortrup, Jens. 1997. "A Voice for Children in Statistical and Social Accounting: A Plea for Children's Right to Be Heard." In *Constructing and Reconstructing Childhood*, edited by Allison James and Alan Prout, 85–106. London: Routledge Falmer.

Rasmussen, Susan J. 1994. "The Poetics of Childhood and Politics of Resistance in Tuareg Society: Some Thoughts on Studying 'the Other' and Adult-Child Relationships." *Ethos* 22: 343–72.

Rauchholz, Manuel. 2009. "Towards an Understanding of Adoption, Person, and Emotion: The Ideal Norm and Reality of Life amongst the Chuukese of Micronesia." Ph.D. dissertation, Institut für Ethnologie, Universität Heidelberg.

Republic of the Marshall Islands. 2010. *Marshallese Language Orthography (Standard Spelling) Act of 2010*. http://rmiparliament.org/cms/images/LEGISLATION/PRINCIPAL/2010/2010-0004/MarshalleseLanguageOrthographyStandardSpellingAct2010_1.pdf. Accessed May 11, 2015.

Reynolds, Jennifer. 2008. "Socializing *Puros Pericos* (Little Parrots): The Negotiation of Respect and Responsibility in Antonero Mayan Sibling and Peer Networks." *Journal of Linguistic Anthropology* 18 (1): 82–107.

Riley, Kathleen. 2012. "Language Socialization and Language Ideologies." In *The Handbook of Language Socialization*, edited by Alessandro Duranti, Elinor Ochs and Bambi Schieffelin, 493–514. West Sussex: Wiley-Blackwell.

Riley, Matilda. 1987. "On the Significance of Age in Sociology." *American Sociological Review* 52 (1): 1–14.

Riley, Matilda W., Marilyn E. Johnson, and Anne Foner. 1972. *A Sociology of Age Stratification, vol. 3: Aging and Society*. New York: Russell Sage Foundation.

Ritchie, Jane, and James Ritchie. 1979. *Growing Up in Polynesia*. Sydney: George Allen and Unwin.

RMI Biodiversity Project. 2000. *The Marshall Islands—Living Atolls amidst the Living Sea*. Santa Clarita: National Biodiversity Team of the Republic of the Marshall Islands.

Robbins, Joel. 2001. "Ritual Communication and Linguistic Ideology: A Reading and Partial Reformulation of Rappaport's Theory of Ritual." *Current Anthropology* 42 (5): 591–614.

Robbins, Joel. 2007. "You Can't Talk behind the Holy Spirit's Back: Christianity and Changing Language Ideologies in a Papua New Guinea Society." In *Consequences of Contact: Language Ideologies and Sociocultural Transformations in Pacific Societies*, edited by Miki Makihara and Bambi Schieffelin, 125–39. Oxford: Oxford University Press.

Roby, Jini, and Stephanie Matsumura. 2002. "If I Give You My Child, Aren't We Family?" *Adoption Quarterly* 5 (4): 7–31.

Rogoff, Barbara. 1981. "Adults and Peers as Agents of Socialization: A Highland Guatemala Profile." *Ethos* 9 (1): 18–36.

Rogoff, Barbara. 2003. *The Cultural Nature of Human Development*. Oxford: Oxford University Press.

Rogoff, Barbara, Martha Sellers, Sergio Pirrotta, Nathan Fox, and Sheldon White. 1975. "Age of Assignment of Roles and Responsibilities to Children: A Cross-Cultural Survey." *Human Development* 18: 353–69.

Rosaldo, Michelle. 1982. "The Things We Do with Words: Ilongot Speech Acts and Speech Act Theory in Philosophy." *Language in Society* 11 (2): 203–37.

Rosaldo, Michelle. 1983. "The Shame of Headhunters and the Autonomy of Self." *Ethos* 11 (3): 135–51.

Rosen, David. 2015. *Child Soldiers in the Western Imagination: From Patriots to Victims*. New Brunswick, N.J.: Rutgers University Press.

Rubinstein, Donald. 1983. "Epidemic Suicide among Micronesian Adolescents." *Social Science and Medicine* 17 (10): 657–65.

Rudiak-Gould, Peter. 2010. "Being Marshallese and Christian: A Case of Multiple Contradictory Beliefs." *Culture and Religion* 11 (1): 69–87.

Rudiak-Gould, Peter. 2013. *Climate Change and Tradition in a Small Island State: The Rising Tide*. New York: Routledge.

Rumsey, Alan. 1990. "Wording, Meaning, and Linguistic Ideology." *American Anthropologist* 92: 346–61.

Rynkiewich, Michael. 1972. "Land Tenure among Arno Marshallese." Ph.D. dissertation, University of Minnesota.

Rynkiewich, Michael. 1976. "Adoption and Land Tenure among Arno Marshallese." In *Transactions in Kinship: Adoption and Fosterage in Oceania*, edited by Ivan Brady, 93–119. Honolulu: University of Hawai'i Press.

Sahlins, Marshall. 1963. "Poor Man, Rich Man, Big-Man, Chief: Political Types in Melanesia and Polynesia." *Comparative Studies in Society and History* 5 (3): 285–303.

Sahlins, Marshall. 1972. *Stone Age Economics*. New York: Aldine de Gruyter.

Sahlins, Marshall. 1985. *Islands of History*. Chicago: University of Chicago Press.

Sameroff, Arnold, and Marshall M. Haith, eds. 1996. *The Five to Seven Year Shift: The Age of Reason and Responsibility*. Chicago: University of Chicago Press.

Sawchuk, Peter. 2003. "Informal Learning as a Speech-Exchange System: Implications for Knowledge Production, Power and Social Transformation." *Discourse and Society* 14 (3): 291–307.

Schieffelin, Bambi. 1990. *The Give and Take of Everyday Life: Language Socialization of Kaluli Children*. Cambridge: Cambridge University Press.

Schieffelin, Bambi, and Elinor Ochs, eds. 1986. *Language Socialization across Cultures*. Cambridge: Cambridge University Press.

Schildkrout, Enid. 1978. "Age and Gender in Hausa Society: Socio-economic roles of children in urban Kano." In *Sex and Age as Principles of Social Differentiation*, edited by Jean S. La Fontaine, 109–37. London: Academic Press.

Schwartz, Jessica. 2015. "Marshallese Cultural Diplomacy in Arkansas." *American Quarterly* 67 (3): 781–812.

Searle, John R. 1969. *Speech Acts: An Essay in the Philosophy of Language*. Cambridge: Cambridge University Press.

Sewell, William H. 1992. "A Theory of Structure: Duality, Agency, and Transformation." *American Journal of Sociology* 98 (1): 1–29.

Sewell, William H. 2005. *Logics of History: Social Theory and Social Transformation*. Chicago: University of Chicago Press.

Shweder, Richard, ed. 1998. *Welcome to the Middle Age! (And Other Cultural Fictions)*. Chicago: University of Chicago Press.

Shweder, Richard. 2003. "Toward a Deep Cultural Psychology of Shame." *Social Research* 70 (4): 1109–30.

Silverstein, Michael. 1976. "Shifters, Linguistic Categories, and Cultural Description." In *Meaning in Anthropology*, edited by Keith Basso and Henry Selby, 11–55. New York: Academic Press.

Silverstein, Michael. 1979. "Language Structure and Linguistic Ideology" In *The Elements: A Parasession on Linguistic Units and Levels,* edited by Paul Clyne, William Hanks, and Carol Hofbauer, 193-247. Chicago: Chicago Linguistic Society.

Small, Cathy, and David Dixon. 2004. "Tonga: Migration and the Homeland." Washington, D.C.: Migration Policy Institute. https://www.migrationpolicy.org/article/tonga-migration-and-homeland.

Sobo, Elisa. 2015. "Anthropological Contributions and Challenges to the Study of Children and Childhoods." *Reviews in Anthropology* 44 (1): 43–68.

Soley, Gaye, and Nuria Sebastian-Galles. 2015. "Infants Prefer Tunes Previously Introduced by Speakers of Their Native Language." *Child Development* 86 (6): 1685–92.

Sorenson, E. Richard. 1979. "Early Tactile Communication and the Patterning of Human Organization: A New Guinea Study." In *Before Speech: The Beginning of*

Interpersonal Communication, edited by Margaret Bullowa, 289–305. Cambridge: Cambridge University Press.

Spoehr, Alexander. 1949. *Majuro: A Village in the Marshall Islands, Fieldiana: Atnthropology*. Chicago: Natural History Museum.

Steedman, Carolyn. 1995. *Strange Dislocations: Childhood and the Idea of Human Interiority, 1780–1930*. Cambridge: Harvard University Press.

Stege, Kristina. 2008. "*An Kōrā Aelōñ Kein* (These Islands Belong to the Women): A Study of Women and Land in the Republic of the Marshall Islands." In *Land and Women: The Matrilineal Factor*, edited by Elise Huffer, 10–34. Suva: Pacific Islands Forum Secretariat.

Stephens, Sharon. 1995. *Children and the Politics of Culture*. Princeton: Princeton University Press.

Stokke, Andreas. 2013. "Lying, Deceiving, and Misleading." *Philosophy Compass* 8 (4): 348–59.

Strathern, Andrew. 1975. "Why Is Shame on the Skin?" *Ethnology* 14 (4): 347–56.

Strathern, Marilyn. 1988. *The Gender of the Gift: Problems with Women and Problems with Society in Melanesia*. Berkeley: University of California Press.

Super, Charles, and Sara Harkness. 1986. "The Developmental Niche: A Conceptualization of the Interface of Child and Culture." *International Journal of Behavioral Development* 9 (4): 545–69.

Super, Charles, and Sara Harkness. 1997. "The Cultural Structuring of Child Development." In *Handbook of Cross-Cultural Psychology, vol. 2: Basic Processes and Human Development*, editors John W. Berry, Pierre R. Dasen, and T. S. Saraswathi, 1–39. Boston: Allyn and Bacon.

Sykes, Karen. 2005. *Arguing with Anthropology: An Introduction to Critical Theories of the Gift*. New York: Routledge.

Tamis-LeMonda, Catherine S., Yana Kuchirko, Rufan Luo, Kelly Escobar, and Marc Bornstein. 2017. "Power in Methods: Language to Infants in Structured and Naturalistic Contexts." *Developmental Science* 20 (6): 1–14.

Tannen, Deborah. 1995. "Waiting for the Mouse: Constructed Dialogue in Conversation." In *Linguistics in Context: Connecting Observation and Understanding*, edited by Deborah Tannen, 198–217. Chicago: University of Illinois Press.

Teaiwa, Teresia. 1994. "Bikinis and Other S/Pacific N/Oceans." *Contemporary Pacific* 6 (1): 87–109.

Tetreault, Chantal. 2010. "Collaborative Conflicts: Teens Performing Aggression and Intimacy in a French *Cité*." *Journal of Linguistic Anthropology* 20 (1): 72–86.

Thayer, Zaneta, and Amy Non. 2015. "Anthropology Meets Epigenetics: Current and Future Directions." *American Anthropologist* 117 (4): 722–35.

Thomas, Deborah, and Kamari Clarke. 2013. "Globalization and Race: Structures of Inequality, New Sovereignties, and Citizenship in a Neoliberal Era." *Annual Review of Anthropology* 42: 305–25.

Thomas, Nicholas. 1991. *Entangled Objects: Exchange, Material Culture, and Colonialism in the Pacific*. Cambridge: Harvard University Press.

Thorne, Barrie. 2005. "Unpacking School Lunchtime: Structure, Practice, and the Negotiation of Differences." In *Developmental Pathways through Middle Childhood*, edited by C. R. Cooper, C. T. G. Coll, W. G. Bartko, H. M. Davis, and C. Chatman, 75–100. Mahwah, N.J.: Lawrence Erlbaum Associates.

Tisdall, E. Kay M., and Samantha Punch. 2012. "Not So 'New'? Looking Critically at Childhood Studies." *Children's Geographies* 10 (3): 249–64.

Tobin, Jack. 1958. "Land Tenure in the Marshall Islands." In *Land Tenure Patterns: Trust Territory of the Pacific Islands*, 1–76. Guam: Office of the High Commissioner.

Tobin, Jack. 2002. *Stories from the Marshall Islands*. Honolulu: University of Hawai'i Press.

Toren, Christina. 1990. *Making Sense of Hierarchy: Cognition as a Social Process in Fiji*. Atlantic Highlands, NJ: Althone Press.

Toren, Christina. 1993. "Making History: The Significance of Childhood Cognition for a Comparative Anthropology of Mind." *Man*, New Series, 28 (3): 461–78.

Trevarthen, Colwyn. 1988. "Universal Co-operative Motives: How Infants Begin to Know the Language and Culture of Their Parents." In *Acquiring Culture: Cross-Cultural Studies in Child Development*, edited by Gustav Jahoda and I. M. Lewis, 37–90. London: Croom Helm.

Urban, Greg. 1986. "Ceremonial Dialogues in Native South America." *American Anthropologist* 88: 371–78.

UN General Assembly. 1989. *Convention on the Rights of the Child*. UN Doc. A/Res/44/25. 20. November 1989. https://treaties.un.org/pages/viewdetails.aspx?src=treaty&mtdsg_no=iv-11&chapter=4&lang=en

U.S. Census Bureau. 2012. *2010 Census Summary File 1*. https://www.census.gov/prod/cen2010/doc/sf1.pdf.

U.S. Citizenship and Immigration Services. 2016. *Federated States of Micronesia, Republic of the Marshall Islands, and Palau*. Edited by the U.S. Department of Homeland Security. https://www.uscis.gov/i-9-central/complete-correct-form-i-9/complete-section-1-employee-information-and-attestation/federated-states-micronesia-republic-marshall-islands-and-palau

Veblen, Thorstein. 1953. *The Theory of the Leisure Class*. New York: Viking Press.

Vygotsky, Lev. 1978. *Mind in Society: The Development of Higher Psychological Processes*. Cambridge: Harvard University Press.

Vygotsky, Lev. 1998. "The Problem of Age." In *The Collected Works of L. S. Vygotsky, vol. 5: Child Psychology*, edited by Robert Rieber, 187–205. New York: Kluwer Academic/Plenum Publishers.

Wakefield, Sara, and Roger Apel. 2016. "Criminal Justice and the Life Course." In *Handbook of the Life Course, vol. II*, edited by Michael Shanahan, Jeylan Mortimer, and Monica Kirkpatrick Johnson, 301–19. Springer.

Walsh, Julianne. 1999. Adoption and Agency: American Adoptions of Marshallese Children. Paper presented at "Out of Oceania: Diaspora, Community, and Identity" conference sponsored by University of Hawaii at Manoa, Honolulu, HI. Retrieved February 8, 2018, from http://poundpuplegacy.org/node/30196

Walsh, Julianne. 2003. "Imagining the Marshalls: Chiefs, Tradition, and the State on the Fringes of United States Empire." Ph.D. dissertation, University of Hawai'i.

Walsh, Julianne. 2018. Personal Communication.

Wardlow, Holly. 2006. *Wayward Women: Sexuality and Agency in a New Guinea Society*. Berkeley: University of California Press.

Watson-Gegeo, Karen. 1990. "The Social Transfer of Cognitive Skills in Kwara'ae." *Quarterly Newsletter of the Laboratory of Comparative Human Cognition* 12: 86–90.

Watson-Gegeo, Karen. 2001. "Fantasy and Reality: The Dialectic of Work and Play in Kwara'ae Children's Lives." *Ethos* 29 (2): 138–58.

Weiner, Annette. 1976. *Women of Value, Men of Renown: New Perspectives in Trobriand Exchange*. Austin: University of Texas Press.

Weiner, Annette. 1992. *Inalienable Possessions: The Paradox of Keeping-while-Giving*. Berkeley: University of California Press.

Weis, Lois, and Michelle Fine. 2013. "A Methodological Response from the Field to Douglas Foley: Critical Bifocality and Class Cultural Productions in Anthropology and Education." *Anthropology and Education Quarterly* 44 (3): 222–33.

Weisner, Thomas. 1996. "The 5–7 Transition as an Ecocultural Project." In *The Five to Seven Year Shift: The Age of Reason and Responsibility*, edited by Arnold Sameroff and Marshall Haith, 295–326. Chicago: University of Chicago Press.

Weisner, Thomas, and Ronald Gallimore. 1977. "My Brother's Keeper: Child and Sibling Caretaking." *Current Anthropology* 18: 169–80.

Weismantel, Mary. 1995. "Making Kin: Kinship Theory and Zumbagua Adoptions." *American Ethnologist* 22 (4): 685–709.

West, Candace, and Don Zimmerman. 1987. "Doing Gender." *Gender and Society* 1 (2): 125–51.

Whiting, Beatrice, and John Whiting. 1975. *Children of Six Cultures: Psycho-cultural Analysis*. Cambridge: Harvard University Press.

Willson, Heather. 2008. "Subject Positions in Marshallese." Ph.D. dissertation, University of California, Los Angeles.

Yamada, Seiji, and Matthew Akiyama. 2014. "'For the Good of Mankind': The Legacy of Nuclear Testing in Micronesia." *Social Medicine* 8 (2): 83–92.

Yamada, Seiji, and Neal Palafox. 2001. "On the Biopsychological Model: The Example of Political Economic Causes of Diabetes in the Marshall Islands." *International Family Medicine* 33 (9): 702–4.

Yamada, Seiji, and Wesley Palmer. 2007. "An Ecosocial Approach to the Epidemic of Cholera in the Marshall Islands." *Social Medicine* 2 (2): 79–86.

Yang, Yang. 2007. "Age-Period-Cohort Distinctions." In *Encyclopedia of Health and Aging*, edited by Kyriakos Markides, 20–22. Los Angeles: SAGE Publications.
Yang, Yang, and Kenneth Land. 2008. "Age-Period-Cohort Analysis of Repeated Cross-Section Surveys: Fixed or Random Effects?" *Sociological Methods and Research* 36 (3): 297–326.
Zelizer, Viviana. 1985. *Pricing the Priceless Child: The Changing Social Value of Children*. New York: Basic Books.

INDEX

Tables and figures are indicated by an italic *t* and *f* following the page number

www.ingramcontent.com/pod-product-compliance
Ingram Content Group UK Ltd.
Pitfield, Milton Keynes, MK11 3LW, UK
UKHW040604210726
13854UKWH00009B/2693

9 780190 876982